DOWN THE RAT HOLE

DOWN THE RAT HOLE

Adventures Underground
on Burma's Frontiers

Edith Mirante

Orchid Press

Edith Mirante
DOWN THE RAT HOLE:
Adventures Underground on Burma's Frontiers

Published by
ORCHID PRESS
P.O. Box 19,
Yuttitham Post Office,
Bangkok 10907, Thailand
www.orchidbooks.com

ISBN 974-524-050-8

Printed in Thailand

Contents

List of Illustrations

The stir and rumour of ten thousand men
Moved in those forests once and shook the leaves,
Sudden and secret, as the hot wind breathes
Tossing the jungle, and is still again.
Silence has taken all. The runways fade,
The jungle marches where our camps were made.
— Steven Bracher, '14th Army'

For John. *Akui nyalam ika*

Author's Note

Not long ago, I brought my husband by light-rail train to a suburban Pacific Northwest nature reserve that I had spotted on my way to an out of town root canal appointment. We wandered the inner trails of the reserve, getting thoroughly lost, until we emerged in a parking lot next to an abandoned drive-in movie theater and found our way back to the train stop. We got off at another station to look at a time line in the form of a core sample which had been drilled when the train tunnel was excavated hundreds of feet underground. Elements of natural history from tree rings to the extinction of the dodo were depicted above the tube of layered rock. After examining that we got on another train, with our transfer tickets expired, risking some $500 in fines for deliberate fare-beating, and rode two more stops.

Emerging uncaught, I commented that our excursion 'had all the traits of a good adventure: a train trip, getting lost, breaking the law, and a core sample.' In the tales of the Burma frontiers which follow here, train travel is rare, but trucks, mules, riverboats, and the dreaded baby taxis may compensate for that. Remarkably, I do not lose my way. Illegal activity, especially the violation of borders and other restricted regions, is rife. And all my explorations constitute a core sample of Burma's oppression, its revolution, its reality.

In my previous book, 'Burmese Looking Glass', I told the story of the fight for survival by the people on Burma's frontier with Thailand, through my experiences there—learning of their plight first-hand, starting an information project to investigate human rights abuse, and getting jailed and kicked out of Thailand because of it. That was the 80's, when I played The Clash in my headphones and wore lucky dice earrings with my camouflage fatigues. When I returned to Burma's insurgent zones in the 1990s, I could not go to the Thai border anymore, so I sought other avenues of approach. This book is about my journeys among the brave people of even less-known frontier regions: Burma's borders with Bangladesh, China, India and Laos.

The events I am writing about here all really happened, and all of the people described here are real. I have changed quite a few of their names for their safety. Conversations are reconstructed from memory, and in some cases from interview tapes.

There does not appear to be a standard way of transliterating Laotian place names, so I have used my favorite variations of names for the towns and villages I visited in Laos.

Two lively and detailed books are especially useful for learning more about the India/Burma frontier: Sanjoy Hazarika's 'Strangers of the Mist' and Dr Vumson's 'Zo History'. For further revelations of life and rebellion in Burma's frontier areas, I recommend the writings of Bertil Lintner and Martin Smith, two intrepid Burma watchers of 'my generation'.

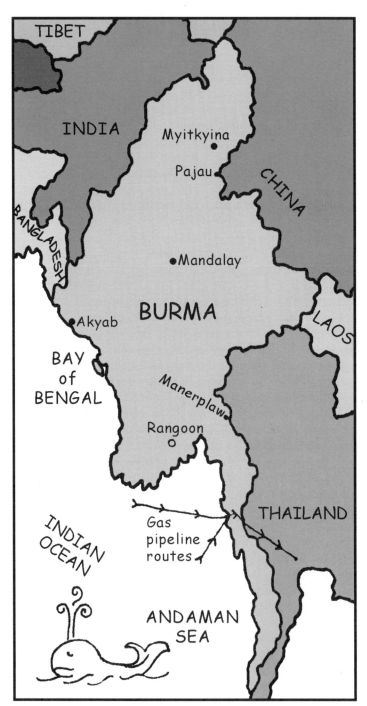

Map 1. Burma.

1

INSURANCE

I did not have insurance. I didn't really understand insurance. I didn't have a car, and had never even had a driver's license. But I was working at what was perhaps America's largest auto insurance company, on one of those temporary jobs that dragged on week after week, month after month.

I found it a very odd company, housed in a concrete bunker-like edifice in the New Jersey woods. Their corporate culture included mandatory blue plexiglass pyramids engraved with customer service goals on everyone's desk. The employees weren't allowed any personal artifacts to compete with the pyramid on their desks, which were all the workspace they had. Nobody had cubicles, let alone offices. I didn't even have a desk, but at least I had the file room mostly to myself as I spent my days putting car crash case folders back in the correct drawers for posterity. Everyone got a half hour break in the morning and a half hour break in the afternoon, as well as an hour for lunch. The rest of the time they were expected to work work work—no hanging around drinking coffee like in other companies. The employees seemed happy. Sometimes they donated blood at the Bloodmobile and got smiley-face stickers to wear on their 'casual day' blue company polo shirts. Sometimes the company treated them all to ice cream sundaes in the cafeteria.

I wasn't happy. It was 1990 and I had been kicked out of Thailand in 1988 because of my investigations of human rights violations in neighboring Burma, and I hadn't made it back to Asia since. I spent my time distributing Burma information to an ever-widening network of individuals and organizations, by photocopy and mail, and doing temp jobs to try and get together enough money to go back. I lived in my mother's house, in my childhood bedroom, surrounded by Burma files in cardboard boxes, and did my 8 to 5 jobs in a different world of files. Refusing to spend any money on warm or 'corporate' clothes, I dressed like some Marshall Plan orphan in my brother's old sweaters over threadbare cotton dresses. My hair was pulled back with an elastic band. I had no social life except for my karate classes at a local *dojo*.

Three times a day I would fill in for the switchboard operator while she took her breaks and lunch. Then, instead of dozing secretly in the file room, I could read a book between calls reporting the latest collisions of the insured. I also read during my own breaks and lunch, outside at a picnic table unless it was raining. I read books about World War II's China-Burma-

India Theater, the combat zone including my old stomping grounds; and 'The Forty Days of Musa Dagh' in which the genocide of the Armenians in 1915 so closely resembled the plight of the ethnic groups I knew in Burma. When the day was over, I'd walk home through the woods. Once in a while I'd find kids playing there as I used to, thirty years before with my friends organized into an 'Indian tribe'. But mostly the children were all indoors playing Nintendo computer games.

It was a fall evening when I got home and my mother showed me the business card a Federal Bureau of Investigation agent had put through the mail slot with a note asking her to call him. The FBI agent's name was Lazarus Simmons. My mother had called the number on the card and it really was the FBI office in Newark, New Jersey, but Mr Simmons was gone for the day. So we had all night to speculate about what it was regarding. We joked about having pulled off those mattress tags that say 'do not remove under penalty of law'. My mother, who always read everything under the sun, thought it might be in reference to her subscription to _Soviet Life_ magazine during the 1950s. We wondered about an uncle who contributed to Noraid, the Irish Northern Aid Committee. Or perhaps my brother had applied for some position pertaining to Operation Desert Shield, the run-up to the Gulf War then in process, something that would require a security clearance background check? All that aside, we really knew it had to be about me.

'I guess one of the Burmese exiles must have threatened the Burma Embassy or some diplomat,' I said. I knew plenty of dissident students who had fled Burma's military regime's bloody crackdown on a nationwide pro-democracy uprising in 1988. I was on the overseas Burma movement's contact lists, in their address books, on their phone bills. Following the passive resistance lead of their scrupulously non-violent heroine Aung San Suu Kyi, the exiles had not turned terrorist. But maybe, I supposed, someone's pent-up rage had gotten the better of him, and the FBI's attention had been drawn their way. The FBI agent would want to hear what I could tell him about Burma's oppression and the resistance to it. With that scenario in mind, we decided that my mother would telephone Mr Simmons, because his 'call me' message had her name on it. I'd check in from work the next day to see what he wanted.

When I called my mother from the insurance company, she said that she'd talked with Lazarus Simmons, he'd told her only that it 'didn't involve crime, just national security', and he was on his way over to the house from Newark. A while later I called back, and he was there.

'He keeps asking about your project,' my mother whispered, 'and _Eastern Europe..._'

'Send him over here,' I said.

I was in the second floor reception area, at the switchboard. Mr Simmons, a middle-aged, stocky African American in a brown suit, arrived. I got a very junior clerk to take over the switchboard for me. Then I brought the FBI agent into a small room to the side of the reception booth. It contained a desk and two chairs, and was normally used for questioning suspected perpetrators of insurance fraud. It was not a friendly little room. I sat behind the interrogator's desk, and motioned Mr Simmons to the fraud chair in front of it.

'I'm from a part of the Bureau that kind of keeps track of different groups, political groups, operating in northern New Jersey,' the agent explained. 'We understand you are running something called Project Maje out of your mother's home.'

'Yes, it's the information project on Burma that I founded in 1986.'

'Burma?'

'Human rights information, mostly, and the environment and narcotics. A large proportion of the heroin here comes from Burma, and the dictatorship over there is completely involved in the drug trade. The junta there is in power illegally. The Reagan and Bush administrations have condemned it for its human rights abuses, and we don't have an Ambassador in Burma anymore,' I added, figuring that an FBI agent would want to know that our Republican government was on the same side as I was, firmly against the thugs holding power over Burma.

'Oh,' said Mr Simmons in a low voice. He looked up from the pad on which he'd been writing or doodling. 'Um, have you ever traveled to Eastern Europe?'

'I spent a couple of days in Poland, in Warsaw, in 1985,' I offered.

'What were you doing in Warsaw?'

'It was just a stop-over, I had taken the Trans-Siberian Express from China through Russia, it was my way of traveling from Asia back here. I'd been all over the Thailand/Burma border that year, exposing the abuse of indigenous ethnic groups by Burma's military, going around the rebel—freedom fighter—bases on the frontier...'

'How about Czechoslovakia?'

'What about it?'

'Have you ever been there?'

'No. Only Poland. Actually, the democracy movement of Burma is kind of like what happened in Eastern Europe last winter, all these people demonstrating peacefully for freedom, only in Burma in '88 they got shot for it instead. Like Tiananmen Square in China, only the Burmese Army killed thousands, not hundreds, and it didn't get a whole lot of international press coverage. No TV cameras there at the time.'

'Are you sure you haven't had any contact with Czechoslovakia?'

'I have not. But their leader, Vaclav Havel, and Burma's democracy party leader, Aung San Suu Kyi, have a lot in common. Both intellectuals, followers of Gandhi and Martin Luther King, strong-willed, articulate. Even though her party won an overwhelming majority in elections last spring, Aung San Suu Kyi is being held under house arrest now, incommunicado, because she won't give up her beliefs...'

'You're saying you haven't had contact with the Czechoslovakian Embassy?'

'No, I haven't. So, anyway, since the '88 uprising a lot more people have gotten interested in Burma. So my information is more in demand. It makes my work a bit harder, but at least I'm not the only one doing it. Now we have to get American companies to quit going into Burma, making investments with the regime. Bringing their money there, which really undercuts US Government policy...'

The FBI agent interrupted me gently. 'What about some communication, a letter you sent to the Czechoslovakian Embassy last winter?'

'What? I don't think so.' Then I remembered something. 'Oh, I know what you mean. The old Communist government of Czechoslovakia, just before it fell, it had an arms deal with Burma in the works. Helicopter gunships, I think. After the Burma democracy uprising was suppressed, the Burmese junta, it calls itself the Slorc, State Law and Order Restoration Council, *Slorc*—if you can believe that, has concentrated on rearming itself. Its army had about 150,000 troops then, now it's going for half a million. So they got all this hard currency from foreign investment—logging companies, oil companies, even a Pepsi franchise. And they've been buying weapons from China mostly. But they also had a deal going with Czechoslovakia. So naturally when the Velvet Revolution and Vaclav Havel came along and overthrew the Czech Communist regime, I wrote to the new Czechoslovakian Ambassador in Washington. To ask her to get her government to put a stop to selling helicopters to a dictatorship like the one they'd just gotten rid of themselves.'

'I see. You were writing to the new Czech Ambassador about Burma.'

'I can send you a carbon copy of the letter.'

Before I could launch into any more explanations of Burma and its international relations, a topic with which I really wanted to acquaint any representative of the US Government, Mr Simmons put his pen back in his pocket and leaned forward in his chair. 'Well, I think that covers it,' he said. 'Thanks very much for your time. Do you have any questions for me?'

I was astounded. That 1985 Trans-Siberian Railway trip had not gone smoothly for me. When the train had crossed from (then Communist) Mongolia to the (early days of Gorbachev but still Communist) Soviet Union, I had been taken from my train compartment to a station building by a pair of Kalashnikov-toting Russian soldiers. In a room with a locked, padded door and a guard, I was questioned by a stern KGB commissar in a gray overcoat and fur hat. A search of my belongings had produced items—a sketchbook, photos—that they considered 'military', and which related to my recent travels in Tibet. The KGB agent seemed oblivious to my Burma involvement, but was fixated on Tibet. My brief interrogation, during which I played dumb pretty effectively, began with the extraordinary query, 'Do you speak Tibetan?' and included the gratuitous confiscation of my Talking Heads cassette tape ('this group is not allowed in Soviet Union'.) It ended with, 'Now do you have any questions for us?'

When an FBI agent in my home state of New Jersey wound up our session in exactly the same manner, I could only wonder, 'do these guys all have the same training manuals?' For the second time, I declined to ask my inquisitor anything. Lazarus Simmons and I shook hands and I walked him to the door, then returned to the switchboard.

Eventually I figured out the reason why the FBI was wasting taxpayer money investigating my little info project, at a time when the US federal budget was in dire straits and the Cold War was really over and done with. Vaclav Havel had been on State Dinner terms with the White House for months, so why the obsession with my contacting his Embassy? I found out that Cuba, which remained a US enemy in the classic Cold War sense, used the Czech Embassy in Washington as a representative office and mail drop. It seemed that somehow the FBI got to look at the return addresses of letters going there, but not to open them, so they didn't know what mine was about. With an envelope showing an unknown-to-them Project Maje, and my mother's address, they made the intuitive leap that we had some kind of Cuba group going. Castro-sympathizers, apparently. Spanish-sounding name, Maje, although it meant a kind of bell in a Himalayan tribal language and 'older sister' in Burmese.

That afternoon, still mystified by the Czech thing, I was back in the dim file room, picking at the insurance claim folders in my usual lethargic way. One of the claims adjusters, a Dilbert type in white shirt and tie, came in looking for a case file. I dug it out of a dusty steel cabinet for him.

'You look tired, Edith,' he commented.

'Well, I've had an interesting day.'

And the claims adjuster just laughed, knowing that no mere temp file clerk trapped in the windowless cell of this smug dull corporation could ever have anything interesting happen to her.

2

VULTURES OVER CHITTAGONG

My stay in Cox's Bazar, on Bangladesh's southeast coast, was brack-eted by the corpses of two children. I saw the first from a bus window on the way there. It lay at the side of the road, wrapped up to its face in a checked sarong and surrounded by grieving villagers. A few coins, funeral donations, had been strewn around the body. Hit by another speeding bus, I supposed. The other child-corpse floated in swollen isolation, caught in the stilt roots of a mangrove forest. It was mottled pinkish, with a rag of red cotton around its middle.

Cox's Bazar had been founded in 1798 by a British officer, Capt. Hiram Cox (who died of fever shortly thereafter) on a narrow finger of land stretching between the world's longest beach and the Burma border. Over that border was a coastal state of western Burma called Arakan, which had Burma's largest Moslem population, the Rohingyas. Those Moslems lived to the north of Arakan's majority ethnic group, Buddhists called Rakhines. In Burma's western mountains (north of Arakan) lived the Chins, a primarily Christian people with many subgroups and clan affiliations.

All of those ethnic groups of Burma's west were less known to the outside world than those whose regions bordered Thailand. Since I was not allowed in Thailand, I had decided to go looking for human rights information on this less traveled border. In particular, I suspected that Burma's regime, the Slorc junta, might be mistreating the Moslem Rohingyas, as they did many other ethnic groups. I thought that documentation of the abuse of Moslems might raise the ire of largely Islamic Southeast Asian countries like Malaysia, Indonesia and Brunei, which were on the verge of providing commercial and diplomatic support to the Slorc.

I had saved up enough money from my temp work to fund my investigations in Asia for a while. Starting out in India in April 1991, in Calcutta I met with the Chairman of the rebel Chin National Front (CNF), which had taken up arms against the regime of Burma. He told me that some of his Chin officers and troops were active in a hill region called Bandarban, on the Bangladesh/Burma border. Unable to get a visa to travel to Bangladesh himself (he thought it was because his travel document listed his occupation as 'evangelist') the CNF Chairman gave me a letter to bring to a CNF staff officer whom I could find at a hotel in Bangladesh's capital, Dhaka.

The next few days' flights to Dhaka were booked out, and impressed with the urgency of my courier assignment, I looked into an arduous bus-

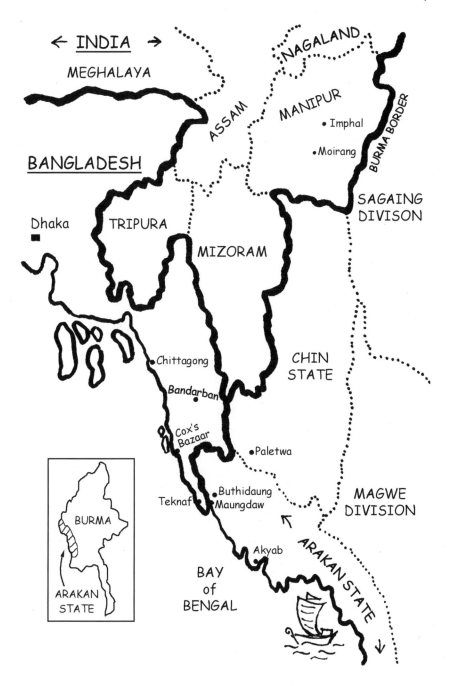

Map 2. The northwest Burma border area.

walking-bus India to Bangladesh crossing. Just to make sure, I telephoned the Dhaka hotel. After a long, sweaty wait in Calcutta's international telephone office, I got through, only to be informed by the hotel clerk, 'They check out.' I decided to open the envelope and see how important the letter was. It was written in English, and consisted of just a very few lines of 'Hello, how are you doing', pleasantries from the Chairman to the staff officer. I waited until I could get a flight to Dhaka instead of using the land route.

I carried the note with me anyway, and I also had several hundred US dollars from a relief agency run by my friend Emma in Thailand, to be given to some exiled students from Burma who had formed a small resistance group near Cox's Bazar. When I converted the dollars to *taka*, the Bangladesh currency, the cash formed a damp, thick wad in the waist pouch I wore under my leggings and loose Indian-style dress. My outfit approximated the comfortable *salwar kameez*—matching dresses and trousers—popular with women throughout South Asia. I had a diaphanous black shawl to add some further Moslem modesty to my look.

I flew from Dhaka to the southern port city of Chittagong. I checked into the shabby pink four-story Hotel Mishka. The Mishka had been built some time between Bangladesh's first independence (from Britain) and its second independence (from Pakistan). First the British left their East Bengal colony in 1947, and Partition made it part of Pakistan, all the way over on the western side of India, because most of the people were Moslems. Then that territory, feeling oppressed by a far-off government that spoke a different language, sought to break away from Pakistan in a 1971 war. Pakistan's army unleashed mass killing, rape and starvation on the Bengalis who nonetheless (with Indian help) won their War of Liberation and became the nation of Bangladesh.

The Mishka had an obliging staff, Victorian furniture upholstered in leopard print vinyl, and an old Pan American advertisement-barometer with the slogan 'Fly Above the Weather' in the lobby. Conscious of my wealth in *taka*, I barricaded my room door with chairs. The sounds of midnight feasting rose from the market below the hotel, as it was the month of Ramadan, when food, drink, cigarettes and betel nut are foregone by the Moslem faithful until darkness falls.

In the morning I took the Cox's Bazar express bus, a ramshackle overcrowded vehicle. Bangladesh's buses, and the ubiquitous bicycle rickshaws, were painted in Fauvist colors, a lot of green, a lot of violet, plenty of pink and red. Darting in and out of the slower traffic were 'baby taxis', metal passenger shells grafted onto scooters with noxious noisy two-stroke engines. Some transport was embellished with hand-painted scenes from musical movies, some with iconic portraits of Saddam Hussein. The government of Bangladesh had sent a contingent of troops to fight Saddam in the Gulf War, which had just ended badly for Iraq and especially badly for the Kurds who were in a mass refugee flight to the hills. But Saddam had won the hearts of average Bangladeshis, with his mustache, his beret and his underdog defiance. His stony visage stared from posters, calendars, and even plastic shopping bags.

About midway on the four-hour bus trip, one of the passengers flung himself up to the front and began pummeling the driver, who swerved to the side and booted him off. A long, loud, Ramadan irritable debate occupied the rest of the passengers for the rest of the trip: was the ejection justified or not? Jammed next to the window, I looked for the 'dense jungle' my 1985 Bangladesh guidebook assured me would be seen on the road to Cox's Bazar, but it had all disappeared, replaced by villages and rice paddies everywhere. Bangladesh was small and packed with inhabitants. More people lived on less land every year. The country was about the size of Michigan, with over 116 million people stuffed into it somehow.

Cox's Bazar was a beach resort, thinly patronized by Bangladeshis of leisure and innocent of foreign tourists. The room boy at my hotel asked me (blonde, green-eyed) if I was Japanese. More familiar ethnic groups were the Bengalis, the main, mostly Moslem, population of Bangladesh; Rohingyas, the Bengalis' cousins from Arakan; the Rakhines, Burmese-related Buddhists who had their own neighborhood in the town, and a few hill tribes such as the Chakmas, who were themselves caught in a web of insurgency and persecution by the Bangladesh Army.

My first contacts for my Burma investigations in Cox's Bazar were Rakhines. One of them, U Kyaw Hlaing, was a survivor of 'the year of the long marches', 1977, when Rakhine rebels who had trained in other parts of Burma returned to their home state and were virtually wiped out along the way in ambushes by Burma's army, the Tatmadaw.

I had linked up with U Kyaw Hlaing (U means 'Uncle' in Burmese and Rakhine) through my old rebel friends on the Thai border. He was immediately enthusiastic about my idea of gathering information on Arakan, so that I might inform journalists, human rights groups, and governments about that hidden area. A fit man in his forties, with a military crew cut and trimmed mustache, U Kyaw Hlaing exuded energy. His English was excellent, and he knew all the players, Buddhist and Moslem alike.

Although they had a common enemy in Burma's dictatorship, the politicized ethnic groups of Arakan tended to mistrust each other. Rakhine activists bought the regime's line that Rohingyas were somehow outsiders, interlopers from overpopulated, threatening Bangladesh. The Rohingyas perceived the Rakhines as lawless, violent types who would push them off their ancestral lands and deny them credit for their role in Arakan's history. At the best times, Rakhines and Rohingyas intermingled perfectly well in the communities of Arakan. But these were the worst times, and the Slorc played ethnic groups against each other skillfully. I found it remarkable that U Kyaw Hlaing was able to ignore the prevalent prejudices and be everyone's friend.

On foot and by rickshaw, U Kyaw Hlaing and I roamed Cox's Bazar, from the teak-towered temples of the Buddhist Rakhine district, where women wore flowered sarongs and sleeveless blouses, doing business in the shops they owned; to the main street and piers, where women were hardly to be seen at all. The Moslem markets were full of men, swaggering Sinbads off the fishing boats, old fellows in white robes and Haj caps, boys vending watermelon and mangoes. Cox's Bazar's roads ended just past a few holiday cottages, at the Sea Beach, as everyone called it. There, by a stretch of fine sand, men swam and fully-dressed girls waded in groups. A fringe of casuarina trees, a couple of large hotels, and a row of shops bordered the strand. There visitors could buy shell bangles, as I did, or have a cowrie shell custom-engraved with the name of a sweetheart or Saddam Hussein.

We went further south, to the Rakhine village where U Kyaw Hlaing's relatives lived in exile from Arakan, which was visible all the time just across the Naaf River. We stayed there for a few days, in the family house. His sisters fed me fish curry and green mango salad in the candle-lit evenings, and put cooling *thanaka* powder on my face. I read the documents of the Rakhine resistance movement, stack after stack of them, from the collections of U Kyaw Hlaing and other dissidents who had made the village their home for years. For a break, in the hot afternoons I would sit on the upper verandah of the stilted house and read a Patrick O'Brian novel, feeling as if I was on the deck of one of his wooden sailing ships.

Meetings with a dizzying array of Rakhine politicians, young and elderly, male and female, saffron-robed and secular, took up most of my days. I tape recorded them all. The Rakhines had a faction for every day of the week, if not more. U Kyaw Hlaing had made it his mission to unite them all in an umbrella group, but his efforts seemed futile.

The Rakhines were very closely related to Burma's biggest ethnic group, the Burmese—who were also called the Burmans. Even the Rakhine and Burmese languages differed only in nuances, pronunciation. Still the Rakhines deeply resented Burmese domination: the overthrow of ancient Arakan empires, the theft of a revered Buddha statue carried off by the conquerors to the central Burma city of Mandalay. The dictatorship over Burma initiated in 1962 by General Ne Win, and carried on since 1988 by the Slorc was a predominantly Burmese (Burman) conspiracy bent on suppressing the rights of all other ethnic groups. That inflamed the old hostilities of the Rakhines. Many of them tried to organize within the narrow confines of non-violence and 'above ground' political parties in Arakan, which as often as not earned them jail terms. Others were clinging to the Bangladesh border and dreaming up revolutions.

Of those hard-core Rakhine dreamers the hardest were the various Communists. Their left-wing revolt in Arakan had peaked and failed in the 1970s. Now scattered splinter groups held onto the notion of a 'People's Republic of Arakan'. I met a Rakhine officer of the Burma Communist Party (BCP) who seemed unaware that the BCP was already defunct due to a 1989 mutiny against its Chinese leaders by its Wa tribal troops in northeast Burma. He was not sure where the BCP headquarters was, knowing only that his ragged guerrillas must keep fighting the old fight somehow in Arakan. Functioning like a reptile with its head cut off, the Arakan BCP's two hundred or so guerrillas led the Tatmadaw, the government troops, on a wild chase through the hills and river delta of Arakan. The counter-insurgency left a trail of villages burned by the Tatmadaw on suspicion of helping the rebels, their inhabitants massacred or marched off to 'new towns' to provide forced labor for the regime. That was 'armed struggle' in Arakan, and it was the nature of the war in much of Burma at that point. One of the region's past rulers had described the futility of an army pursuing hill tribe raiders as an elephant trying to 'enter the hole of a rat'. But in modern Burma, the elephantine Tatmadaw trampled everything in its path, rat holes, nests of insurgents, peaceful villages, alike.

Confused by the liberation of Eastern Europe and the break-up of the Soviet Union, and excessively impressed by American victory in the Gulf War, some of my Communist contacts actually were gazing wistfully towards my country in hope of aid. 'Why does the USA not help us?' an officer of the Arakan Communist Party, a non-BCP faction, demanded to know.

'What would you want from the United States?' I asked back.

'Assistance. Military assistance for our struggle.'

'You mean the US Marines landing in Arakan?'

'Oh, yes!'

'Well, you may be the only Communists in history who ever wanted that to happen.' I tried to explain why it wouldn't come to pass, and how American 'help' for indigenous peoples' fights usually ended up with those people becoming abandoned refugees like the Montagnards of Vietnam, H'mongs of Laos, and now Iraq's Kurds.

When I met Comrade Thaw Da, he gave me a letter on thin paper, stamped with the hammer and sickle seal of the Red Flag Communist Party, a once powerful faction in Burma of which he was General Secretary and one of the only living representatives. His letter was to President George Bush. It included a critique of 'revisionism' by Chinese Communist leaders in Beijing, as well as an impassioned appeal for US support for the Red Flag Communist Party against the military overlords of Burma. Decrying the Slorc's fascism, the letter to President Bush ended with 'We consider it vitally important to embark the whole world on the due course of a new and peace-keeping era during the life times of the distinguished world leaders who had ever painfully passed through the bitter experience of tragically calamitous catastrophe of war, particularly Second World War. May God bless you!'

Comrade Thaw Da, a compact sixty-year-old man with bristly white hair, had lived a hard committed life. I tape recorded his thoughts on Burmese politics. 'Ne Win's government is not socialist, it is feudalist, so it cannot help but breed a democratic movement,' he commented. I asked him about the 1988 protests, if the way it ended had surprised him. 'We had no surprises. The Burmese political condition is very confused. The backbone's the Army. Without breaking the Army we cannot topple down this Ne Win regime.' About the weakened insurgency of western Burma, the old comrade said, 'On the Arakan side there is only one need: leadership unity. Without it, this front cannot develop. They cannot organize their people, it is sure.'

Continuing the dream and adding another faction to it were a group of Rakhine students who had barely escaped the 1988 Slorc crackdown. U Kyaw Hlaing and I hiked a narrow path to the hideout they called 'Eagle Camp.' The students were members of the All Burma Students Democratic Front (ABSDF), a romantic attempt by the young fugitive urban elite to join the decades-old frontier war of Burma. ABSDF units took up what weapons they could procure, wore uniforms, and tried to participate in battles and skirmishes against the Tatmadaw along Burma's borders with Thailand and China. Only a few of the ABSDF's young men and women, fresh out of city universities and high schools, had what it took for jungle warfare. Malaria and malnutrition decimated them. Many ended up hiding in the slums of neighboring countries, and eventually some lucky ones were able to resume their studies overseas. In other cases, they became teachers or medics among the civilian population of the war zone.

Eagle Camp was tucked onto a hill in a patch of jungle. When I arrived there I gave the group the *taka* supply that I had brought for them from Emma's relief organization, which looked after such stranded students. The Eagle Campers were nearly out of food. They had been surviving for months on watered-down rice gruel, river snails and bamboo shoots. This branch of the ABSDF had badges and olive drab uniforms, but no guns. U Kyaw Hlaing pointed out that rifles would only attract better-armed Bengali bandits, looking to take away the weapons. The students spent their time writing political pamphlets to be smuggled back into Arakan, and monitoring Tatmadaw troop movements by radio. Someone had a guitar, and the boys played chess using a tree stump for a table. They had planted a rice crop in hopes of managing to stay at the camp long enough to harvest it. Sometimes they had to bang on pots and pans to keep wild elephants out of the paddy field, they told me.

Among the twenty or so student rebels was Khai Htun, a poet-adventurer who had roamed the wildest border mountains disguised in Buddhist monk's robes. He gave me a poem that he'd written in English, to put in my report on Arakan:

'Our Journey'

Under the blow of the storm
We travel;
The waves are as high as the mountains,
And the day is so far as the sight.
The night is so dark,
And the cloud is so thick;
But some stars are shining soft,
And with the light of hope,
We travel.

Another ABSDF member recalled 1988 at its worst: 'They shot many monks, students and workers the 19th of September. I saw them fire and hit someone in the stomach, and blood and organs falling out. People's sandals and schoolbags were all dropped on the roadside. Soldiers would order us not to stand up more than three feet off the ground, they were firing that high. So I was crawling on the ground, saying "No! No! No!"'

I tape recorded Mrat Kyaw, a tall physics near-graduate who had been detained in Burma's infamous Insein Prison in the spring of '88. 'They question and torture, and then they question and torture again,' he told me, 'They called me again and again, and they tortured me like "riding motorcycle". We stand and bend our knees, and we must make a motorcycle sound, "rrrrhh". Every time they call me and make me do that. And they make a very rough road with pieces of gravel, and we must walk it "like a tortoise", on our knees and elbows. Again and again they do this. And beat me, also. Sometimes they held my head in the big water ponds.' Mrat Kyaw had escaped from Arakan to Bangladesh, hidden out on the India/ Burma border, and eventually came back to Bangladesh to help form this student group.

The ABSDF members hadn't all been university students. The oldest was actually a bespectacled twenty-seven-year-old bank clerk who had turned democracy activist in the ancient city of Mrauk-Oo and now endured repeated attacks of malaria. The youngest was a boy who'd been only eleven years old when he'd 'manned' the democracy barricades, slingshot in hand, against the Tatmadaw's machine guns in 1988s savage denouement. A young Rakhine deserter from the Tatmadaw was also a member of the band of brothers. He told me that in 1988 he'd been in northeast Burma fighting rebels of the Pa-O ethnic group, and had known nothing of the demonstrations shaking Burma's cities at the time.

Eagle Camp also harbored Thein Maung, a Rakhine black-belt karate champion whose real life was like a Bruce Lee movie. He recollected the way all kinds of people had worked together in Arakan during 1988 to form civil administrations without the police or army; they had gotten away with it for several months, but when the crackdown came that September in Arakan it was ruthless and very thorough. Now, like the other escapees at Eagle Camp, he placed his remaining faith in warfare: 'We must achieve democracy by fighting. If we must fight without weapons, we can fight with our bare hands.' After the interview session, Thein Maung and I gave a martial arts exhibition. I had been taking a tough style of Japanese karate for several years, so I had some presentable *kata* (formal patterns of fighting moves) to show in the dirt clearing. Thein Maung did his *kata* too, and they were remarkably similar, as if we had a common language.

U Kyaw Hlaing and I treated the young rebels to chickens purchased from a neighboring village to put in their forest curry. When it got dark we went to a cleared spot on the hill for a bonfire. We discussed whether the 'armed struggle' was preferable to nonviolence. The ABSDF members all felt that nonviolence had been tried in 1988 and had not worked against the guns of the Tatmadaw, so now they would try to be an army. But in '88 they had come so close—nearly toppling a dictatorship through underground organization and popular protest. Their forlorn attempt to latch onto the ethnic style of frontier warfare didn't seem much more promising to me. I was all for fighting, but would have left it to Burma's hardy, experienced hill people, while hoping the students could turn their intellectual abilities to reorganizing less-violent resistance in the urban zones.

Our discussion shifted from political turmoil to Phoebe Cates. A cute, dark-haired American movie actress not terribly well-known in her own country, Phoebe Cates was the poster queen of Burma. Her pouty teenaged face adorned walls everywhere in the country, and haunted the reveries of young men from jungle border to jungle border. Next to democracy leader Aung San Suu Kyi, she had to be the most famous woman in Burma. After their nation's liberation, the Eagle Campers agreed, the best thing in life would be 'to meet Phoebe Cates'.

I slept among the soldier-students, under one of their few mosquito nets, on the wooden platform that was their barracks. In the morning U Kyaw Hlaing and I went to a nearby Buddhist monastery to talk to an extraordinary 38 year old monk, another escaped 1988 activist. Kyaw Mra Thein, a hyper-articulate English-speaker, was tall and thin. Faded orange robes hung loosely from his left shoulder. We sat in the shade under the first story of the stilted wooden building. Kyaw Mra Thein had a pot of tea and two glasses set out, but the tea went unpoured. As soon as I turned on my tape recorder, he went into a seamless, breathless description of his political history—school teacher, freedom marcher, student of Buddhist doctrine, international activist—and the recent tragedy of Arakan. His eyes gleaming, he reeled off outrage after outrage committed by the regime. 'You see,' he said, 'in 1990 our famous historian Mr U Tha Htun, was arrested. He was a candidate of Parliament. People respected him very much. He was a very gentle man. And he was brought into the Akyab prison. We suspect regarding his death, he was dead in the prison. It is not easy to forget for us.' Winding down, still tea-less, Kyaw Mra Thein went into a reverie about nonviolence, peace and the brotherhood of man. Spotting some local children creeping up to have a look at us, or at me, the monk grabbed a matchbox from the tea-tray and hurled it at them with directions to get the hell out of the monastery courtyard, then went back to peace and light without missing a beat.

Those last patches of southern Bangladesh's forest were a strange never-never land, sheltering Burma's lost generation and other runaways. After saying farewell to Kyaw Mra Thein, we hiked into a Chakma village. I was conscious that due to that tribe's insurgency against Bangladesh and the heavy-handed campaign to suppress it, few outsiders would see such places, where ordinary people of the Chakma tribe lived. On the high porch of a bamboo and thatch Chakma house, we found another refugee from Arakan. The brown-haired young Rakhine woman was living there with her three children, one a baby snoozing in a cradle-hammock. She was a Communist, as was her husband. I taped her story, and after she described Burma Communist Party politics, I asked her where her husband was. 'Actually the facts are not sure,' she responded. 'Whether he was killed, or missing, or just going for a long trip.' She would have to stay in the Bangladesh hills with the children and 'some revolutionary friends', and wait for his return or the bad news.

U Kyaw Hlaing and I continued south to Teknaf, a scruffy town which seemed to exist solely on the smuggling trade to and from Burma. Years of military control of Burma's economy had given rise to a free-wheeling illicit border trade in consumer goods. Not only Arakan's rice and cattle came into Teknaf, but also Chinese and Thai goods brought all the way across Burma by traders who paid off rebel tax posts and Tatmadaw officers alike. In exchange, from Bangladesh to Burma went medicines, and precious powders: the Ovaltine and Horlick's tinned drink mixes which were much-loved British nostalgia products in Burma.

In Teknaf we stayed in a low sprawling bungalow owned by hospitable friends of U Kyaw Hlaing's. We were there to get the Moslem side of the picture of Arakan, and our Rakhine hosts did not mind at all when Rohingyas showed up one after another to be tape recorded by me on their verandah. The Rakhine family's eccentric transvestite servant, in iridescent sarong and frosted lipstick, would sashay out with the tea tray, proffering the biscuit plate with his nailpolished right hand and a bow. Even though it was

Ramadan and the Moslem guests could not partake of such things all day, it would have been unthinkably rude for the Rakhines not to offer any refreshments.

I spoke to Rohingyas who had fled Arakan in 1978 and managed to stay on in Bangladesh. That was the year when more than 200,000 Rohingya refugees had ended up in the Teknaf area. The dictator Ne Win considered the Rohingyas aliens, a substandard group foisted off on Burma as laborers by the British Raj. An ethnic registration program in 1978, with accompanying human rights abuse by the military in charge, had made Rohingyas run for their lives to Bangladesh. Their existence wasn't much better there, as they were deliberately starved out of the refugee camps, their relief food shipments held up by Bangladesh, and then they were forcibly repatriated to Burma. Some of those Rohingyas had made it further overseas, others hung on in Teknaf or Chittagong, but most had ended up back where they started. Under the thumb of the Tatmadaw in the northern Arakan regions of Buthidaung and Maungdaw.

Ever since, Rohingyas had been trying to melt quietly over to Bangladesh, seeking safety. I interviewed Moslem refugees who had come to Teknaf years ago, and those who'd arrived just months before. Even though they knew they were not very welcome in Bangladesh, they wanted me to use their real names in my report. They were proud of giving me the true information, they said. But I didn't write their names down, in case the Bangladesh police might confiscate my notes and use them to go on a refugee sweep.

A very recent refugee, who gave his age as 'about fifty', told me of the hardships in his native Buthidaung: 'The soldiers just come and demand rations, food, as they like. And sometimes they just make us do work for them, so we have no time for our own work. So it is just too difficult for our own survival to stay any longer.'

'Is this a new situation?' I asked.

'Only recently it became worse than before. It started last spring. They demanded our hard labor so we had not enough time to reap our paddy and we lost it. And they wanted to build some buildings on our farmland. So we lost everything.' The Tatmadaw troops' harassment was constant and gratuitously cruel, he told me, his voice rising in indignation. 'When I was going to the market, with some money in my shirt pocket, the military officers met us, and they just took away the money from my pocket. And they asked me the question, "Whose money is this?" And I said, "This is my money." The soldiers said, "Where is your *name* on this money? Do you see any name on this money?" I said, "No, there is no name..." "So you must know that this is the government's money, here it says, *the Bank of Burma*, and so on. So this is *our* money!" And they took it away just like that.' The refugee added that worship in the Rohingyas' Moslem faith was nearly impossible in Buthidaung. 'As of now, they have burned down most of the mosques.'

I began to realize that in April 1991 the refugee curve was rising, with hundreds, perhaps thousands, of Rohingyas arriving that month from Buthidaung. Apparently there was a huge Tatmadaw build-up going on in northern Arakan, just across the Naaf River. Rohingya homes, farms and mosques were being confiscated by the Slorc's armed forces and were being demolished to be replaced with Tatmadaw bases and security roads. The refugees told me of a *gulag* of forced labor camps in Buthidaung. The increased Tatmadaw presence intensified the incidence of rape, torture and murder of Rohingya civilians. The Rohingyas knew the way out, and so were hiring small boats to take them across the river to Bangladesh.

With U Kyaw Hlaing's help, I was able to talk to the refugees and collect documents on their plight. He was the rare Rakhine who was not suspicious of Rohingyas and actually sought their friendship. The two groups had derogatory names for each other. Rakhines called the Rohingyas '*Kalas*' (foreigners.) Rohingyas referred to the Rakhines as '*Maghs*', an old term which implied that the Buddhists were pirates. The preferred names, 'Rohingya', 'Rakhine', 'Arakan' itself, seemed to be related, especially if one said them out loud, but nobody knew the names' origins for sure. The intellectuals of both groups, who were in no short supply, were much given to gazing into the past glories of Arakan's ancient empires for their roots. They stayed up nights trying to prove which ethnic group was truly indigenous to the region, and which its rightful rulers, usually at the expense of the other group.

More worrisome to me was the present situation in Arakan. I thought that the Slorc's troop build-up there might be on behalf of foreign oil or logging companies invited by the Slorc to come in and exploit resources with forced labor, as had happened on other frontiers of Burma. Or perhaps the Tatmadaw was just there to secure Burma's border with Bangladesh, which had recently overthrown a dictator, General Ershad, and replaced him with a democratically elected woman, Begum Kaleda Zia. Maybe the Slorc feared that Begum Zia might naturally back the efforts of Aung San Suu Kyi to bring democracy to Burma. Whatever the reason for the heavy military occupation of northern Arakan, it was all too obvious that Rohingyas, perhaps the most looked-down-upon ethnic group in Burma, were being driven out of their homeland in an eerie replay of the 1978 exodus.

Everyone, refugees and Bangladeshis alike, was crammed onto such a slim wedge of land. It was only about twenty miles from the Burma (Arakan) border to the sea at Cox's Bazar, and less than five miles at Teknaf. As U Kyaw Hlaing and I took the bus from Teknaf back to Cox's Bazar, a commotion arose. The passengers, instead of fighting among themselves this time, were shouting and pointing out the right side windows. I saw a farmer pulling his cows off the road. Then I saw a larger shape, no cow, charging us. A wild elephant, one of the less than three hundred left in Bangladesh, had just rampaged through a village and taken an instant dislike to our bus. 'Elephant! Elephant!' the passengers shouted in Bengali. 'Elephant!' registered in my brain in response to the sight of an enormous gray animal running towards my side of the bus, its ears billowing. The driver floored the gas pedal and drove on our collective adrenaline the rest of the way. We got to Cox's Bazar half an hour ahead of schedule.

'That elephant has no jungle left to feed it,' U Kyaw Hlaing told me. 'He turns bandit, he is now a thief to steal the rice from villages.' I thought that the elephants were the ones being stolen from. Once they had ruled forests in Bangladesh, but now their realm was gone. Velvety green and gold rice paddies took up just about all the flat land in Bangladesh's countryside, but I wondered if their carefully tended crops could feed all the millions of people, let alone a few doomed mad wild elephants.

Cox's Bazar was festive when we returned. For the first time U Kyaw Hlaing could remember, Buddhist New Year and the Eid celebrations that marked the end of Ramadan were coinciding. Moslems bought new clothes for their families and gave alms to the poor. Buddhists gave scented baths to their temple statuary and the Rakhine teenagers splashed water on each other, sang and danced. I took pictures of children in their best holiday outfits, white frangipani blossoms in their hair.

I had been unable to link up with the Chins. I couldn't go to their lair in Bandarban, an area which was closed off to foreigners due to the Chakmas' hill rebellion, and I still carried the CNF Chairman's letter. I sent it by messenger to the CNF camp, with a request for a representative to come down and meet me in Cox's Bazar. While waiting for a reply, I went back to Chittagong. In the port city I contacted a cordial Rohingya businessman, Anwar Hussein, who arranged for me to meet the two Moslem rebel factions. Anwar Hussein sent me to a house on the outskirts of the city which served as the office of the Rohingya Solidarity Organization (RSO). The RSO leader, a medical doctor named Mohammed Yunus, was away, so I met with their second in command. He gave me the RSO newsletter and brochures in English, from stacks they'd printed up in a number of languages for international Islamic conferences which they attended in hopes of drumming up international enthusiasm for the Rohingya cause. Which was, he told me, 'self-determination.' At its simplest, a sort of regional autonomy for Buthidaung and Maungdaw, within an autonomous Arakan, within a federal, democratic Burma, some time in the future that they found so worth fighting for.

Nurul Islam, the smooth-talking lawyer who headed RSO's rival group, the Arakan Rohingya Islamic Front (ARIF), met me for tea in the Hotel

Mishka's restaurant. I asked him my standard lead-off question, 'When did you come to Bangladesh?' and, sitting right across from me he told my tape recorder, 'Actually we have not come to Bangladesh. We are in the jungles. This is not that we are here. We are taking shelter.' Another basic inquiry, 'What is ARIF's current membership?' was met with 'Thousands upon thousands. In every nook and cranny of Arakan.' He waxed wonderfully eloquent on his vision of the true Burma: 'This is one point to be stressed—Burma is a multi-national state. Many people live in it. This is a place where various streams of culture and civilization have joined together. Just like a garden where many flowers grow. And this is the beauty of the country. To be different, to have different cultures...'

Continuing with a torrent of English idioms, Nurul Islam then dissected the regime's attempt to destroy that multicultural paradise. 'They thought that within fifty years they could make the whole of Burma a country with one culture, same similar type. But in Arakan they found our people a stumbling block. A hard nut to crack. In the way of assimilation of the region. Because we, as Moslems, the Islam demands some sacrifice from us. If we are going to retain it, we cannot be easily put into the Burman melting pot. So when they saw it is not possible for them to assimilate, to Burmanize us, that's why they have adopted for us a national policy of exterminating our people till the last one.'

With his neatly trimmed beard and Western clothes, Nurul Islam was the model of Moslem moderation, although his ARIF and the rival RSO seemed both to have courted any Islamic extremist group from Libya to Iran that would give them the slightest hope of support. Both Rohingya organizations had some troops in the field and in guerrilla training camps just over the Burma border, capable of little more than riling up the paranoia of the Slorc's dreaded Military Intelligence torture squads. The ARIF and RSO newsletters pictured their fighters in training, or as holy warriors at prayer: 'Mujahideen Beseeching Almighty Allah, the Omnipotent and the Merciful.' Most of the warriors' support seemed to come from the successful refugees who had become tailors in Saudi Arabia or ditch-diggers in Pakistan and sent contributions to keep an armed struggle for Rohingya self-determination alive.

Both RSO and ARIF were politically sophisticated and reasonably well-funded, by Burma standards, and I found it a shame that they weren't talking to each other. It was also a dreadful shame that the Rakhine rebels wanted nothing to do with them, and since the Rakhines were already members of Thailand/Burma border based opposition alliances like the post-1988 Democratic Alliance of Burma, the Rohingyas were shut out of those 'united fronts'. Somehow I had a natural sympathy for the Rohingyas. It quite possibly came from reading 'Revolt in the Desert' and seeing that movie about T.E. Lawrence when it opened on the big screen, at a very

impressionable age, so I wouldn't be really happy until the revolution in
which I was involved had an Islamic component.

Anwar Hussein had told me of some very recent refugee families from
Buthidaung who were camped out near Cox's Bazar, and he gave me
directions so I could find and interview them. So I went back to the beach
resort with that in mind, as well as the hope of finally meeting up with the
Chins. I had started to want to leave Bangladesh. I liked a lot about the
country. I enjoyed buying mangoes from fruit-sellers whose stalls were
plastered with pictures of Saddam, but said 'America—very good country!'
when they learned I was not, as they guessed, Turkish or Japanese. As
congenial a place as it was, and as well as my interviewing had gone, I had
begun to feel too confined. I was spending so much time in dingy hotel
rooms, or riding around in hooded rickshaws, or wrapped up in my black
shawl. I set a time limit for the Chins and my last refugee encounters. I
began counting the days until I would fly out of Dhaka.

Before I left Chittagong, I visited by rickshaw what was probably the
most beautiful place in the city: the World War II Cemetery. Beneath the
flame trees and purple bougainvillea lay rows of bronze tablets, the graves
of Allied soldiers from Britain, India, Africa, North America and Burma. A
stone marker listing names for a mass grave of Japanese soldiers, their enemies,
stood at a distance uphill. Every Allied grave had flowers planted on it.

Walking from Scottish names to Nigerian names, to names I recognized
as being from the Karen tribe of Burma, I perused the inscriptions. I had a
favorite. It read: 'Escaped a Japanese gaol, to die gloriously with the Chindits
in Burma.' Glory in the Chindit campaign—a terrible slog through the
jungle with massive British casualties—was probably in the eye of the
beholder, not the participants, I thought. The Chindits were a long-range
penetration force, devised and led by a brilliant manic-depressive, Maj.-
General Orde Wingate, who was known for eating raw onions like they
were apples, straining his tea through his socks and scraping his skin rather
than bathing. He had survived a throat-slitting suicide attempt before the
culmination of his military career in Burma. Controversy still exists as to
whether the Chindits' marches deep into Burma and straggling crawls back
out were tide-turning successes or, as Wingate's commanding general put
it, 'an expensive failure'. All accounts agree that casualties, as much from
disease and exhaustion as hostile fire, were appalling, the Chindit missions
nearly suicidal in themselves.

When I returned to Cox's Bazar, on Sunday afternoon, April 29th, a
dreary intermittent gray drizzle had started. 'Is this an early start to the rainy
season?' I asked U Kyaw Hlaing, my eyebrows raised. I had hoped to avoid
that kind of weather, which might bring Bangladesh's notorious flooding.

'Oh, no, it's just the lead-in to this cyclone we're supposed to have
Monday night,' he replied off-handedly. Between spatterings of rain the air

was densely humid, but the word 'cyclone' didn't seem like anything to worry about. I knew that it didn't mean 'tornado' as in my country, but was some sort of hurricane brewing offshore in the Indian Ocean.

I was more concerned about the Bangladesh intelligence police than about the weather. As yet, no one had bothered to question me, even though I was apparently the only Westerner in Cox's Bazar and had been rather conspicuous on my research mission. Still, I thought I might have overstayed my welcome, and I hid my film and interview tapes as best I could in my minuscule corner room at the Panowa Hotel. When I had returned to the Panowa, an unpretentious place just off the main road at the center of Cox's Bazar, the desk clerk had greeted me with, 'You're back. *Why?*' In reply I had only smiled.

On that Monday I still had no word from the Chins, so I visited some of the Rakhine students in their unfurnished cabin near the fishing piers. Eagle Camp could barely support the students who lived there, so a few of the ABSDF members were usually to be found in town, earning money for everyone's rice. They stayed in the cabin while working as apprentices of a local goldsmith, and had declared it the ABSDF office, stocking it with newsletters, revolutionary statements, and magazine articles about the 1988 uprising.

In the evening I rickshawed back to the Panowa. It began to rain viciously. The electricity went out and stayed out. A room boy brought me a candle along with my rice and goat curry dinner. The wind started to build, flogging the palm trees overlooking the sea-channel which went from the Sea Beach to the piers, less than a mile from my hotel. The wind whipped an Iraqi flag which someone had flown from a palm tree. I wondered if that flag would still be there by dawn.

The storm's real violence began around 9:00 that night. My room had an attached bathroom with a small, high, unglazed window and a steel door. The wind invaded the bathroom through the window and started slamming against the door. It was like something big and angry was trying to break through it. Next to my bed was a glass window with anti-burglar metal filigree on the outside. I put the mosquito netting down as if that would keep some of the glass out of my bed, should the window break.

I tuned in the BBC on my battery-powered shortwave radio. In awesome synchronicity a British actress was reading this passage from Henry James' Gothic governess tale, 'The Turn of the Screw': '...it came in the form of an extraordinary blast and chill, a gust of frozen air and a shake of the room as great as if, in the wild wind, the casement had crashed in. The boy gave a loud, high shriek, which, lost in the rest of the shock of sound, might have seemed, indistinctly, though I was so close to him, a note of either jubilation or of terror. I jumped to my feet again and was conscious of darkness...' The candle went out on the BBC, but the one in my room still flickered light, and glass plus casement held on. The steel bathroom door was pounded and pounded, but the bolt held it shut.

The noise outside—wind keening, trees groaning, and then human screams and ambulance sirens—increased. I put my face to the window. Just below, I could see the wind slowly but inexorably peeling the tin roof off a woven bamboo house, like a sardine can being opened. Rain slashed the black sky, wind tore trees asunder. The wind was all over the place. It was not just coming from the direction of the Sea Beach, it was pushing hard from the opposite direction as well. Every so often, the room boy or the hotel's owner would come to my door with extra candles or matches, and ask, 'Is there any problem?' They told me that there was some flooding on the hotel's ground floor, but no damage had been done, all was secure so far.

I had grown up in New Jersey, an Atlantic Coast state through which hurricanes sometimes ripped in the late summer or fall. In the 1950s one of those hurricanes had picked up the large wooden play-airplane my dad had built for my brother and I to sit in, and crash-landed it (unpiloted) across the street. I knew I was in a hurricane in Cox's Bazar, even though it didn't have a name like 'Hugo' or 'Andrew', or any name at all. 'Cyclone' was what they called the same kind of storm—a rogue merry-go-round of low air pressure causing torrential rain, gale-force winds and tidal waves— when it occurred in the Indian Ocean. In the Pacific, they're known as 'typhoons'. I knew the cyclone wouldn't last forever in Cox's Bazar. Soon it would rampage elsewhere on its self-appointed course. At around midnight, the noise—the wind, the crashing trees, the roof-metal, the screaming—seemed to peak, then it waned. I fell asleep before 1:00 AM.

In the morning I lifted the mosquito netting and opened my perfectly intact window, and the Iraqi flag was gone. So was the palm tree from which it had flown, and at least half of every other palm tree, and half of the neighboring house's roof. A woman in a blue sari ventured out of that house, climbed a broken fruit tree, and tried in vain to push the twisted tin back onto the sodden crushed bamboo wall.

I took a rickshaw to the Rakhine section of town. Most of Cox's Bazar's shops were open, although the streets were mud-soaked and the buses weren't running. The lack of traffic made the town oddly quiet, and the weather was unbearably beautiful, as if the air had been scrubbed clean and flooded with pure light. There wasn't the slightest breeze, but the day felt cool and fresh.

The storm had damaged all of the bamboo houses and some of the wooden dwellings in town, but not the brick or concrete buildings. The ABSDF students told me about the tidal surge. They had been sleeping on mats on the floor of their cabin when neighbors had shouted at them, 'Run away!' They awoke thinking they were back in 1988 with Tatmadaw troops about to fire at them. The students had opened their door and a five-foot wave rushed in, coming straight down a creek from the sea-channel. Escaping, they spent the rest of the night piggybacking children and old people to safety in the upper stories of concrete buildings. In the morning they had begun to salvage their possessions. A *Time* magazine cover photo of Aung San Suu Kyi, a waterlogged paperback of *War and Peace* in Burmese, were placed carefully in the sun to dry.

U Kyaw Hlaing went down to his village to see how it had fared. Tun, a Bangladesh-born Rakhine college student would act as my translator in his absence. Tun told me about the damage in central Cox's Bazar: homes ruined, fishing boats wrecked, but only three deaths (all children drowned in the flash flood). We went up on the roof of a concrete building and could see fishing boats flung up on land along the sea-channel, and people everywhere trying to dry out their rice supplies, clothing, and books on rooftops.

Back at the Panowa, the desk clerk told me that '300 people died last night near the Sea Beach.' 'They were all from Burma,' he added, having figured out my interest in the neighboring country. But on the short-wave radio, the national death toll stood at only 120, with much congratulation about Bangladesh's effective new early-warning system. Then, as the night went on, newscast after newscast, reporters began to tell of tremendous damage in Chittagong near the airport, with a broken bridge and shipwrecks, and the death count increased ten-fold. A candle cast the shadow of a plastic water jug on the wall of my room, its curved handle forming the beak and the rest of it the hunched body of a giant vulture. 'Vultures over Chittagong,' I thought.

The buses were running the next day, and in Cox's Bazar, all was calm. Soda-pop was being served without drinking straws for some reason, and the electricity was still cut off. The sellers of roofing metal were raking in *takas*. My Rakhine friends were making jam and pickles from an unprecedented windfall of green mangoes. Townspeople began to raise money and collect supplies for storm victims, especially those on islands just offshore, Maheskhali, Kutobdia, which had been very hard hit. Although there had already been talk on the radio of Bangladesh government relief operations, or even international help, Cox's Bazar had seen no helicopters, no truckloads of rice. So every Moslem group in town set up collection booths, and the Rakhine students from Burma called a relief-raising meeting at a Buddhist monastery. When I went to the meeting, I happened to run into the messenger I'd dispatched to the CNF. The Chins were all gone, he told me, off on a guerrilla operation to the north.

That night the radio death report rose into the six figures in a matter of hours. Bangladesh suddenly took precedence over all other news, even the US space launch which had been keeping it in second place on the Voice of America broadcasts. The radio informed me that we in Cox's Bazar had just lived through the worst catastrophe to hit Bangladesh since a previous cyclone in 1970 had killed as many as 300,000 people. This one Monday night in April 1991 had seen at least 139,000 perish. The cyclone had hit shore right at Cox's Bazar, but it had done its worst damage up the coast. The radio said that the districts of Chittagong near its port and airport were strewn with corpses and animal carcasses; starvation and cholera epidemics were anticipated. Reporters spoke of communications breakdowns hindering relief efforts. Telephone lines were out all over the country. But I knew the road to Cox's Bazar was clear—where were the relief trucks? Ordinary boats were going out to Maheskhali Island, why weren't government supplies?

On Thursday I wandered Cox's Bazar's poorer neighborhoods with Tun, the college student. We found hundreds of people from the Sea Beach area, their huts having vanished in the storm, camped in hungry squalor at a high school, making fires from the wood of fallen trees. An old Buddhist temple, its stucco gates crumpled by the cyclone, sheltered Moslem and Hindu women and their children. The temple roof had blown off, but none of the serene gold-skinned Buddha statues from Arakan sitting under it had been so much as nicked by debris. We stepped around ruined muddy matting that had once been humble but safe family homes. Now people were living on top of the former walls, or propping up the old roofs for lean-tos. Tun and I wandered around in the mud, talking to the people, taking some pictures, and the storm survivors with their gracious innate hospitality gave us coconut milk, or tea. If they had nothing else, they gave us water, germ-laden disaster water, which we drank, and it did not hurt us.

The next morning, Tun and I set off by bus to search for the Rohingya refugees I'd learned of from Anwar Hussein. As we left Cox's Bazar I saw three children from a settlement of squatter huts which had been demolished by the storm, playing, swinging from the downed wires of an electrical pole. The cyclone had hit the last night of April, and the happy urchins played with the lethal May pole it had left them.

The paddy fields just outside of town were full of frenzied people trying to harvest rice which was ripe or near-ripe but soaking wet and in danger of rotting. Crushed houses and fallen trees sagged all along the roadside, but markets and teashops were functioning and road traffic seemed normal. We got off the bus at the side path I'd been told to look for, and after much asking around, we were directed to a group of Rohingya families who were taking refuge in the home of an old Bengali widow.

The families had fled Buthidaung for Bangladesh about two months before. The cyclone shredded the bamboo and thatch hut they'd built for themselves on a corner of the widow's land, and only its center post was left. Now they lived crowded into one room of the lady's house, absolutely

dependent on local charity for their food. I photographed them posed around
the house post, and tape recorded interviews. The new refugees, all barefoot
and simply clothed in cotton sarongs and shirts, spoke matter-of-factly of
forced labor for the Tatmadaw: 'Whenever we are sick or tired, they will
not treat us well, but they will just take a rod or branch or any kind of wood
and beat us to make us work.' They said that if they complained about the
work, or the land confiscation, the soldiers told them 'You can go to
Bangladesh.' They told me they really wanted to go home to Arakan, but
only if 'the military' went away.

Nearby I found another Rohingya family, who had taken a small boat
across the Naaf River to freedom only three days before the cyclone hit.
Having nothing to lose in it, they were not at all fazed by the storm and still
seemed to prefer this unpredictable new country to the homeland where
they'd been used as pack-animals by the Tatmadaw. The main impetus for
their flight had been the safety of their thirteen-year-old daughter. 'Why did
your family come to Bangladesh?' I asked her. 'The Burmese soldiers wanted
to take me away and rape me,' the round-faced little girl replied.

That evening I went to the Sea Beach to see what had happened to it.
So did most of Cox's Bazar. Bangladesh being a predominantly Moslem
nation, Friday was the weekly day off, and it was customary for townspeople
to visit the Sea Beach around sunset on Fridays. On that particular Friday
evening, everybody drifted over there. I met up with Rakhine students,
Rohingyas, Bengalis, even the messenger I'd sent to the Chins.

The cyclone's tidal surge had sucker-punched the Sea Beach area. The
tourist hotels were storm-scarred, with broken windows and ruined gardens.
Even some concrete buildings had been smashed into rubble. Many of the
casuarina trees and shell shops had disappeared. Kids had begun digging
for trinkets from the shops, urchins and schoolchildren sifting the sand
together, finding broken bangle treasure.

Cox's Bazar had by now realized that it had survived true catastrophe,
and survivor joy elevated us all; we were all smiling, laughing in the wreckage.
A puckish beggar capered about, demanding one *taka* from each visitor,
and getting more. Strangers came running up to me, congratulating me in
Bengali and English, for just being there with them. Women skipped in the
surf in their saris, holding hands. Townspeople were still arriving as I left in
a rickshaw that bumped over the beach road, which was fissured as if by an
earthquake and swept with sand.

The Bangladesh newspapers, which still arrived each day in Cox's Bazar,
were by then full of terrible pictures of dead people. The half-naked corpses
of children lined up in rows. The bodies of men, women, babies, washed
ashore, caught in trees, stacked up or sprawling. From my month there, I
knew that Bangladeshis were rarely ugly. They walked gracefully, they
wore their clothes or rags with great style, their eyes flashed brightly, they

smiled generously. But now the cyclone had reduced them in the eyes of the world to exposed, bloated corpses.

The Rakhine relief group had chartered a boat for Saturday. A well-off group (university kids in sunglasses, ladies in Indonesian batik sarongs, merchants flashing rings of jade or pearl) they had contributed numerous sacks of rice, bread, potatoes, used clothing, and boxes of medicine. The boat would take them directly to offshore Rakhine villages, including those on Maheskhali Island. I went along, and as we waited for all the supplies to arrive at the jetty, one Rakhine businessman mentioned to me that 'thousands also died in the cyclone over in Buthidaung'. The radio had carried no mention of storm damage on the Burma side of the border. I supposed that the Slorc would be pleased that the Rohingyas, whom they were out to obliterate, had been beaten down further by the wind.

Ordinary passenger boats were arriving and departing as we boarded our relief boat, an old fishing craft with an open deck. The sky was bright blue and the sun felt hot. I sat among the rice and potato sacks with the Rakhines, who opened umbrellas for shade. We had to wade ashore to reach the first island village, avoiding several large yellow and black poisonous sea snakes floating dead—we assumed—in the shallows.

We made our way through muddy lanes and the torn up sticks and thatch of village houses, to a Buddhist monastery. A sturdy building on concrete stilts, it had sheltered the whole village population on the night of the storm. Rakhine fatalities had been relatively slight because their traditional buildings were up on stilts (unlike the ground-level architecture of the Moslems), so the Rakhines had places to perch above the flood surge. The villagers had all lived through it, but their fishing boats were lost and crashed, salt-gathering and shrimp-raising ponds washed away, house walls collapsed.

The island village had fallen like a house of cards and now it was being reconstructed like one. Families were stacking salvaged fragments of wall and roof together to form A-frame shacks. One such fragile new shelter had a miraculously intact poster of Phoebe Cates fastened to its entrance. Under the charismatic gaze of their Phoebe, the villagers cut bamboo poles and hammered and mended.

At our next stop, where the wind and waves had knocked even wooden buildings askew, I went to a teashop. The shop had no milk for the tea, but their sugar supply had stayed dry. Moslem fishermen were sitting in there without any tea, which they suddenly couldn't afford. A handsome older man named Alam told me that all the fishing boats there had been lost or damaged. The two he had owned were lost. 'We didn't know about this,' Alam said angrily. 'This damned government did not warn us, and where is their help? We have nothing.' I asked him about the radio broadcast storm warnings, of which the government had been bragging. The fishermen in the teashop laughed contemptuously. 'Radios? We have never had the money for a radio!'

Our boat went on to Mody Saura, where a huge fishing boat had plunged into the village on the ten foot height of the tidal surge, breaking in half, knocking palm trees onto buildings and crushing the wooden house where a sixty-five-year-old woman, Mou Marhee had lived for forty years. Gesturing with her arms flung out, her silky white hair flying loose, she showed the destruction she had witnessed from the shelter of a Buddhist temple. 'The water came in, and the ship, boom! boom! boom! We prayed, we asked Buddha for help.'

A little girl with a pixie haircut and almond eyes stood nearby in tears, amid the uprooted palms, posts and pilings. I bent down to talk to her, with Tun as translator.

'I am afraid of the wind,' she told us.

'What's your name?'

'Ma Thin Aye.'

'And how old are you?'

'Seven...'

'Where is your house, Ma Thin Aye?'

'The wind has taken my house away.'

It was on the mangroved edge of Mody Saura that a dead boy of about Ma Thin Aye's age had been deposited by the cyclone. The villagers told us about the boy, who must have floated there from a fishing boat or another village. Our boat went past him on our way out to sea. As we neared the small, pale form, the only people with cameras, a student and I, raised them to take the newspaper kind of photo. When we were alongside, we both lowered our cameras, no pictures for us. The boat was silent until we landed again.

We visited two more storm-swept places on Maheskhali Island. Boats had crashed into houses, trees had fallen down, everything had been thrown around. The villagers, all fishing people, sat on mats that had been walls, under floors with the walls blown away, in A-frames of roof pieces, in new shelters made of fragments of fishing boat cabins. They were hungry and thirsty and angry. A village well was full of salt water. Their goats had drowned. They could not fish—no intact boats, no nets.

A teashop near the Maheskhali jetty was open for business amid the debris, and rickshaw drivers were waiting for passengers to take to the island's interior. As our boat pulled away we watched a Japanese man supervising the unloading of his own relief effort, bags of rice and big tins of biscuits he had brought to distribute to the islanders. It was the first 'foreign aid' and it arrived like all the other help that week: purchased in Cox's Bazar and delivered on a rented boat. The Bangladesh Government was asking the world for helicopters. But areas accessible by truck and boat were being officially ignored.

I took the bus to Chittagong the next day. I saw no sign of anything like disaster relief going south. I went on to Dhaka by train. The Chittagong railway station had a ratio of about one professional beggar for every five actual passengers. The beggars' ranks would probably soon be increased by some of the storm victims, and so would the endless warrens of cardboard and rattan huts built all along the train tracks in Dhaka by previous disaster survivors.

Before the cyclone happened I had planned to entice journalists to visit Bangladesh and write about Rohingya refugees by suggesting that they also could reveal undiscovered tourist spots like Cox's Bazar's Sea Beach. Now tourism in Bangladesh had been set back for decades. Instead it was the disaster that was drawing in the world press, *en masse*. Reporters were helicoptering over Chittagong with their TV cameras and Sheraton box lunches. They were taking the pictures that might inspire an outpouring of international sympathy and charity. Bangladesh was again a basket case, a beggar, a victim nation. The United States would respond with 'Operation Sea Angel': eight US Navy ships on their way back from Gulf War duty stopping off in Bangladesh to lend a hand in repair work and chopper pallets of bread to the islanders. That would inspire orgiastic rumor-mongering among Arakan's resistance, to the effect that the task force's next stop was going to be Burma and a democracy-restoration mopping-up mission. That was never to happen. Arakan's Communists would not get their Marine allies.

On the way into Dhaka, my train passed a Bangladesh Army base which was having a Sports Day—hundreds of soldiers running about in shorts before a reviewing stand. So much for 'all available military personnel' being involved in the relief effort, as the government said. I noticed a dozen flat-bottomed boats stacked up in a weedy corner of the base, apparently forgotten. In the government's appeals for foreign assistance, urgent requests for flat-bottomed boats, for sending aid to the islands, were second only to pleas for helicopters. It seemed that the recently departed dictatorship had left a legacy of aid-siphoning corruption, and the new government was thoroughly disorganized. Genuine warnings, more shelters, better transport, could have saved so many lives. Burma was part of the problem too. The refugees added to the overcrowding of southern Bangladesh that forced people onto sand-flat islands in the storm path.

In Dhaka I played journalist by going to the office of *The Daily Intafaq*, a Moslem fundamentalist newspaper that had been the first to cover the latest influx of Rohingya refugees from Arakan. I provided them with black and white photos of the refugee families near Cox's Bazar and wrote a story about their travails before and after the storm, which *The Daily Intafaq* translated into Bengali and published. They gave me a *Daily Intafaq* ballpoint pen and a photo credit.

My direct flight from Dhaka to Hong Kong kept getting canceled, due to a shortage of airplane fuel. Instead I ended up with the worst possible route, on Bangladesh Biman Airlines to Bangkok with a twelve-hour layover there before the next connection to Hong Kong. I would have to sleep on the floor in the Bangkok transit lounge, as I remained *persona non grata* in Thailand. No going past the Thai immigration counters for me.

Despite rampant flight cancellations on other airlines, the Biman flight was half empty. The jet rose and headed east. A flight attendant in a beige sari slid a dinner tray in front of me. We were flying over Chittagong, above the weather. Then the dark night of Burma was in view. I cursed General Ne Win and the Slorc and their Tatmadaw from above, a witch in their own airspace. I thought about dying, that this would be my most perfect death: 'Escaped a Bangladesh cyclone, to die gloriously in a plane crash in Burma.'

In the Bangkok airport I read a Reuters report about Chittagong: 'Many bodies have been eaten up by dogs while many more were devoured by vultures.' In the three weeks following the cyclone, Bangladesh endured three tornadoes, storms of hailstones weighing up to two pounds each, a minor earthquake, two huge floods, and warnings of another storm to come from the ocean. Rohingya refugees stubbornly continued to cross over from Burma. Their numbers grew from thousands to tens of thousands, and eventually about 250,000 huddled in dusty camps near Cox's Bazar.

3

KACHIN WARPATH

I dyed my blonde hair black in Hong Kong. I had not exactly gotten the go-ahead from the Kachin rebels to enter their territory, but I dyed my hair anyway. The Kachins fielded what was probably Burma's most effective insurgent army, far more powerful than the Chin, Rakhine or Rohingya rebels whom I'd sought on the Bangladesh border. Kachin soldiers had turned their guns on Burma's government back in 1961, pushed from disgruntled-but-loyal to ready to die for independence by an effort to make Buddhism the state religion of Burma. Few Kachins were Buddhist—they were Christians or Animists. They wanted freedom, religious freedom, cultural freedom. As the decades went by under General Ne Win and then his Slorc, the fight grew more bitter, and the Kachin Independence Organization (KIO), unlike most other ethnic rebel groups, grew stronger.

Burma's far north, the partly rebel-held Kachin State, was the Kachins' home, a mountainous region that bordered China, Tibet and India. I had long wished to go there, but it was a hard place to infiltrate. The frontier regions of the neighboring countries were themselves off-limits to foreigners, unlike accessible, tourist-porous Thailand's border with Burma. Still, a dozen or so foreign adventurers had made it to the Kachin Independence Organization's headquarters, a place called Pajau. In 1985 a Swedish journalist, Bertil Lintner, with his Shan wife Hseng Noung and their baby daughter, had made an epic trek there from the India border. A Japanese botanist, Tanaka, and a Japanese anthropology professor, Yoshida Toshihiro, had found their separate ways there on foot by other routes in the '80s. Now, in 1991, China's border with Burma had become a bit more penetrable, although crossing it was still completely illegal. A frontier town called Ruili in China's Yunnan Province had recently been opened to foreign travelers. From there, with my hair black for Asian inconspicuousness, and a great deal of luck, I just might be able to sneak across to the Kachins.

I got over the mirror shock of my mass of what the dye box had called 'Natural Black' hair, and decided to ignore a message from a Kachin colonel, an old friend of mine from my Thai border days, telling me 'it would not be convenient' for me to go to Pajau. I sensed that the letter was a ritual barrier, an indication for the faint hearted to turn back. Coal black dye showed that I wasn't faint of heart, and I told the Colonel that I'd at least go to Ruili anyway. He replied that in that case, I could meet the wife of the Kachin Independence Organization's Chairman Brang Seng. She was living

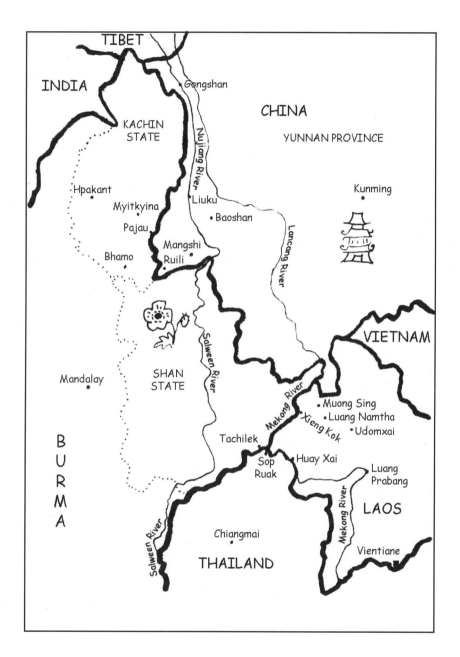

Map 3. The northeast Burma border areas.

in Kunming, the Chinese city nearest to Burma, in Yunnan Province. I flew to Kunming in early August, on the day after my 38th birthday. From my hotel I telephoned the Chairman's wife, and she said she'd come right over.

When I opened the door, in walked the Chairman's wife, and also Chairman Brang Seng himself. I had met the Chairman, an unprepossessing man with glasses and wavy dark hair, before at a Burma conference in the United States. In Kunming he was casually dressed, while his wife looked elegant in pearls and a turquoise silk suit. They were accompanied by Maj. Zau Bom, another old acquaintance of mine from a post the KIO had maintained on the Thailand/Burma border. I made no mention of my desire to go to Kachin headquarters. Our small talk rambled around China, Bangladesh and Burma for a while.

Then, out of the blue, Madame Brang Seng asked, 'Are you the first, or second or third, daughter in your family?'

'Well, I'm the only daughter, I just have one older brother,' I replied, and the three Kachins began an animated discussion in their own language, leaving me mystified by their very specific inquiry. Finally, Maj. Zau Bom reverted to English.

'The Chairman wanted to know so he could give you your Kachin name. Our Kachin names have a word in front according to what order the girl or the boy was born in the family. You are the first girl, so you are "Hkawn".'

'We've named you: "Hkawn Shawng",' said the Chairman with a smile. 'The name "Shawng" means "a pioneer".'

They added that since Chairman Brang Seng and his wife were naming me, I was in effect adopted by them, and would be part of their clan, the Maran, which went well with my own Italian last name. Clan links were of intense importance to the Kachins. A famous anthropology book, *Political Systems of Highland Burma*, by Dr E.R. Leach, had described Kachin clan structure and other aspects of their lives back in the 1950s when foreigners could still enter the region freely. The Kachins had strict rules about intermarriage from clan to clan, and extremely complicated lineage patterns. Now I would be one of them, after a fashion. I knew, from Bertil and Yoshida and the Morse family of old time missionaries, that the Kachins had this possessive streak. If foreigners showed any interest in them, the Kachins had to gather them into their very extended family. Since I'd started wandering the frontier areas back in the early '80s, I had usually avoided becoming too associated with one ethnic group of Burma or another, in order to maintain a semblance of impartiality. But with the Kachins that would be impossible.

My name, Maj. Zau Bom proceeded to explain, would allow their Kachin Army to discuss my progress to their KIO headquarters without any Chinese surveillance agents knowing they were referring to a foreigner. 'I know how you are from the Thailand border,' the Major added. 'You can do things the hard way, you can walk or ride a horse. This trip you will make that way, going up the hard trails from the south. It will be difficult but I think you can do it.' So just like that, I was 'in'. Of course actually getting there was another matter, but I now had my permission from the highest level.

The next day I left for Ruili, taking what the Chinese called 'the sleeping bus'. An ordinary old bus fitted with rows of bunk beds, it careened around the hairpin curves of the Burma Road all through the night. The Burma Road was a mule track transformed into a motor-road by wartime desperation. Hundreds of thousands of Chinese forced-laborers had hacked the Road out of mountainsides and paved its way through northern Burma and southwest Yunnan Province to Kunming in 1938, in order to transport supplies to the Chinese Nationalist forces arrayed against Japanese invaders during World War II. The Burma Road was still a miracle, a wonder and a horror. Above the precipitous gorges, switchbacks formed loop after loop with the sinuousness of a Celtic manuscript page. Freshly crashed truck carcasses hung off cliffs along the way.

At Ruili, I found a decent, new hotel. I had a couple of days to contact a Burmese student group (an ABSDF chapter that operated in Kachin rebel territory) and explore Ruili's border bazaar, before backtracking to a jade trading town called Mangshi where the Kachins were going to fetch me. Night and day, Ruili was a decadent scene right out of 'Bladerunner'. Muddy market streets were lined with stalls selling jade trinkets, patent medicines, leopard skins. Food stalls staffed by Moslems from Burma cooked up spicy Indian dishes. Squatting on the footpaths, old women sold pineapples, or would wrap up a bit of opium, a bit of heroin in plastic or banana leaf, for their steady customers. Seedy-looking stores had signs painted in Chinese, Burmese, and sometimes English—'The South Pole Cold Drink Den', 'International Viand Shop'.

Ruili was China going through a Weimar Republic phase. Neon-lit saloons and creepy *karaoke* dives flourished there. The lanes were trolled by heavily made-up girls of various nationalities, heavily made-up boys, boys dressed as girls and girls dressed as boys too. Lycra stirrup pants, slingback high-heeled white patent-leather pumps, see-through blouses, the black leather miniskirt, were all the Ruili rage. Botanical and zoological goods, endangered, dangerous, came into town by pony or ox cart. Every afternoon a line of trucks decorated with blue and white penguin pictures cruised through town. Refrigerated, they carried seafood caught on Burma's Indian Ocean coast all the way to China for sale.

Walking around the next day in one of my Bangladesh *salwar kameez* outfits, I was generally mistaken for another Indian in town from Burma. On the street where unofficial traders changed bags of Burmese currency for much smaller bags of Chinese money, I noticed a pair of teenagers in shorts and T-shirts, and by their hairy muscled legs I guessed them to be Japanese, maybe some more Japanese bent on getting to the Kachin region. I didn't talk to the boys, but they were turned around looking at me when I turned to look back at them.

I went on to a Burmese teashop, really a perfect replica of the kind of hangout found all over Rangoon and Mandalay. It was presided over like Rick's of Casablanca by an all-knowing expatriate Burmese proprietor. I had been instructed to ask him about my ABSDF contact. He said he could pass a message along to him, so I wrote one down. I sat there for a while, sipping tea thick with milk and sugar. I watched the Burmese customers' intrigues hatch and fly away. The only Chinese person to enter the teashop was a tourist type, who stared at me while he drank his coffee. When he got up to leave, he leaned over to me and inquired, 'Do you speak English?' I shook my head vaguely and looked down at my tea, and he then said, firmly, definitively, 'You are Burma.' He left and I felt like my hair and I had passed a test.

I took a share-taxi minibus to Mangshi, and waited there in my corner room at an old guest house. The KIO contact showed up right on time. He was Lt. Khun Nawng, a pleasant man in his thirties, short in stature like most Kachins. 'We have heard so much about this Mirante, who goes to all the frontier areas of Burma, who rides horses, who knows karate,' the Lieutenant said. I smiled.

'So,' he continued, 'when do we meet this husband of yours?' The Kachin language didn't have gender in its pronouns.

I broke it to him. 'Actually, Mirante is me, Hkawn Shawng. I don't have a husband. I ride horses. I do karate.'

The Lieutenant recovered admirably from his preconception and went right into our trip plans. He had accompanied Bertil and Hseng Noung on their journey years ago. He had also taken a Swiss reporter, 'Mr Bernard' up to the KIO headquarters a couple of months before, and that had gone well. But now, he warned, the regular paths to Pajau were washed out by recent flash flooding. We'd have to cross and re-cross the border. He didn't know if the terrain was even passable anymore, but we'd give it a try. He disapproved of my shoes, a pair of nearly treadless Reeboks. 'Leave those here,' he said, 'We'll get you the Chinese Army shoes, the best for our mud.'

I had one day to wait. I was all keyed up. I'd read for a while, then pace the room, then do a karate *kata* (bumping into furniture), then dance around. I thought bad thoughts about my photojournalist ex-boyfriend. Then I thought good thoughts about mud, and horses, and the Kachin forests and mountains. I spun around in circles. I was nearly deliriously happy. At some point in all this an ABSDF student knocked on my door. Wearing a green beret, a too obvious military touch, the student had somehow tracked me to Mangshi from Ruili. He was the right one, the contact to whom I had sent the note, but I was still wary of him. The ABSDF group in the Kachin State was composed mainly of Burman students who had fled the 1988 crackdown in cities such as Mandalay. Not sure how close the Kachins were with the ABSDF, I told him nothing of my impending departure. I flat-out lied and said I'd be headed back to Ruili the next day.

In reality in the morning a local Kachin picked up my backpack for safe-keeping. I'd bring only the minimum with me in a canvas shoulder bag: warm clothes, a 4"x6" sketchpad and pocket watercolor set, first aid stuff, serious bug repellant, two cameras, some film. I left behind my books, my short-wave radio, even my tape recorder. I planned to write down my interview notes. I checked out of the guest house and waited at a nearby noodle shop. In the evening, a Chinese-made jeep showed up there, and I got in the back with Lt. Khun Nawng. 'This jeep will carry us up to the border,' he told me. 'Do not worry yourself about checkpoints, they are taken care of.' We drove away, heading west, then northwest.

At one or two in the morning, we stopped next to a darkened farmhouse and said goodbye to the driver. Our next mode of transportation awaited: what was known as an 'iron horse', a farm wagon pulled by a small tractor. Chugging along a rutted dirt road, at some point we crossed into Burma, the Kachin State. My earliest memory, from before I was two years old, had me up against the baby gate at the top of the stairs in my family's old house, demanding in whatever speech I had to be let out, to be let through. I still loved a border violation. Evading a checkpoint, busting a gate, climbing a fence would always make me happy. It got me into Burma.

A pre-teen boy in an olive drab uniform illuminated us with the beam of his flashlight. He had a rifle. Lt. Khun Nawng told him in Kachin to get lost. 'He's one of our local patrols,' he explained. Some time later the Lieutenant and I got out of the wagon and walked uphill. Eventually we reached a big stone farmhouse. The people there had been expecting us. I tried on green canvas Chinese Army boots until I found a pair which, although a trifle wide, fit well enough. I was shown to my private bedroom which featured all the Burma border comforts: a plate of cookies, a glass of milk, a baby blue blanket, and somebody's holstered pistol hanging on a hook. I cleaned up on the back porch, above a rushing stream. In this medieval, or timeless, dwelling, I was as happy as I could possibly be.

At dawn, I was told, 'Your horse is waiting.' It was actually a mule, but a nice one, tan, with a thick neck and a narrow reasonably intelligent face. I rode the mule, while Lt. Khun Nawng and a few accompanying men from the Kachin Army walked. We headed up into the mountains on narrow trails, and in the afternoon we reached the KIO's 3rd Brigade headquarters. Cold mist swirled around the military base's low-slung bamboo buildings and obscured the surrounding landscape. The camp was capable of vanishing like Brigadoon in white clouds, good protection from the Slorc's Air Force which occasionally attempted a bombing raid against it. Sitting close to a wood-burning stove in the cabin of the base commander, Maj. Zau Tang, I drank tea. The Major drank his 'medicinal wine'. He kept his special home-brew in a jeroboam-sized bottle, marinating pieces of roots, forest herbs and slices of deer antler in it. He claimed that the wine had healed his various war wounds.

'Your travel north to Pajau will not be easy,' the Major warned me. 'That trail was completely washed away in a water-flood last June. So you will have to climb through the jungle with no road. And no more mule!' The Major and the Lieutenant gave me the option of backing out. I told them that I certainly wanted to go through with the trip, but not if it created a problem for them. 'No problem for us Kachins, just for you,' Lt. Khun Nawng assured me. We laughed together and there was no more talk of my not going further.

We would proceed directly north, following the Chinese border. Along the Burma side of that border the region was largely in Kachin rebel control. When the Kachins had first revolted in the early 1960s, their leaders had advocated complete independence for their region, but over the years that demand had been downgraded to full autonomy within a federal Burma. I knew that the KIO's Chairman Brang Seng, encouraged by old missionary friends and international conflict resolution groups, was working towards some kind of formal peace talks with the Slorc. But meanwhile his 10,000 or so troops fought the Tatmadaw relentlessly and controlled a vast territory of northern Burma.

Maj. Zau Tang's 3rd Brigade base was one of the KIO's southernmost outposts. It bordered a breakaway Kachin area held by a commander named Matu Naw. In a surprise move, much reviled by the KIO, Matu Naw had cut his own cease-fire settlement with the Slorc, like the Wa armies to the west, who had quit fighting after they overthrew their Burma Communist Party commissars. The KIO considered Matu Naw a traitor for literally breaking ranks.

For our trip north, Lt. Khun Nawng and I borrowed ten young commandos from the 3rd Brigade. The escort included two army nurses, Lau Mae, very compact and energetic, and Roi San, who had tea-brown hair in long braids. Lau Mae spoke some Chinese, as I did, and I could manage minimal Burmese conversation with Roi San, who carried a tin box full of pills, powders and glass ampoules in her bulky knapsack. I understood not a phrase of Kachin, a collection of dialects distinguished by the 'aw' sound, a language that could be well spoken by a raven, orated by a parrot, sung by a hornbill.

Our rebel band headed off across ridgetops and detoured to a bamboo tea shack to talk to some ABSDF members. Lt. Khun Nawng didn't think it was a good idea for me to visit the students' nearby base—one never knew how good the security was with those Burmese kids, he cautioned me. We rode and walked on, and stopped for the night in a mountain village nestled among huge boulders. It boasted a Baptist church and a Catholic church, bamboo houses for the two main Christian faiths of the Kachins. Rain had been pounding down since late afternoon. Our wet clothes were hung up to dry by a log fire. Roi San toasted her Kachin Army hat, a distinctive sort of engineer's cap, over the fire on a stick. Eventually the downpour ceased, and fireflies zipped around outside.

The next day the hill paths were still clear enough for me to ride. My mule was cranky on the climbs, and had to be kicked a lot, but he broke into a spirited near-gallop on the occasional downhill stretch. The Kachin soldiers, marching along briskly, carried packs and rifles, and short swords in red wooden scabbards. Their uniforms were plain olive drab with red cotton patches bearing the Kachin Army insignia of crossed swords. Some wore a kilt-like fringed burlap apron over their trousers, with pockets for carrying grenades and ammo clips.

The soldiers were as tough as any I'd ever seen, marching for hours without stopping once. They ate handfuls of rice with pounded chilies and thorny wild plants. I never noticed a complaining or argumentative tone from them. Lt. Khun Nawng, a generation older, was just as fit and good-natured, and kept up a swift stride, his spotless civilian sportswear augmented by a pair of borrowed Chinese Army boots like mine. He carried an airline flight bag over one shoulder. It held his military necessities, including a camouflage-pattern Mag flashlight. 'You don't look like you're out in the jungle,' I chided him. 'You look like James Bond checking in First Class at some airport counter.'

For my part, I was in World War II uniform, a roomy khaki shirt and trousers like those worn by the pilots who had not infrequently crashed/parachuted into those very mountains. The China-Burma-India Theater of that war had been distinguished by its daredevil aviators: the Flying Tigers, the Hump Pilots, and others. The Flying Tigers, American quasi-mercenaries based in Burma, then Yunnan with their shark-painted P-40 fighter planes, raided Japanese airfields in China and elsewhere, inflicting great losses. Other Americans flew over 'The Hump', the Himalayan foothills, from India to China and back, in ungainly C-46 transports. They provided the only outside supply route to Chinese Nationalist forces between the shutdown of the Burma Road by Japanese ground troops in Burma, and the against-all-odds creation of another land route, the Ledo Road across northern Burma.

The risk of crashing or being shot down was always with those men, and the lucky ones were pleasantly surprised to be rescued by friendly indigenous people. Kachin units located and took care of hundreds of American flight crew members, escorting them back to safety in India. I could clearly visualize them marching or limping to safety with their tribal rescuers.

We kept mostly to mountain ridges. Other mountains were visible in the distance, endlessly blue. Sometimes we ducked into the shadows of upland rainforest. Mid-afternoon we ended up at a hunter/farmer's house. The nurses and some of the young soldiers and I tromped through his pig yard to bathe in our sarongs at a water-spout. The Christian soldiers had tattoos done by Buddhist spirit-doctors, body-calligraphy of sacred inscriptions. I too, had such tattoos, simple circles inked with a magic potion, three over each elbow, that I'd gotten in 1985. They were supposed to keep me safe from ghosts and bad people.

After the sun left, we sat around the fire in the hunter/farmer's main room, beneath drying ears of corn and animal skins. Roi San, the older of the two nurses, mentioned that she had almost completed the five years service required by her enlistment in the KIO, and was considering calling it quits, getting married, having children. 'Oh, you might as well re-enlist,' Lt. Khun Nawng advised her. 'We are going to get Democracy this year. The Slorc can't hang on much longer—all of Burma even voted against them. Soon we will have Democracy, then we can all enjoy civilian life.' I had thought the same thing myself, every single year since I'd first gotten involved with Burma's resistance. Ever since 1983. Every year I sent my Christmas cards to rebel friends with best wishes for the 'New Year of Victory and Peace'. I could never imagine Burma's military dictatorship lasting much longer. But somehow it did.

I conducted my first Kachin State interview by the hearth, with a twelve-year-old boy. He told me that the Tatmadaw had come there 'one time— they shot our pigs and took our chickens'. I had decided that my journey's project would be to interview children like him, the most unknown element, the most helpless, in that hidden war zone. I'd ask each child a few basic questions, and at some point I would try to get children to draw pictures to put in my report.

The family on whom we were imposing that night was of the Lisu tribe. The people called 'Kachins' were a conglomeration of seven tribes—the Jinghpaw, Maru, Lisu, Lishi, Azi, Nung, and Rawang. Most of the soldiers I was with were Jinghpaw, and the KIO seemed rather Jinghpaw-dominated. The seven Kachin tribes spoke similar dialects and had many cultural traits in common, and all traditionally preferred to live in mountain villages, while the Shans (a mainly Buddhist group with a much larger population) dwelled in the valleys far below. The Kachins were renowned for their prowess in hunting and war. Both vocations were in evidence that night, as I bedded down on a bearskin under a borrowed army blanket.

My mule was left behind when we set off again. It was bad going on foot. The path had narrowed to a slick little trace through rainforest and

1. *Rohingya refugees after the Bangladesh cyclone, 1991.*

2. *Rakhine children, cyclone-swept island, Bangladesh, 1991.*

3. Kachin nurse Roi San on the trail to Pajau, 1991.

4. Aiming front line artillery, Kachin State, 1991.

bamboo thickets. It went up up up and down down down. Then it went, lung-ripping, up again. During a rare brief pause for gulping water from canteens, I asked one of the soldiers to use his sword to cut me a bamboo walking stick, to help me balance on the slippery climb. Everyone had a good laugh about that. 'They say, "like an old lady" about that stick,' Lt. Khun Nawng helpfully translated. Then the trail got really awful. Lau Mae tried out the walking stick concept, and found that she liked it. Soon thereafter the soldier boys began cutting bamboo staffs for themselves too.

We reached a clearing and crouched down for lunch, gobbling chunks of sticky white rice in a steady drip of rain. The leeches found us that afternoon. Apparently the leeches, innumerable, had been waiting, waiting in that remote forest, waiting for some warm-blooded mammal to happen by, the Kachin Army, for instance. Lau Mae was the number one leech bait, and she was mosquito bait too, but she took it well, with giggles. We all wore our trouser-legs rolled up, so we could spot our leeches before they inched higher up to someplace where we'd never find them. I had enough Off DEET spray on me to send all but one extremely desperate leech elsewhere. That one vaulted onto my leg from the foliage and a soldier yanked it back off. The Kachins didn't bother with sissy niceties like salt or cigarettes for leech removal. They just pulled them off and flicked them back into the bush for the next in line, stoically ignoring the streaks of blood from their bite marks.

Despite the leeches, I was glad to find such dense forest in the Kachin State. So much of Burma had been denuded by logging, especially by Thai timber companies which had been granted clearcutting concessions by the Slorc. The Kachin farmers cleared land by slash and burn, but they still had enough room to move around and do that on a rotating basis, and it seemingly hadn't caused much harm in that particular area yet. While the neighboring Shan State had lost its forest cover, the KIO-held territory of Burma's north still included old-growth, never logged regions of evergreen and teak. Just across the border in China, such stands were gone. Severe deforestation there had led to erosion, which had caused floods like the one that had rushed down the river border in late June.

Our path met the river, then disappeared. Before the flood it had followed the west bank, which now was covered by the water or collapsed into it. In single file we found our way gingerly along ledges. Landslides had sent rocks, soil and trees tumbling down to the rushing river, and we stepped across the debris stone by stone. We passed the decomposing head of a brown-maned horse which must have been swept away in the flood. We crossed over to the China side on a long cable bridge, and back on another. The soldiers amused each other by jumping up and down on the flimsy bridges. Back on the Kachin side of the river, we sought another crossing. The jungle and rock slides were getting harder and harder to penetrate and it looked like better footing over in China. But a third cable bridge was gone, destroyed in the flood. We scraped along until we found an enormous gray-barked tree which had—a miracle, the Kachins exclaimed—fallen directly across the river to form a perfect bridge for our use.

The divine intervention tree-bridge brought us over to a settlement of Kachin refugees from Burma living in bamboo stilt houses on the China side. A schoolteacher brought two boys, eleven and six years old, for me to interview. They were often sick with malaria and colds, they told me. When I asked them my last question, 'What do you like to do for fun?' the older boy said 'singing' and the younger replied 'feeding the pigs and chickens'. I gave them colored elastic bands for their wrists as their interviewee reward, to go with the rubber band collections Kachin kids always sported.

I squirted Bactine on the soldiers' leech bites and the nurses fixed up various cuts and scratches. The woman whose house I was staying in sat down in front of me and gave my feet and legs a long, soothing massage. I realized that it was the most prolonged physical contact I'd had since I'd been cold-shouldered by the photojournalist back in Thailand. I had entered into a celibate, pure, fanatical, political existence in the years since then. Other than the punches I took in karate class, nobody touched me much. Now I was on the edge of a flood zone, in a place dead to the world, having my feet brought back to life by a refugee stranger.

My feet were feeling fine when we set off in the morning, which gave me strength to face the day. The morning was full of leeches. We stumbled along wild animal paths in the forest, then in and out of the river shallows and across streams. Leeches waved avidly on the leaves. I kept the Bactine in my pocket so soldiers could spray it on their bites; tough as they were they enjoyed the sting of antiseptic. A leech got inside my shirt and drank blood from my armpit like a bubonic plague lump. Once they get in your clothes you always feel like you're on the verge of an 'African Queen' leech freak-out. I suspected every dribble of sweat down my back of being a leech. Then one parachuted out of a tree to fasten itself right to my jugular vein. My throat-leech filled up fast, a big fat slug when plucked away. I poured *Yunnan Bai Yao*, a Chinese botanical powder, on the bleeding wound to close it up. 'That one was an assassin leech, sent by Ne Win to kill me,' I joked to Lt. Khun Nawng. The Lieutenant was as usual hiking along nonchalantly without a speck of dirt or sweat or blood on his slacks and polo shirt.

It was the kind of day that gives leeches a bad name. Once I had been presenting a 'save the rainforest' lecture in Philadelphia with an entomologist who believed that every creature has its useful place in the ecosystems of the world. 'What about leeches?' I challenged him. 'Oh, leeches exist to keep humans out of the forest,' he explained.

At last our beleaguered party reached a roaring jungle waterfall. La Jong, the cheroot-smoking, heavily-tattooed 3rd Battalion sergeant, over-ruled Lt. Khun Nawng and made it a rice and weed picnic stop, a frolicking in the delicious cool waterfall spray stop. Then we pushed on for just another hour and reached our village for the night. It was Sunday, and the villagers, in bright-colored sarongs and jackets, were returning from their afternoon Baptist services.

Devout though they were, theirs was an opium-growing village. The KIO had pressured them to try a little crop substitution with potato fields on a hillside, but mostly they harvested the opium poppy pod gum, the raw material for heroin. Their opium was gathered up and bought by itinerant Burman merchants who took it down to Hpakant, a jade mining town, they told me. Anything could be bought or sold in Hpakant. The Kachin State was the world's main source of jadeite, the most precious form of jade, and that town was the center for its mining and transport. Although the Slorc controlled Hpakant, the KIO had a piece of most of the jade trade, which was its primary source of income. Kachin rebel customs officers took a cut of the revenue from raw jade rocks going to China and elsewhere in Asia. Translucent imperial jade in pure shades of green, or lavender, smoke gray, pale blue, white, even honey gold, would be carved out of the heavy rounded stones.

The wooden house where Lt. Khun Nawng, the nurses and I would stay belonged to a Kachin World War II veteran, who reminisced about an American training officer he'd had back then. By firelight I played tic tac toe with Roi San and one of the younger soldiers. 'Tomorrow—no leeches!' Lt. Khun Nawng promised us. At around midnight, as everyone else slept, I heard the World War II veteran's ancient-looking father creep out to the adjacent kitchen building. 'He was ashamed to smoke opium in front of us,' explained Lt. Khun Nawng in the morning. 'He is a mission school boy, taught by Catholic nuns when he was small. So he thought the KIO and the foreigner lady would not approve his narcotic. Actually, we KIO allow such old ones their smoke. It is a kind of medicine for their health. We just want for opium growing and heroin refining to stop in our area.'

As soon as we set off in the morning we waded right through the river, which had become wider and shallower, without taking our shoes off. I had bandaids over blisters formed on my heels by my too-wide boots. River sand got in between the bandaids and the blisters, rubbing my heels raw quickly. We kept going through water and up hillsides, gathering thirsty leeches as we went, but the day was not so dreadful. We stopped for lunch, and later for glasses of hot tea in a village, and then we climbed rocks to another village where we would spend the night. It was sunny enough to bathe there. Lau Mae had head lice, perhaps from sleeping on a bearskin, which prompted me to undo my hair from its week-old braid and wash it.

Some of the soldiers had leech bite infection sores, prickly heat rashes, septic blisters. Roi San tried moxibustion, an old Asian therapy, on a few, trapping smoking pieces of paper in tea glasses over their sores to cure them. The soldiers bandaided each other and sat arm in arm, a happy, affectionate group. Probably they would have rather been out fighting the Tatmadaw, but they didn't seem to mind escorting me and Lt. Khun Nawng north through the flood zone, even with the leeches infesting the way.

The flash flood had struck violently at that village on a June night, sweeping away riverside rice paddies, homes and the one school. It had also wrecked the only civilian hospital in the area. Serious cases now had to be carried far away to a KIO military hospital. Our nurses handed out aspirin powder and vitamin C tablets to the villagers. I noticed that some women there had pus-filled sores or rashes on their upper arms. 'That is from the injection doctor,' Lt. Khun Nawng told me. 'It is not really a doctor, just a man who will go from village to village and give injections for their health. His needle is not so clean so she gets like that.'

'Injection doctors—that has got to be stopped!' I said, shaking my head, 'Tests were just done near here, down in the city of Bhamo. More than 80 percent of the heroin users there are HIV positive now. An "injection doctor" could spread that far up into these hills very easily. Don't they know about AIDS?'

'They heard of it, I think. Many in our land have it now. But they don't know so much how they get it.'

I asked the man in whose house we stayed why the flood had occurred, expecting an answer involving China-side deforestation. 'Because we are getting very near to the end of the world,' he replied, without hesitation. I thought of the devastation I'd seen from the cyclone in Bangladesh a few months before. 'Maybe you're right,' I told the Kachin farmer. That night Lt. Khun Nawng got his short-wave radio out of his airline bag and tuned in the BBC. We received a report of a *coup d'etat* attempt in Russia, Yeltsin holding out, Gorbachev missing. Maybe the end of the world starts in Moscow, I speculated.

The world, leeches and all, was still around in the morning. I took group photos of our tattooed, cheerful, hard-bitten band by another waterfall. We crossed the river and again sand chafed my blistered heels. We were on a flat area, following the river bank on the China side, so I took off the canvas boots and put on a pair of sandals. Immediately I picked up the pace, keeping up with the strongest soldiers in my comfortable footwear. We marched jauntily down a long stretch of beach and the sun came out. A Chinese sawmill appeared, and nearby a proper bridge spanned the river. I walked quickly over it among the soldiers so I wouldn't be identified as a foreigner. Trees were few now, and as I followed the shadeless logging road on the Kachin side of the bridge, I began to feel exhausted, dog tired, dead tired. I realized that I wasn't sweating anymore. I began to stagger along in a dull state. I tried to think of waterfalls, of standing under waterfalls, of drinking ice-cold Champagne. Our group had spread out, so on some parts of the road I was alone for a while. Left by myself, I would crumple to my knees, then force myself back up and trudge forward.

Eventually I caught up with the others, who were sitting in the shade of a few remaining trees. Back in 1988, while marching across far southern Burma with another ethnic army, the Mons, I had decided that the best way to make it through was to keep all complaints to myself and keep going no matter what. This time, even though I didn't say anything, the Kachins knew I was in trouble. Lt. Khun Nawng went back to the China side, and returned with a can of *Jian Li Bai*, a Chinese orange soda-pop 'sports drink' for me. Roi San got out a hypodermic syringe, ready to revive me with something from her box of ampoules. 'I feel better already,' I assured her, imagining the orange pop tuning up the electrolytes and not at all eager to get any kind of shot in the Kachin State.

'A Chinese police, plain clothes, was at the shop where I got your orange drink,' Lt. Khun Nawng commented. 'We have to be careful around here.' Our group headed uphill along more logging roads. I drank another *Jian Li Bai* and kept moving. We went over to the Chinese side again, and walked right into a timber camp. Sun-addled though I was, I grabbed the autofocus camera out of my shoulder bag and snapped a couple of photos of stacked-up Burmese teak wood. I noticed a crimson Chinese flag flying over the sawmill. We closed ranks and hurried through as fast as we could without actually running. A bridge over a stream took us into a town. 'We are here. This is Laiza. This is a KIO town,' Lt. Khun Nawng said to me with a broad smile.

The nurses and I were given a room in the Laiza township office building. Roi San braided white flowers into Lau Mae's hair. I donated a gold ribbon with which to tie her braids. My energy was thoroughly depleted. For hours I sat in a deck chair on the second floor balcony, staring out at the rain-swept town and eating plate after plate of juicy pineapple. Work elephants with umbrella-carrying Kachin soldiers on their backs lumbered down the street like a circus parade. The town consisted mainly of thatched bamboo houses and was freely roamed by ducks, mules, pigs and cattle. A bustling market sold trade goods from China to be smuggled further into the Kachin State and beyond. Laiza held some 700 families, mostly Kachins and Shans who'd fled Tatmadaw controlled regions deeper inside Burma. I'd spend three nights there, resting up, Lt. Khun Nawng told me.

At a noodle shop run by a Shan, Lt. Khun Nawng gathered a few adults who wanted to be interviewed by me. Watched over by the inevitable Phoebe Cates poster, I tape recorded a Shan woman who traveled back and forth between the China border and the Kachin State city of Bhamo, trading in smuggled Chinese goods—flashlights, batteries, soft drinks. It was not a safe way to make a living. 'It is very difficult for people to go out trading anywhere,' she told me. 'If the traders go out to buy and sell, the Slorc soldiers are on the riverboats, and some are on the way, we have to stop, they search our articles and ask where we go. They ask, "This kind of merchandise, where are you going with it?" They ask for money. They disturb the merchant traders in every way. So we feel very upset about it. A very difficult life.'

I spoke with another Shan woman in her twenties who had fled her home village for Laiza. Where she came from, 'the Slorc government, every time they took porters. Until there were no men and boys in the village. They took all to be porters! And in Shwebo district there's a ruby mine, the Slorc government has secured, and they took porters to work in the mines.' About pay for the ruby miners, she reported, 'they give nothing'.

I also interviewed two brothers who were of the Gurkha ethnic group, descended from Hindu Nepalese soldiers brought to Burma during the British colonial period and World War II. As Gurkhas, the brothers had been issued Foreigners' Registration identity cards (the kind the Rohingyas were stuck with) instead of Burmese citizenship. 'We suffer so many tortures,' one of the brothers said of their ethnic group. 'In my village, one of the Gurkhas was just going to gather some bamboo and wood, and the Slorc military personnel met him in the jungle and they took him, and broke his jaw. Just like that, we suffered so many troubles. They always take Gurkhas for porters. If we don't go, they beat us.' The brothers said that they personally had been taken as porters by the Slorc 'many, many times' and that the Slorc confiscated much of their rice crop in their old village. They had just arrived in Laiza, leaving one step ahead of the Tatmadaw.

I visited the military hospital, which was occupied by skeletal malaria patients on IV drips, soldiers and mothers with children. I went by the Laiza high school, which was said to be the best in KIO territory, and I looked in on a rambunctious kindergarten. I asked Laiza middle school teachers to collect kids' drawings for me, and they produced a sheaf of expressive pictures, all in pencil on lined copybook paper. Many were idyllic picture-maps of Laiza or the villages the children had left, with homes on stilts, flocks of chickens, elephants and extravagant flowering plants. War scenes depicted not only infantry skirmishes and jet bombers, but civilian porters being beaten with sticks by the Tatmadaw. The picture that revealed the most pain was not the most facile in its drawing—crude wobbly people shaped like bowling pins with legs were Tatmadaw soldiers (in derby-looking hats) and their captive porters. The porters had baskets on their backs and some of them were children and black spots of weeping projected from their eyes.

Many of the young artists sketched scenes of malaria, the bane of their childhoods: little patients shivering under blankets and mosquitoes the size of hawks hovering overhead. The drawings were heartbreaking. 'I will treasure these and I'll display them in my country,' I promised the teachers. A few of the refugee schoolchildren came to the township office for interviews, perching primly on the meeting room chairs, hands folded. They told me about the Tatmadaw coming to their old villages, some very far away from Laiza, and their familes' flights to safety. Someday, the children hoped, they would study to become teachers themselves, or doctors, or pursue whatever profession Bible school might produce.

Following the interview session, the local chapter of the Kachin Women's Association appeared at the office and presented me with a black sarong embroidered with the interlocking diamond patterns favored by the Jinghpaws. They told me that when I got to Pajau, other Association members would be my hostesses. The women also brought a basket of traditional welcoming packets of sticky rice wrapped in leaves, which I shared with my 3rd Brigade companions.

With one of the Laiza teachers providing English translation, I asked my friends, the 3rd Brigade infantrymen and military nurses, to tell me about their lives, their aspirations. When I questioned her, Roi San (who had always been the most lighthearted of the unit) turned solemn. A free spirit undaunted by every obstacle, who wore golden fan-shaped earrings with her olive drab uniform, Roi San frowned, near tears, when I asked her what I'd meant to be a funny question, what didn't she like about being in the army. 'The worst is seeing the drug addicts,' she told me. 'The opium and heroin addicts in the villages. I couldn't believe people do that do themselves.' Other soldiers told me they were depressed by constant requests to bury the corpses of heroin overdose victims, which the villagers would not touch.

I also interviewed a couple of young school teachers and two female doctors. The doctors said that they had no way of knowing how much HIV and AIDS infection had reached their area, as they had no tests for it, although with plenty of heroin addicts around they supposed the disease was increasing. A KIO education official who was translating added, 'We heard the American movie star Rock Hudson died of AIDS,' to show me that they weren't completely uninformed.

The school teachers asked me for English pronunciation advice about the words 'situation', 'condition' and 'circumstance'. They told me that 'thanks to American missionaries we Kachins have a written language'. Those missionaries had indeed introduced the Kachins to the Roman alphabet, but had unfortunately neglected to add tone marks, making the highly tonal language extremely hard to read. Even native speakers had to decipher and guess their way through Kachin texts.

Roi San and Lau Mae cried when we had to say goodbye. Lau Mae's canvas boots were falling apart, so I gave her mine—I'd be riding the rest of the way. They would be jungle-marching back to their base the way we'd come. I walked down to the Laiza bridge with the 3rd Brigade group and watched until they were gone.

The morning after they left, I continued on my way north with Lt. Khun Nawng, a few Laiza troops and a new mule. We took an easy path up into the mountains. My obstinate bay mule treated the landscape as a salad bar and I constantly had to pull its face out of the weeds. As I rode through leafy tunnels, low overhanging branches attacked my face so I got off and walked. We went uphill for several hours, then slept in a quiet little village.

The next day we found ourselves in a dark rainforest, lined with slender ribs of black bamboo. The forest floor was carpeted with moss and tiny violet-like flowers, other miniature blossoms, delicate ferns. Orchids and other epiphytes dangled from the mossy trees. I saw no wild animals, but I felt it must be the realm of the tiger, and the red panda. It was a medicinal forest. The Kachin State had been known to plant-hunters in the British colonial days for its wealth of flora, and had long been a source of botanical cures. I hoped that this shadowy paradise could be preserved from the depredations of the timber trade and investigated for new drugs, new magic potions.

Out of the moss forest and still climbing, we crossed a meadow of thistles, which my mule did not disdain, and entered the cold zone. On the highest peak of our route, Padang Hkawn, we entered a KIO base which had been seized from the Tatmadaw, then defended in a series of bloody battles throughout the previous winter. The base commander, Lt. Hkyet Naw Lar, an English speaker in a pea-green pullover, welcomed us to his zigzag bunkers of earth and woven saplings. Fog wrapped the edges of the base so we could not see the Tatmadaw's positions below us to the west, and they presumably couldn't see us. The trees on the peak were all broken, blasted by artillery, but Padang Hkawn hadn't been shelled in a whole month because of the fog.

Lt. Hkyet Naw Lar showed me their old Chinese anti-aircraft gun, which resembled a Victorian dentist's chair. He told me about the Tatmadaw sieges of his base, showing me two collages of snapshots that he kept framed under glass. One frame held photos of dead Tatmadaw soldiers, sprawled on the hillsides, stripped of their boots and anything else useful. The other displayed a collection of wallet pictures taken from those enemy bodies. He was especially fond of a studio portrait of a Tatmadaw captain and his wife. 'High rank. My troops killed him,' he said with a slight smirk, 'and we buried him somewhere on the mountain. I suppose his wife wonders what happened to him.'

'They don't care much about their soldiers,' Lt. Hkyet Naw Lar said. 'They favor the "human wave" against us, that sacrifices so many.' Hundreds, even thousands, of the regime's troops would throw themselves against rebel forts like Padang Hkawn. The Tatmadaw's casualties would be grievous, but eventually the attackers might break through and over-run the base, especially when the Kachins' bullets were depleted. 'We run out of ammunition all the time,' Kachin soldiers had told me. The Kachin Army had previously bought their weaponry from the neighboring Burma Communist Party, which had obtained plenty as revolutionary aid from China. But then China had quit backing the BCP, and the BCP fell apart. So since 1989, the Kachin Army had suffered an arms shortage, and particularly an ammunition shortage.

Lt. Hkyet Naw Lar gave me a look at his homemade arsenal. 'We don't have enough ammo, so we make our own bombs to throw,' he said, gesturing to an array of primitive pipe-grenades and a landmine improvised from a hollowed-out rock. 'We put plastic explosives in pipes and Heineken beer cans.' They purchased the green cans of beer in China, along with the 'agricultural' explosives and pipe. The Kachins' main defense was straight out of the forest, though. Padang Hkawn bristled like a porcupine with punji stakes. Sharpened fire-hardened bamboo, sometimes poisoned with rotten pigs' liver or other substances, the stakes were thrust in the ground to pierce the feet and legs of advancing troops. Kachin guerrillas had taught their American comrades the use of punji stakes, and much else, during World War II.

When the British, American and Chinese forces fought on land to drive the Japanese back out of Burma in World War II, they could not have done it without the Kachins. Jungle warfare outfits such as the British-led Chindits and the American combat unit known as Merrill's Marauders penetrated deep into Burma, completely dependent on Kachin scouts and guides. The Kachins led the way into forbidding terrain, a process described by the acerbic American commander of Chinese troops, Gen. 'Vinegar Joe' Stilwell: 'We have to go in through a rat hole and dig the hole as we go.'

Kachins had been prominent in the pre-war Burma Rifles, a colonial military force, and they fought on for the Allies, enduring punitive village destruction and killings of Kachin civilians by Japanese soldiers. The Kachins formed the Kachin Levies, and also participated in the Americans' clandestine Office of Strategic Services Detachment 101, gathering crucial intelligence, rescuing bailed-out aviators, raiding and ambushing the Japanese. The Kachins' attacks were so subtle that most Japanese soldiers never saw a Kachin face while falling prey to their bullets and artful traps.

Paid their war wages in silver coins and sometimes in opium, the Kachins managed to keep parts of their northern land wholly free of the Japanese invaders. Of course they fully expected more of a reward when peace finally came—not just medals, but autonomy, if not independence. Forty-four years later, some of the Kachins' old comrades in arms still felt guilty about leaving the indigenous people of Burma high and dry after the war. Aging British officers wrote letters to their Parliament demanding condemnation of Ne Win and the Slorc. A group of old American veterans of the Office of Strategic Services tried to play along with the Slorc junta in order to build a school for the Kachins, but were only allowed into Burma's Shan State, not the actual land of the Kachins who had served their cause.

The Kachins had taught the foreign soldiers everything they needed to know to survive—how to find water in the dry season, how to snare and grill a jungle rat for protein, how to make bamboo weaponry. Charlton Ogburn, a lieutenant with Merrill's Marauders, wrote, 'the Marauders took an immediate fancy to the Kachins...they made us think of a Robin Hood version of the Boy Scouts'. Now I was among the Kachins in the 1990s and they were still whittling bamboo and hardening it in the fire for war. 'I'll show you our new device!' Lt. Hkyet Naw Lar said, grinning proudly. 'The triple punji stake!' Three bamboo stakes lashed together, its sharp points stuck out in all directions, making it harder to avoid than the classic model. I stared at the new device, and the landmine. The Kachins were fighting the Tatmadaw with sticks and stones.

We spent the night in a bunker at Padang Hkawn. Lt. Hkyet Naw Lar showed me the book he was reading, *The Sicilian* by Mario Puzo. He broke out the medicinal Chinese wine to share with Lt. Khun Nawng. It was so medicinal it even said 'Shake Well Before Using' on the bottle. A wood-stove heated our hiding hole. I had my own room with a paraffin lamp and two army blankets and I got only one flea bite.

Leaving Padang Hkawn, we made our way down into another extraordinary rainforest, like the most hallucinatory botanical garden. A flat path wound through its corridor of moss-coated trees, ferns, vines, orchids, flowering herbs, vaults of a rare kind of thin bamboo, medicinal plants with flat red-veined leaves. Not only tigers but elves, *djinns,* celestial dancing *apsaras,* had to live there. I had never been in a forest so exquisite, and I had been in many.

The rainforest gave way to open country. Former opium poppy fields, abandoned at the command of the KIO and not yet planted with substitute crops, were abloom with wildflowers. Queen Anne's lace, buttercups, dusty miller, or their Asian counterparts, grew there in profusion along with thistles and many other flowers I couldn't start to name. The meadows smelled like the penny candy counter in an old general store. My mule, somewhat subdued in the dark forest, went hog-wild in the meadows, stuffing its jaws with messy bouquets.

We traveled on for a few hours through more forest and more high ex-opium meadows. And then Pajau came into sight—many low woven bamboo buildings nestled among scruffy hills. The place had a distinctly shabby appearance, particularly because of the roofs made of leaf-thatch overlaid with ragged plastic sheeting. In the mid-1980s Bertil and Hseng-Noung Lintner had stayed at a well-established Kachin headquarters called Pajau, but since then the Tatmadaw had managed to destroy that place. The KIO had relocated and applied the old name to a decidedly downscale camp. I rode up to an empty reception hall, where Lt. Khun Nawng and I waited for a while, drinking the tea that was brought in for us and chewing our way through a bowl of White Rabbit vanilla taffy.

When the Kachin Women's Association had assembled to welcome me, I was brought uphill by jeep. The women were all very soignée in their sparkly embroidered sarongs and colorful handknit sweaters. Among them was Ja Seng Hkawn, one of the younger Kachin Women's Association members. Ja Seng Hkawn was the daughter of Chairman Brang Seng. She was in her twenties, married to a young KIO officer, and quite obviously pregnant. She had Phoebe Cates-style short thick hair. An English Literature graduate of Mandalay University in central Burma, Ja Seng Hkawn would be my translator at Pajau, as well as my sister due to my 'adoption' by her parents in Kunming.

The English curriculum at Mandalay had been 'rubbish', Ja Seng Hkawn told me, but only her brother had been allowed to go overseas for higher education. It would have been considered politically unseemly for all the Chairman's children to get such a privilege. Ja Seng Hkawn was close to her parents, but had been raised much of the time by relatives in Myitkyina, the largest city in the Kachin State. It was a city firmly under the dictatorship's control. Ruthless as Burma's military authorities were, I could not figure out why they hadn't held hostage the children of one of their most formidable foes, Chairman Brang Seng. The police had harassed them, Ja Seng Hkawn told me, but it had never gone too far. It seemed as if there existed some weird understanding between the two sides, in spite of the battles always raging in the region.

Ja Seng Hkawn had joined the Kachin rebel army after university, worked as a War Office clerk at the Pajau headquarters, and retired from the service due to a strange illness that dragged on for two years. She'd finally recovered after ritually changing her name. Now she spent a lot of time on Kachin Women's Association projects. Her mother, Madame Brang Seng, had started the Association as a vehicle for charitable works by the wives of Kachin Army officers. A member of the women's group, Lu Ra, would host me in her bamboo cabin during my stay at Pajau. Lu Ra, another Mandalay University grad, was married to General Zau Mai, a famous Kachin Army commander now off on the western front near the India border. Awaiting his return, she stayed at Pajau with their small boy and girl. Lu Ra spoke English well, laughed often, and like many of the Pajau women, wore her long hair in a sort of 1940s back-sweep with ornamental combs.

Lu Ra's cabin was dirt-floored and drafty, but it had a roaring wood-stove. Soldiers kept it stocked with pine logs. The camp generators powered electric lights until about 8:00 each night. I had a bed in an alcove off the main room, with a heap of warm quilts and embroidered pillows. Someone asked me what else I needed. 'Could I have something to read, something in English?' I asked them. A compulsive reader, I had been reduced to perusing the labels on my clothes and the printing on candy wrappers on the way to Pajau. I expected my request to be met with a stack of political and human rights documents, or maybe a stray Puzo novel. Instead I was provided with two fairly recent issues of *Newsweek*, and coffee-table picture books about Berlin and France.

Ja Seng Hkawn appeared for tea and cookies with me just after sunrise. She mentioned that people were rather amazed that I had made it to Pajau 'the hard way' from the 3rd Brigade base. Lt. Khun Nawng was telling everyone that I was like 'the sister of Rambo', so tough, that I was much stronger than Mr Bernard, the Swiss reporter who didn't have to walk on his trip. He was making me much more Rambo in the telling of it, how brave I was to cross through the Chinese logging camp and even take photos—when in actuality I'd been just following along in a daze.

I learned from Ja Seng Hkawn that a pair of Japanese university students on an elaborate video class project were now visiting the nearby main camp of the Kachin State ABSDF. Those two boys I had seen in Ruili, all right. Being Asian, they'd been able to pass for Chinese and cross right over the border near Pajau to go visit the student rebels. 'We find those ABSDF people a problem, in a way,' Ja Seng Hkawn told me. 'They fight each other, even shoot each other. They all want to be the leader, it seems, being of the same age and education, and arrived at the war zone at the same time. Also, they can behave very badly in Kachin villages, so the villagers think they are just more bad Burmans with guns. Our KIO gave those people their ABSDF uniforms and some weapons, but they won't take leadership from us.'

Late in the morning, Lu Ra and I were joined at the front room table by some KIO officers for the main meal of the day, a glorious repast of white rice, fried pork, potatoes, and forest vegetables. Like the soldiers on my trip north, the Kachins at Pajau ate fast and ate massive amounts of rice. They were taken aback that I managed only one bowl of rice at a sitting, and urged me to have two or three more, to keep my strength up. I was too thin, they said. They were also appalled that I was unmarried. That was nearly unheard of among the Kachins, they said, to be single after the teens or early twenties. Ja Seng Hkawn told me there was a lot of pressure to 'reproduce'. The Kachins were not a big ethnic group, estimated at only a million or so. They had large families for the most part, either because of lack of birth control availability, or (among the revolutionaries) with the political goal of increasing the Kachin population.

'I really just hope I have twins and get it over with,' Ja Seng Hkawn sighed. 'I know I must have at least two children, but I don't want do go through the pregnancy again. It is tiresome for me and I still have four months more.'

'You're getting big already,' I noted. 'Maybe it's triplets...'

Young officers from all the areas of KIO control had gathered at Pajau for a refresher training course in strategy and command. Maj. Pan Awng, a legendary guerrilla tactician much feared by the Tatmadaw, was in charge of the course. The Major, a slightly built, multi-faceted man, believed in trying out new things, so he had procured a Chinese 'Learn Ballroom Dancing' videotape and sprung it on the young officers. In between the classes in map reading and reconnaissance and demolition, the officers (all male) pushed the assembly hall benches back and paired up. Following along with the tape by glancing over their shoulders, with Maj. Pan Awng translating the instructions, the officers counted steps in the most awkward cotillion imaginable. Soldier girls from the headquarters offices hung around the sidelines to giggle and catcall. The videotape ran over and over, repeating the basic steps, but nobody seemed to get any better. 'Let's go,' Ja Seng Hkawn said, after we watched for a while. 'We'll come back to the hall for church later this afternoon. Better music, I promise you.'

The benches got put back in place and a visiting Kachin Catholic priest with a bad cold presided over an ecumenical service. It was mostly singing, Catholic and Baptist hymns translated into Kachin and given a whomping disco beat by Maj. Pan Awng who played an electronic keyboard equipped with percussion effects.

In the evening at Lu Ra's cabin I had my formal welcoming. The Kachin Women's Association members brought in their traditional baskets filled with sticky rice packets. I exchanged toasts with the KIO's Central Committee, glasses of harsh rice wine and Chinese-brewed Steinlager beer. The Kachins adored Chinese beer and the bottles, buried neck down, made decorative green borders all around the buildings of Pajau. For Baptists, they sure didn't mind drinking. It seemed to be considered 'medicinal' by most people, and women as well as men took their 'medicine' regularly. I gave a speech about the miraculous tree that fell over the river and made a bridge, and I promised to stand with the Kachin Army when they took the city of Myitkyina away from the Tatmadaw. It didn't seem so impossible then. The Kachin Army was strong, it was aggressive, it was tactically more sophisticated than the Tatmadaw. 'Tonight we will launch attacks at nine different places at the same time,' I was told.

I put on the sweater and jacket I was glad I'd packed, to go for a walk in the morning. Cold wind always blew through Pajau while I was there—and it was August. In the wintertime snow would sometimes sugar the ground. Wearing sweaters layered over sarongs, Ja Seng Hkawn and other Kachin Women's Association members hiked out of the headquarters camp with me, up a dirt road to their rehabilitation settlement for badly wounded soldiers. I was shown a row of sewing machines they'd purchased for some of the men to use. The women introduced me to the amputees (missing hands, feet, legs) who stayed there in bamboo barracks insulated with cardboard and plastic. The soldiers had no artificial legs, using crude heavy wooden crutches instead. The Chinese artificial limbs were not good, the soldiers said—too uncomfortable, and probably too expensive anyway. I promised to send them information on the limbs that were being manufactured by Cambodian landmine victims in low-tech workshops.

As I met the wounded soldiers, who included Shans and Gurkhas as well as Kachins in their maimed ranks, it became clear that their own homemade pipe grenades had wounded as many as had Tatmadaw bullets. I talked with a gruff forty-year-old Kachin sergeant who estimated that he had killed 'two or three hundred' Tatmadaw soldiers in his time with the Kachin Army. His killing days had come to an end when his own lead-pipe grenade had blown both hands off at a frontline base. 'When it happened, I held steady, asked God for help, and walked over to find a nurse,' he told me. Walked over. With his hands blown off.

I asked the Kachin Women's Association members about psychological casualties among the soldiers in their project. They didn't understand what I was talking about. I tried to explain shell-shock, post-traumatic stress disorder. That was apparently an alien concept in the Kachin warrior universe. Finally one of the women seemed to catch on and said, 'Oh, yes, there is one officer who was wounded and he went quite mad. Never quite right since then. He must be looked after all the time now.'

'How was he wounded?' I asked.

'In a battle with the enemy he got shot in the head.'

As wind howled around Lu Ra's cabin that night I took an anti-malarial chloroquin tablet. Immediately after our arrival at Pajau, Lt. Khun Nawng had come down with an attack of malaria, the fever-inducing parasite injected in his bloodstream by a mosquito he'd encountered on our way north. He was treating it with a new Chinese remedy. So far the malaria pills I habitually took were suppressing any symptoms. No mosquitoes infested Pajau itself, it was far too cold for them. I didn't see any kind of bugs there, but furry rats scurried around in the rafters of the cabin. I could hear them running through the bamboo roof poles, using them as tunnels from room to room. I had wild *Alice in Wonderland* dreams, perhaps from the chloroquin.

Following the rehabilitation settlement visit, I went on an overnight Kachin Women's Association field trip to a village further down the same dirt road. We walked there with a couple of soldiers carrying AK-47s to guard us against any sudden Tatmadaw raid, or particularly foolhardy bandits after the jade jewelry. The officers' wives always wore precious jade rings and earrings, all their families' portable wealth. Some of them had enough money to go shopping in China from time to time. Ja Seng Hkawn had even invested in her own little sweater-shop business in a Chinese border town. Still, none of them were strangers to revolutionary hardship. Most had spent their younger years in cold frontline outposts, planting rice, tending the wounded, being soldiers themselves. Lu Ra, who seemed so serene and good humored, was really constantly worried about the health of her children. Because it was up above the mosquito zone, Pajau was more salubrious than most of Burma, but Lu Ra's son and daughter had suffered from kidney problems and tuberculosis, and often coughed all night. Her third child had fallen ill and died only months before.

In the village, we visited a kindergarten where toddlers bundled up in layer after layer of clothing were started off on their educations. The children bounced around a bamboo platform in the unheated kindergarten hut, and chanted their ABCs for me and sang a song or two. Most of them had circles and stripes of *thanaka* or baby power applied to their faces as decorations by loving mothers. The two Kachin Women's Association funded kindergarten teachers laughed constantly, delighted with their incredibly cute pupils. But the wide-eyed three and four year olds were completely serious in demeanor, so intent on the tasks of memorizing and reciting all those letters and numbers and rhymes.

Ja Seng Hkawn and I entered a maternal health clinic that the Kachin Women's Association had recently set up. 'The village women have a meeting here each month,' Ja Seng Hkawn said, 'and they can all be Kachin Women's Association members. They don't have to pay dues.' An American health worker from a missionary family long associated with the Kachins had visited Pajau earlier that year, and the women were putting her advice on mother and child health care into practice. Posters on nutrition and how to make oral rehydration salts to treat diarrhea were tacked to the clinic's woven walls. A sling scale hung from the ceiling, so babies could be weighed in order to assess their development. A local mother set her healthy-looking red-cheeked baby girl in it. The baby wore a bib made of camouflage material, an old uniform scrap, over her fuzzy jacket. A lot of the village kids were dressed in bits and pieces of old Kachin Army uniforms, as well as the cartoon flannels and ruffled pinafores available from the China trade.

We went on to the village middle school, a long building where the drafty bamboo slat walls were decorated with world maps and wild orchids. Some of the teachers were in the ABSDF. When they asked if they could correspond with me, Ja Seng Hkawn, untrusting, gave them my Kachin name, Hkawn Shawng, and the Pajau War Office as my address. 'The ABSDF camp near Pajau has sixty people,' she commented as we left the middle school. 'We've heard that twenty of them have now been jailed as spies by the others! We must beware of them.'

A Kachin Army officer's family put us up for the night, and I interviewed the children for my report. They played in the dirt yard afterwards, taking bunches of rubber bands off their wrists and looping them into a jump rope. That game of rubber band jumping was by far the most popular Kachin children's pursuit, rivaled only by kicking a soccer ball around. Their complete lack of toys surprised me. I knew that even the poorest children in the world devised dolls or cars or guns from whatever materials they might find around. But not one Kachin kid I'd met had anything like that. Even the Pajau elite's children had scarcely an item from the gigantic Chinese toy industry. It appeared that the young Kachins had a cooperative culture, much more interested in group games than ownership of things. Rubber bands were their only material currency, their echo of the adults' jade ornaments.

I roomed with Ja Seng Hkawn that night. As we lay under thick pink Chinese blankets in a war zone room decorated with puppy and kitten posters, she whispered, 'I must tell you something else about those ABSDF. Some of them plotted to kill our KIO Central Committee. Earlier this month, they invited our leaders to a feast at their place. Just before, though, one of their spies confessed, and we found out that they had planned to poison the soup. The Slorc has very cleverly sent them here. Poisoning is one kind of plot. Also, sometimes in the winter when the fog clears, the Tatmadaw will try to shell or bomb us at Pajau. Now these ABSDF with their spies know all about our position. It will be the worse for us.'

I wasn't yet sure if the ABSDF infiltration was a real concern, or a figment of Ja Seng Kawn's own prejudice. At Pajau, I had visited the quarters she and her husband shared with other young officers, and we'd snacked on *laphet thoke*, a delicious, caffeinated Burman salad made with pickled green tea leaves and crunchy nuts. 'We hate the Burmans, but their food is not bad,' Ja Seng Hkawn had commented. In some areas of Burma, the flight of idealistic revolutionary students from the cities to the borders had convinced other ethnic groups that not all Burmans were all bad, but that certainly hadn't happened among the Kachins.

Back in Pajau, having read every single word of the *Newsweeks*, even the sports and the masthead and the subscription information, I got into the photo books, lingering over captions about cheese-making in France and the Wall formerly bisecting Berlin. For a more intellectual diversion, Maj. Pan Awng asked Ja Seng Hkawn and me to come to the assembly hall to observe a debate held between two teams of young officers. The debating topic was 'Is the armed struggle or political action more important?' To further challenge the officers' mental agility, the debate was held not in Kachin but in Burmese, which Ja Seng Hkawn translated for me. We were rooting for the pro-armed struggle side, and not just because her husband

5 (right, top). The Heineken can grenade at Padang Hkawn, 1991.
6 (right, bottom). Lau Mae with her leaf umbrella, 1991.

was on that team. But the 'political action is more important' group won the debate, citing Gandhi, Aung San Suu Kyi, Jane Fonda's anti-Vietnam War activities, and peace accords in the Middle East in the course of their arguments. The other side tried in vain to counter them by saying, 'OK then, why don't the four of you leave your guns here and go to the frontline with only propaganda?'

Interestingly, both sides considered cease-fire agreements with the Slorc to be a danger of the other's approach. The 'armed' side asserted that being too caught up in politics could lead to terrible mistakes such as a compromise with the enemy, while the 'political' side believed that being politically naive even if militarily strong would cause a group to be manipulated by the Slorc into a cease-fire. The latter point was expressed by the 'political' team leader, a captain who had been in a unit commanded by Matu Naw, so despised for having broken away from the KIO and thrown his lot in with the Slorc.

The debate confirmed the mood I had sensed among the Kachin military. Although their Chairman Brang Seng openly sought a 'peaceful solution' to Burma's warfare, his soldiers seemed to reject any thought of stand-down or compromise. They were in this to fight, and they looked to their leaders for a way to win the war, not merely survive it. Kachin officers had assured me that their Chairman was traveling overseas all the time because he was 'looking for arms for us', when I knew full well he was looking for a broker for peace talks between the ethnic groups of Burma and the Slorc. After all, I had first met up with him in Atlanta, home of ex-President Jimmy Carter's 'Conflict Resolution' think tank.

Following the debate a talent show was presented, with various singers backed by a War Office rock and roll band. Ja Seng Hkawn went up on stage and took the microphone, announcing, 'I dedicate this song for our special guest from America,' and proceeded to croon the Carpenters oldie 'There's A Kind of Hush' to much applause. Ja Seng Hkawn was known for her singing, and a couple of locally produced cassettes of revolutionary pop tunes featured her voice, with her picture on the labels.

Ja Seng Hkawn was a celebrity at Pajau, and another celebrity, a Kachin traveling under the German name Sigrid, had just arrived from Kunming. A member of the traditional Kachin aristocracy, Sigrid had married a German who later died in an airplane crash in Burma. Sigrid had raised their son in Europe, but had become increasingly involved in Kachin politics as an assistant to Chairman Brang Seng since 1988. Ja Seng Hkawn introduced her to me at the talent show.

7 (left, top). Manipuri dancers, Imphal, 1992.
8 (left bottom). AIDS prevention billboard, Manipur, Northeast India, 1992.

'I hear your trip was very hard,' Sigrid said, her English tinged with a German accent. She wore jeans and an oversized blue pullover, and her hair was piled up haphazardly, all very un-Kachin, very Euro. 'I am really dying for a cappuccino,' she told me.

'Well, we are about 3,000 miles from the nearest espresso bar. You'll have to settle for instant coffee with condensed milk. But we have some chocolate biscuits at Lu Ra's place,' I offered. We climbed the hill to the cabin and talked long into the night there. Sigrid was planning to pay a visit to the ABSDF camp. 'Don't order the soup,' I cautioned, but I also asked her if she would arrange for the ABSDF leaders to come over to Pajau so I could meet them.

The Kachin Women's Association held another ceremony for me in the morning. This time I was dressed up in traditional Jinghpaw finery. Lu Ra borrowed the outfit for me to wear. The Jinghpaw women's garments were so elaborate that they had become heirlooms, brought out only for special occasions like weddings and dance performances. I put on the knee-length woven red wool sarong and matching leggings, and the black velvet jacket trimmed with silver disks the size of silver dollars. Then I was trimmed like a Christmas tree by Lu Ra, Ja Seng Hkawn and Mai Mai, one of the girls from the War Office. They pinned my hair up and tied an embroidered headdress over it. Necklaces of silver fringes and silver circlets, plus pearls and coral, wound around my throat. Hoops of rattan rested on my hips and a red sash bound my waist. Somebody's pink lipstick, a swoop of eye-liner, and I was worthy of photo ops. I posed with the Kachin Women's Association members, and with the KIO Central Committee. For my 'Kachin wedding photograph' they produced the only bachelor around who was older than me, a stout, genial officer well into his sixties. At least he was inches taller than me, unlike most Kachin men who leveled out below my imposing 5'3".

All dressed up, I made and received speeches. 'During World War II, my father and one of the Flying Tigers devised cameras to be mounted on airplanes and take surveillance photos of the battle zones, like the Kachin land,' I told my hosts. 'I thought of that as I came here to Pajau on foot with your soldiers. I thought of how that war so many years ago, before I was born, has linked your people and Americans together to this day. I hope that my country will help the Kachin people in the future, and show its gratitude in meaningful ways at the present, during this troubled time of oppression.' The Kachins in turn told me how I was their own relative now and I was given a pair of bagel-sized embossed silver bracelets.

The officers and ladies lunched on noodle soup and we discussed women in the military, a topic of some controversy back in my country following the Gulf War earlier that year. Maj. Pan Awng said that the Kachin Army's female combat troops were 'very good, very brave indeed. They will never retreat! At one time, a man combat unit and a woman combat unit were on the same attack against a Tatmadaw post. The woman troops got into there first. Our soldier women killed the Burmese sentries and captured the guns.' Maj. Pan Awng had a request for me: 'Could you ask your President George Bush to send us some of his woman F-16 pilots? With their own airplanes, of course. We would be most happy to see them.'

Someone else's ceremony took place that evening, a gathering of Kachin Army officers to bid farewell to three Jinghpaw men from one of India's Northeast states who had been visiting Pajau. KIO officers hung a Kachin embroidered red wool bag and a silver sword over the shoulders of each of them, and then the feasting began, in a meeting hall decorated with crossed iron broadswords and a dramatic painting of stampeding horses. We sat on benches at long tables, eating rice and chicken and toasting with Steinlager beer and a milky rice wine and caustic white liquor, as a fire blazed in a pit in the dirt floor. It was *Beowulf* country, that hall full of warriors, and as the night went on, I half expected Grendel, or his fiendish mother, to materialize in the dark doorway.

I spent the next morning conducting a group interview with young officers from the training course and then answering the questions they had for me. They mostly wanted to know how other oppressed peoples from Eastern Europe to Ethiopia had achieved liberation in recent years—and why Burma hadn't. For my report on children, I convened their much younger counterparts in the afternoon: soldier boys and girls aged fifteen to seventeen. Almost all of the boys had been conscripted into the Kachin Army, as had a petite, sweet-faced fifteen-year old girl who was the most non-military looking person conceivable. The KIO had a quota in some of their areas of control: one sibling, boy or girl, from each family had to serve the revolution. A few of the girls at Pajau had joined up of their own accord, because 'the people were oppressed and tortured by the Tatmadaw'. and because they 'wanted democracy'. The girls were mostly studious types who were taking medical training. The boys were either in the medic course or were runners of messages up and down the headquarters hills.

Sigrid and I visited the Kachin Army video squad. The rebels had gone crazy for video, taping every speech and ceremony, plus many a battle. The office was piled high with dust-coated stacks of such tapes and more were mildewing in an adjacent shed. One of the video squad soldiers told us of charging up a battlefield embankment with his camcorder: 'I was seeing there a Tatmadaw infantryman right in front of me through my viewfinder. The enemy soldier is in much much confusion—he thinks, "what can be this new Kachin weapon with the red light on it?"—so I had just the time to take up my pistol and shoot him down dead.'

The video office collection included tapes documenting heroin use in the Kachin State and new KIO efforts against drugs. The video squad played some of them for me. In the jade-mining center, Hpakant (a place essentially under Slorc jurisdiction) heroin addicts did the zombie walk or crawled around in the mud, with festering needle-sores visible on their bony frames. The addicts were shown using shared needles to inject themselves and each other right out in the open, in the town bazaar, in the daylight, in the rain. Then more videotape showed KIO soldiers reading anti-drug ultimatums to assembled villagers, and next rounding up heroin dealers and questioning them. The dealers (heroin users themselves) were given a summary hearing by a KIO officer and offered rehabilitation, probably by Shan Buddhist monks or traditional spirit-doctors, if they would promise to cease their commerce in heroin. At least one of them flatly refused to change his ways, apparently lacking any instinct for self-preservation. After that, horrifically, a dozen or so men and women, the dealers, could be clearly seen lashed to posts along the shore of a lake or river. KIO soldiers stood in front of them and with their rifles gave each a few shots in the stomach—not the heart, not the head—leaving them to die a painful slow death slumped from their poles.

'They'll make you a copy of the drug tapes on one video to take home with you,' Sigrid said. 'You can show it to the US Drug Enforcements to show them we Kachins are sincere about ending drugs.'

'I'll take it, but it doesn't make the KIO look so good in a way—human rights groups aren't going to like this use of the death penalty.'

'I know, but it got people's attention in those villages. The KIO only had to make those few executions and everyone knew it was a real policy to end the drugs. Anyway, Europe has already seen this tape. That journalist Bernard got one and put it on Swiss TV. They didn't run the rest of it about the drugs, just the shooting part to show how savage and Third World we are here.'

While we waited for the tape to be copied, we watched some Burmese television. Slorc TV, a turgid revue starring generals and colonels of the Tatmadaw, was enhanced only by amateurish commercials for cosmetics and patent medicines. In one of the ads two Burman girls in glitzy fake Jinghpaw outfits ('I'm not a Kachin but I play one on TV') hawked a botanical cure-all salve.

One of the KIO cameramen told me that the Japanese students had visited the office and left an expensive gift: their pair of top of the line camcorders. Unfortunately, the equipment was Betamax format, still popular in Japan but incompatible with everything the Kachins had, and not even worth selling in China. The Japanese had already gone home, summer break was over for them. I had no idea when I would be leaving Pajau. It didn't seem like I'd have to go back the way I came, but nobody had come up with a plan for any other route avoiding the Chinese checkpoints. Chairman Brang Seng was expected at Pajau in a couple of days, so I figured I'd just wait and see what he thought was best.

In the meantime, Sigrid and I put together a videotaped appeal for funds to rebuild the civilian hospital that had been demolished by the flood. I gave the introduction on the video, showing the locations of the Kachin State and the flood zone on a wall map. Then we cut in footage of the flood itself: injured victims, elephants carrying relief supplies through the torrent. Lu Ra spoke about the Kachin Women's Association and how they would be involved in the resurrection of the civilian hospital, and a doctor who had barely survived the night of the flood, when his assistants had been swept away and drowned, told of the need for health care in the area. I would bring the videotape to Hong Kong and the United States, for church groups to distribute, in hope of inspiring some contributions.

Chairman Brang Seng arrived at his headquarters, Pajau on the second day of September, and I was summoned to a cabin higher up the hill from Lu Ra's. There Ja Seng Hkawn and I sat with her father and a few Central Committee members as a wood-stove warmed the room. The Chairman showed me anti-narcotics material he'd had printed in Thailand for distribution throughout the KIO region. On large square stickers a red opium poppy had a slash over it, with the legend, 'Crush Out Opium Growing and Use' in Chinese, Burmese and Kachin. Posters using the no-poppy graphics declared the KIO area an 'Opium Free State'.

Chairman Brang Seng gave me a copy of the KIO's new anti-drug ordinances, and I spoke up against summary execution and in favor of as much rehabilitation for addicts as possible. One of the Central Committee members insisted that the KIO's executions were not going to continue: 'We Kachins have a low population, so we don't like to use the death sentence. The civilians asked us to execute those criminals.'

Prior to their new 'Crush Out' policy, the KIO had itself profited from the drug trade by charging an 'excise tax' on opium. The poppy growers were charged a small license fee and then a percentage tariff based on their fields' annual yield. The farmers were poor, the crop didn't thrive that far north, so the revenue usually didn't amount to much, especially compared to the Kachin rebels' lucrative jade trade. Sometimes the farmers, lacking cash, had to pay their fees to the KIO in opium, which was then used for medicine or resold, KIO officials told me.

Along with the farmers, opium traders who transported the gum of the poppies to markets also had been compelled to pay a license fee to the KIO. During the 1980s refining of opium into heroin became more and more prevalent in the Kachin region. In 1986, the KIO had banned the use or sale of heroin, while still tolerating and taxing the raw material, opium. Now in 1991 both opium and heroin were supposed to be completely eliminated by the Kachin rebels wherever they were in control.

The Chairman thought the new KIO anti-drug plan had a good chance of succeeding. 'For a long time, opium was justified because it could be used as medicine,' he said. 'But it isn't even good medicine. Aspirin is better. Something had to be done. I have met with the villagers since we announced our new program. I expected them to be grumbling. But they all supported it. They know the effects of the drugs.'

I was familiar with the ins and outs of wars on drugs from investigating and lobbying against a spectacularly counter-productive chemical spraying binge the US had sponsored in Burma's Shan State in the 1980s. I knew that growing bans followed by crop substitution programs, like the KIO plan, were thought to have little chance of success without all sorts of foreign development funding, which seemed unlikely in this rebel territory. Unlikely, but not impossible. 'Oh, the Chinese are very much with us for this, but quietly,' Brang Seng confided. 'They are giving seeds and advice for crop substitution here. They want to stop the heroin coming to Kunming, to Ruili. Those places have the most AIDS in China. They have so much problems with these drugs and AIDS disease, but this December they will see that all the poppies are grown in Slorc government area, not KIO area. And as for us, we are so concerned about AIDS. That is why we have this opium free plan. If everyone has AIDS, where may we recruit our soldiers?'

Sigrid had brought word of my presence to the student camp, and two ABSDF leaders came to see me at Lu Ra's cabin early the next morning. Not wanting to interact with the KIO at all they brought their own translator. Young, intellectual revolutionaries who had grown up in the Burmese city of Mandalay, they spoke quietly but forcefully. They needed more weapons—that was all, they insisted, if they had enough guns they could defeat the Slorc.

I had heard new nasty rumors about the ABSDF camp: that the 'spies' there were confessing after beatings and torture. I'd seen one of the confessions on a tape at the KIO video squad office, and the young Burmese female 'spy' did look disoriented and bruised. Supposedly, of the thirty prisoners now held for spying, at least three had somehow died. My ABSDF visitors didn't bring up the spy issue, preferring a broader political discussion, so I asked them about it point blank. They giggled nervously. 'It is under control,' was all they would say about the infiltration and purges. Actually it was anything but. Not long after our meeting, one of the two ABSDF leaders whom I met would end up executed himself, another 'spy' casualty in the Burmese student movement's equivalent of the Salem witch trials. I had never met the ABSDF where they were strongest, on the Thai border, but on the Bangladesh and China borders their 'student army' was looking more and more like a failed experiment to me. I wished for a Malcolm X 'by any means necessary' revolution in Burma, but one where students used their intellects to good effect instead of imitating militarization in the worst way.

After the Burmese students left, Mai Mai from the War Office showed up with a Kachin Army uniform for me. A big anti-drug rally was going to be held that afternoon. Chinese police officials from across the border had been invited to attend it. I'd gotten word that the Chinese knew 'a foreign woman' was at Pajau. In order to avoid detection by the police guests, I would view the rally from a building up above the parade ground, in uniform, disguised as just another Kachin soldier girl. I put on the olive drab shirt and trousers. Mai Mai French-braided my hair and I borrowed a KIO cap. When we got to my observation post I gave Mai Mai (the only female soldier as tall as me) my cameras and sent her out in the crowd of hundreds of villagers and troops, to pretend to take some photos. Mai Mai was my decoy, so that if the Chinese guests saw me up on the verandah snapping pictures, they'd assume nothing was amiss.

Rain fell on the crowd and soon everyone, soldiers and civilians alike, opened umbrellas as they stood there chanting anti-opium and anti-heroin slogans. Speeches to the sea of black umbrellas were mercifully brief. A hand-painted billboard depicting the evils of narcotics—an ominous field of skulls, a half-naked addict one foot in the grave—was unveiled to oohs and ahs. I took its photo. I thought, 'I should be working for the Drug Enforcement Administration. No DEA agent ever bothers to come here. Instead I go in disguise and get this information and give it to the US Government for free.' It wasn't the first time it had occurred to me that CIA agents, DEA agents, got paid to bring off the kind of covert operations I did for nothing. They probably even got health insurance and other benefits that I went without. Not that I could handle working for some outfit that would just take whatever truth I handed them and twist it for their own bureaucratic ends. As I left, the rain was slacking off and the parade ground was being reclaimed by off-duty soldiers for soccer and badminton.

Ja Seng Hkawn and I went to a Central Committee member's house to watch some television. Slorc TV presented the usual array of military honchos inspecting the 'voluntary labor of the people'. Then an incredibly listless pop band in sarongs and buttoned-up jackets played a song. That was followed by the Slorc's 'slogans' filling the screen in Burmese and English.

'Down with the minions of colonialism' appeared. 'That would be you,' Ja Seng Hkawn said to me.

'Crush all unruly and destructive elements' followed. 'And I believe they are referring to you with this one,' I told Ja Seng Hkawn.

Somebody turned off the Slorc TV and put a tape in the VCR, a video drama home-produced in the Kachin city of Myitkyina. With Burmese state-run television so un-entertaining, people who could afford a camcorder recruited their friends and created their own soap operas, to be copied and sold throughout the Kachin State. This one was called 'Like A Dream', and it told the story of a young man losing his girlfriend, his family ties, and eventually his life, because of his heroin addiction. It was not badly acted, and seemed to get the point across as well as the KIO's billboard, posters and stickers.

Soon I was going to go back across the Chinese border, one way or another. So I spent the better part of the next afternoon filling my sketchbook with imaginary watercolor paintings of the landscape around Ruili. I was anticipating some Chinese checkpoint guard inquiring as to just what I'd been doing in Ruili for a month. '*Hua de huar*,' I would tell him. 'Painting pictures.' The Chinese always seemed to admire aesthetic pursuits, the Cultural Revolution being a cultural anomaly.

While I had my miniature paint set out, I made watercolor sketches of male and female Kachin Army soldiers in uniform with their various rifles: old Chinese AK47s and M22s, and an even older American M18. I also converted a spare War Office ledger into a guest book for Pajau. Decorated with paintings of Ja Seng Hkawn in Jinghpaw red and Mai Mai in uniform, the book was to be filled out by whatever foreign visitors would follow me. I wrote in the names of those who had been in the land of the Kachins before me—Bertil, Tanaka, Yoshida, an American named Shelby Tucker, Bernard, a few others.

The young officers' refresher training course was over. Still innocent of the mysteries of the tango, they were given a marathon banquet with the usual talent show entertainment. To Ja Seng Kawn's amazement, I had no song to sing. I tried to explain to her that in my country there are singers and then there are non-singers, and the latter do not even burden themselves by learning the words to popular tunes. It was not that way in Asia. Who couldn't sing? Who wouldn't love *karaoke*?

In lieu of 'Walk Away Renee' or 'Diamonds Are a Girl's Best Friend', which would have been my choices if only I'd had it together, I gave yet another speech. I told the hundreds of officers, troops and civilians in the hall about a dream I'd had one (chloroquin) night in Pajau. The Kachin Army crossed a river, besieged and took a Tatmadaw-held city in that dream. Even poison gas (which the Tatmadaw was known to use in real life battles) did not hold the Kachin troops back. The Kachin Army took and held that city and then would capture another, I had dreamt. This would happen very soon, I predicted. A similar theme was voiced by Brigadier Tu Jai, of the Central Committee, in his speech: 'We've been fighting a long time, but now we're getting close to the end. We're getting very close to our victory—so don't make any mistakes now. This is going to be our time.' Heads nodded in agreement, and applause for the victory messages was enthusiastic and sustained.

My departure from Pajau really was imminent. I was invited up the hill the next day to say goodbye to Chairman Brang Seng, who was himself off to points unknown again, and the Central Committee was there for a formal farewell to me. All apologies for the 'poor quality', the Central Committee presented me with a little oblong of leaf-green jade, and a darker jade cabochon which they'd had set into a gold ring. A craftsman at Pajau had fashioned the ring setting, a pair of hearts. I thanked them and assured them that 'this fine jade ring shall bring me back here to Pajau. I'm sure it will get homesick for the Kachin mountains and tell me to return'.

Such fancy presents were awkward for me. The KIO had done their best to draw me into their ranks, from my naming to the ceremonies, the uniform, the gifts. I had always tried to stay away from being taken over by one of Burma's ethnic groups or another, so I could continue to be trusted by all of them. But now I was, in effect, a Kachin. The hearts on my ring did not mean I loved them like a family, like my own family, though. My feelings for the Kachins were more of immense respect. I admired their strength, their perseverance in warfare, their unfailing good humor in an often difficult life. They ate bones and thorns and enjoyed every meal. They drank like fishes but never seemed drunk (aside from Maj. Pan Awng). They were utterly unmaterialistic except for jade, which they shared anyway.

In exchange for my adoption and my ring, all I could do was (as foreign aid workers always said) try to help them help themselves. I would send the Kachins manuals about growing roses—for the Chinese market, and viniculture—for their own wine consumption. I would mail off books on handicrafts to the Kachin Women's Association. I'd send baseball equipment (Dwight Gooden Throw-down Bases, aluminum bats, etc.) and instructions for the game, to give the soldiers a variation from soccer and shuttlecocks. Most importantly, I swore I'd stay in touch with an elderly lieutenant named N'Chaw Tang, a chronicler of The Kachins' political history who also knew all about the medicinal plants of their beautiful forests. Perhaps I could encourage foreign botanists, conservationists to visit him, make studies and encourage the KIO to keep that forest heritage out of the clutches of the Chinese loggers.

One more festivity was programmed for the young officers the next day, my last at Pajau. 'Put on your sarong,' Ja Seng Hkawn commanded me. 'We're having the traditional Kachin *tonga* dancing at the hall, and you will dance with us.' I balked at the idea of being dressed up and paired off with some 'bachelor' again, to be a freak at a dance. I had gotten tired of being the spinster at those things, too old to be attractive but still young enough to have a bit of hope. That wasn't how I normally saw myself at all, I just considered myself between dashing boyfriends. But at Pajau I was an Old Maid on display. Ja Seng Hkawn told me to get over it, it was just a folk dance, I'd have a good time. So I got done up in a glittery sarong outfit the Kachin Women's Association had given me, and went to the hall and people said how nice I looked, even though I was too skinny from not eating enough rice. As one of the officers put it, 'She eats like a Kachin, but not as much as a Kachin.'

We watched a dozen of the really good dancers do the *tonga,* all in traditional Jinghpaw clothing, the young women decked out in red wool and silver, the men in dark plaid sarongs. Then everybody else lined up, forming a boy-girl circle all around the hall. We each held the corners of handkerchiefs with both hands. The dance was simple: a step, a raised knee, a turn, a bend. Its drum-beat was so repetitive that it was somehow soothing. I had to concentrate on the steps at first, but after a while I became part of the pattern formed by all the dancers. Bending and turning, we danced our circle into an opening flower or the respiration of an undersea creature.

In the afternoon Ja Seng Hkawn, Sigrid and I strolled over to the parade ground, where a soccer match had just commenced between two teams of female soldiers. One side was comprised of War Office clerks, including tall, athletic Mai Mai, the other of girls from the uniform-sewing department. In shorts and T-shirts they played with gleeful brutality and complete incompetence. They collided into each other, they kicked each other and wildly kicked the ball, which was constantly flying out of bounds. Zero-Zero. We left in the second half. The soldier girls were bedraggled and mud-spattered. They still laughed and their comrades in arms, girl friends and boy suitors still cheered them on. The score was still tied at nothing.

At Lu Ra's cabin I was told that I'd be going to China by car that very night, as soon as it got dark. Ja Seng Hkawn and Lt. Khun Nawng would accompany me. Mai Mai showed up after cleaning off her soccer mud, to help me with my disguise. She French-braided my hair into apparent straightness and cut bangs to cover my pale forehead. *Thanaka* powder was applied to the rest of my face. I put on a sarong, sweater and sandals. The drug video, the flood video, the precious drawings by the children in Laiza, my interview notes and film were put in a plastic bag to be carried by Ja Seng Hkawn, who was unlikely to be searched. The Chinese allowed the Kachins cross-border access to as far away as Mangshi for a few days at a time. The Kachins even had special ID cards to show at the checkpoints.

I said my goodbyes to Lu Ra, Maj. Pan Awng, Lt. N'Chaw Tang and the others, and my party set off in a jeep with a Kachin Army driver, who brought us over the Chinese border. After plenty of bumping over dirt and paved roads, we eventually stopped on the outskirts of a village. 'A Chinese police check point is here,' Ja Seng Hkawn said. 'You and I will walk around it.' A young Kachin boy was waiting for us beneath a big black umbrella. It was very dark, and raining hard, and Ja Seng Hkawn and I walked under umbrellas too, which was most fortuitous for my disguise. We began wending our way along the slippery back alleys of the village. We followed the boy's black umbrella up ahead.

Then Ja Seng Hkawn halted abruptly. 'Oh no,' she whispered, 'that's not our boy anymore! We lost him!' We'd somehow ended up trailing another village kid with an umbrella. Our guide realized we were gone, though, and doubled back to find us. We kept walking, crossing through pigstyes and hoping the village dogs wouldn't get too excited about our trespass. Our perambulation was so roundabout that it seemed like a convoluted city rather than a village, and we were so tense that it felt like we were going around in circles for hours. The umbrella boy, Ja Seng Hkawn and I were joined by a man who followed along in back of us. He was complaining about something in Chinese. I began to wonder if he was turning us in. Lights blazed ahead: a market street, full of business that night. I took off my glasses, which would only have drawn attention to my face, kind of squinted my eyes, kept my head down, and stumbled across the lit-up market street to another dark alley.

The alley led right to a yard where a passenger van was ready to take us all the way to Mangshi. Ja Seng Hkawn and I went off to pee in a corner of the yard. 'The man who was following us is our new driver,' she explained. 'He is not supposed to know you are a foreigner, so don't speak English in the new car, only Chinese.' We got in the van and drove off. Ja Seng Hkawn and I fell asleep in the back. The van drove for hours along mountain roads, passing checkpoints manned by snoozing Chinese soldiers and police without having to stop at all.

The sun came up and we arrived in Ruili. As a foreign 'tourist' I was legal there, but it still was very possible that Chinese intelligence agents were looking for me, to confiscate my film and notes, if not arrest me. We got out of the van to have breakfast in a little café on the edge of town. I hoped the Kachins would not order noodles for breakfast, since that would require chopsticks. Being left-handed (a great rarity in China) my grasp of the chopsticks would expose my identity. Sure enough, bowls of noodle soup were brought out for everybody. I gripped the pair of chopsticks in my right hand and tried to get them to work. Our driver who was not supposed to know looked at me with sympathy, and called out in Chinese to the waitress, 'Please bring a fork and spoon for our foreign friend!'

As we were finishing our noodle soup, a cluster of Burmese student refugees came into the café. From their table across the room, they stared at me. Eventually one young Burmese student rose and walked over to us. 'Good morning!' he said to me with an ingratiating smile. I just looked down at my soup bowl. Enunciating very carefully, he tried, 'Do...you...speak...English?' I glanced at him in absolute mystification, and went back to examining the noodle dregs. He sighed and went back to the student table. 'No, she's not,' he told them in Burmese. 'Of course not,' one of his friends said, 'She's just Chinese. If she was English, she would have said "Good Morning" to you.'

The van stopped at a checkpoint just past Ruili, where a Chinese soldier examined ID cards. He took a look at my passport, comprehending only the Chinese writing of my still very much in order Chinese visa. He let us go on our way without questions. Road crews had begun improving the road from Ruili to Mangshi, and the work in progress made it horribly corrugated. Ja Seng Hkawn felt like every van lurch was being met from the inside with an irate fetal kick. I felt guilty for making her come so far in her condition, and kept apologizing to her and 'the triplets'. I also felt sorry to leave her, as she had really been my sister at Pajau. I hoped that her political abilities, at least as sharp as those of the older men who ran the show there, would be recognized.

Arriving at last in Mangshi, our party checked into a jade traders' inn. We reassembled for farewell meals—boneless chicken and Steinlager beer and *Jian Li Bai*, the Chinese sports drink that had 'saved my life' on the route north. I gave Lt. Khun Nawng my unused snakebite treatment kit, just the kind of jungle gadget he liked, to take on his next adventure. He and Ja Seng Hkawn saw me off on the bus to Kunming in the morning. A young Kachin friend of theirs was taking the same bus, so he got custody of my tapes, film and notes. He sat next to me, though we would pretend not to know each other at the checkpoints.

It was not a sleeping bus. It was barely a sitting bus, with hard school bus seats and everyone crammed together for the overnight trip. A bad checkpoint awaited us past Mangshi on the Burma Road. On my way in, I'd had to get off there and write down my passport number at the booth. I was braced for questions about what I'd been doing in Mangshi for a month, and had my bogus sketchbook ready. Just before the bridge leading to that checkpoint, our bus stopped. Its way was blocked by a truck clinging half off the Burma Road, the truck cab in the air over a steep gorge. Getting around the truck required a cooperative effort by the passengers. We actually widened the other side of the Road by moving rocks away. That took so much time that when we started up again, our bus driver told the checkpoint guard that he was too off-schedule to have him come aboard. We were allowed to proceed without inspection.

At another guard booth further down the road, the police did board, and they shook down a few passengers for their hunting knives. I showed my passport, opened to the Chinese visa page, and that was quite adequate. I was home free. Now we only had to survive the bus itself. Afternoon rain started, and it began to leak in through assorted rust holes and loose window frames. The worst hole was just in front of me, in the roof above a young Chinese couple. They tried to plug the drip of water by stuffing some toilet paper into the hole. After not too long, the toilet paper fell down on their heads in sopping pink globs. Then the couple tried covering the hole with a plastic bag, which soon filled up with rain and became a water-balloon plummeting onto them. I dug around in my shoulder bag for the duct tape (never leave anywhere without it) and handed them the roll. They got tape in their hair somehow, and managed to tape the hole diagonally so that water still dripped through, though at a lesser rate.

The bus pulled up to a rank-smelling stone hostelry for our evening meal. The bowls of greasy cabbage and dry broken rice were so unappetizing that even my Kachin companion was only able to finish half of his. Back on its way in dark hard rain, the bus swerved along until it broke down right in the middle of the Burma Road in the middle of the night. The driver sent someone to a town up ahead for a necessary replacement part, and we passengers sat there and dozed. We dozed until jolted awake by the thump of a logging truck unable to brake in time to avoid our black obstacle. The truck, carrying valuable teak wood undoubtedly ripped out of a forest in Burma, didn't ram into us very hard. Just hard enough to knock all the glass out of our bus's back window.

Eventually, things got patched together, and stalling much, the drafty, leaky bus limped on into Kunming. I got my contraband back from my Kachin companion, and walked away from our miserable mud-crusted coach. After I exited the Kunming bus station, within a block I nearly bumped into the first pale-skinned European travelers I'd seen in a month, so tall with their cheap gaudy clothes and their expensive backpacks. Just a little further down the crowded city street I noticed a Chinese sidewalk vendor with a hank of furs for sale. The pelts were deep russet with white faces and black tails. The man was peddling the furs of endangered red pandas, hunted in a Kachin forest.

4

SHOOTING IN THE DARK

Rumor had it that Manipur might be 'open'. One of the Northeast frontier states of India, bordering Burma, Manipur had long been forbidden to foreign travelers. So had India's other Northeast states: Mizoram, Nagaland, Arunachal Pradesh, Tripura, Assam and Meghalaya. As if being adjacent to Burma was not trouble enough, each of those territories had some level of insurgency against the Indian Government, as well as intertribal conflicts. In the Northeast, small wars were wrapped within other wars.

I wanted to go to the India/Burma border states where Chin-related people lived, Manipur and Mizoram, to meet with the Chin National Front (CNF) rebels from Burma who had proven so elusive in Bangladesh in 1991. A year after that trip, the rumor surfaced that Manipur would welcome tourists. I wrote to the CNF Chairman, whom I'd met in Calcutta in '91, and he sent back the names of CNF representatives on the India/Burma border and how to contact them. He also enclosed the Tourist Map of Imphal, the main city of Manipur. It seemed like a good start.

One summer day in 1992 I took the train from New Jersey, where I was living, to New York City, to see my friend Holly Morgan. We had lunch at a Mexican restaurant in Soho, and that's where the Manipur 'expedition' really began. The petite, sandy-haired Holly and I had first met in a hotel dining room in Urumchi, Chinese Turkestan, in 1984. Back then she had been on her way back from the fabled desert city of Kashgar, and I was just about to embark on a four day ordeal by bus to get there. Holly had skipped the land route, instead flying on the Chinese airline, and been rewarded with a passenger favor: a small box containing pink and green glitter-plastic cocktail glasses. Admiring those, I asked Holly what she did back in New York. She was a sculptor. Something to do with pieces of wood, and fish-eye lenses and glued-on line drawings. Being a painter myself, I wrote down her number so I could see what kind of artwork she was talking about. We had stayed friends and would meet every so often to mull over Asian destinations.

In the Mexican restaurant we talked about India. Holly had been there three times, including a year as an artist in residence amid the palaces of Rajasthan. I had made briefer India trips, two of them. I told her about the Northeast states. Neither of us had ever heard of any foreign tourists going there, but now there was a chance. We realized that we had to make the attempt, and the time was exactly right for it. My first book, *Burmese*

Looking Glass, would be published in January, and Holly's sculpture would have a gallery show that same month. Until then we were free to go traveling to India, and we even had enough money to get there.

I telephoned the Indian Government's travel bureau in New York. The Northeast states were completely open, they assured me. Permits were not required. That was far too good to be true, so I checked with the Indian Consulate. Actually, permits were very much required, I learned. Getting them would take ten weeks in New York, four weeks in New Delhi, India's capital. To cut the time down, Holly and I obtained the permit forms at the Consulate, filled them out and air-expressed them to Tibetan friends of hers who ran a New Delhi travel agency. The Tibetans were to run the permits over to the Home Ministry for approval. We waited. We waited some more.

Holly called New Delhi, and Pema from the travel agency told her our first really bad news. The forms had been delivered to the Home Ministry, but the rest might not be so easy. To go to the Northeast you were supposed to be a 'group'—which meant at least four people. And even then, it was difficult. Pema had been trying to obtain permission for a group of Japanese to go to Mizoram, for nearly a year without success.

I was willing to play the long shot, to go to India anyway. A regional conference on Asia's AIDS epidemic was scheduled for November in New Delhi. I wanted to attend it and network about Burma. I had been trying to raise awareness of Burma's HIV/AIDS situation: the routes of infection, the high rates among the Kachins, the way the Slorc kept it all hidden (reporting zero cases to the UN.) Articles I had written on the subject had appeared in specialized publications like *AIDS and Society* and *Cultural Survival Quarterly*. I could publicize Burma's hidden epidemic more at the conference, and if I could get to Manipur I could find out plenty about one of the main AIDS routes from Burma. Manipur was thought to have the highest rate of HIV/AIDS infection in India, rivaled only by red light districts of Bombay.

Holly and I got visas from the Indian Consulate in New York, and because we had filled out our occupations as 'artist', we had to go upstairs and receive special approval from someone who said he reviewed the suitability of 'all artists, journalists and film producers' who wanted to visit India. We bought cheap tickets on Gulf Air, and settled in for the twenty-four-hour flight from New York to New Delhi, being woken up and fed dates with mint tea every so often by the 'I Dream of Jeannie' blonde flight attendants, and stumbling drowsily through transit lounges at Abu Dhabi and Bahrain crowded with oil sheiks and masked Omani women. A Tibetan from Pema's travel agency met us at New Delhi's airport to take us to our artsy bed & breakfast. On the way, he told us we were going to need to see a certain Mr Bala, reputedly formidable, to plead for our Home Ministry permits.

As soon as the jet lag let us, Holly and I got in a cab and found Mr Bala's Home Ministry office. He was in charge of Restricted Area Permits. His office hours were very restricted too, and we had to wait outside the building until a guard let us in at exactly 1:45 in the afternoon. Then we waited for a while in the office. Tea appeared, and finally Mr Bala, a heavyset, taciturn official. Launching a charm offensive, Holly (who could be very perky) and I (who could be very persuasive) informed the esteemed Mr Bala that we had sent our applications through a most reputable local travel agency the month before, in August. Would we not then be able to visit Manipur and Mizoram, our cultural, artistic goals in this particular life?

'No. No Mizoram. No foreign tourists there. The only states permitted are Manipur and Meghalaya. Only five days there.' That seemed reasonable to us—we would go to Manipur, then.

'No. Two people are not going. It must be a tour group. A tour group is a group of four. It may be more than four people, but it may not be less than four people. This is for security purposes.'

It occurred to me that this wasn't necessarily bad news. Four people would be harder to keep track of than two people. There could be decoys, diversions, while I met Chin contacts or did AIDS research. Once we had our full compliment of tourists, Mr Bala informed us, we should go to the Foreigners' Regional Registration Office and they would issue the permits.

Our task was clear. Holly had numerous friends in New Delhi and they were all asked to help find two people who would go to Manipur with us. Mr Bala had informed us that 'Indians do not count'—our companions had to hold foreign passports to be part of the tour group. Initial phone calls didn't pay off. It became obvious that few foreigners were interested in going to India's Northeast. The tourists and expatriates were more focused on the big culture locales. Nobody had heard much about the Burma-related tribes of the Northeast frontier, except that they were embroiled in constant messy political bloodshed. Even adventurous travelers didn't want to blow money on an air ticket (the 'group' had to fly in) to an obscure place with no known attractions, spend a few days there doing God knows what and fly back out. We tried the dreary doss-houses frequented by long-term India drifters to no avail.

Discouraged, we repaired to the elegant Imperial Hotel for Cold Coffee with Ice Cream in the garden lounge. Holly asked a pair of tourists at a nearby table if they'd like to go to Manipur with us. Certainly not, they replied, and we shouldn't be bothering either—we could go trekking in lots of perfectly decent places where one didn't need a Restricted Area Permit. The more opposition we ran into, the more convinced we became that Manipur would be completely worthwhile, of course.

One day we had lunch with Vikram Seth, the writer of miniaturist verse and epic novel, a friend of a friend of Holly's. We obsessed away about

Manipur to him, and he recalled that his brother who ran tours to Buddhist holy sites had mentioned a German who was trying to get to Meghalaya. It was our first hint of any other petitioner seeking entry to the Northeast. We arranged a rendezvous with the German, at Pema's agency. He showed up with his girlfriend, not another foreigner but an indigenous person from Meghalaya. The purpose of his visit was to meet her family. It was an impasse. He had no need to go to Manipur and we wouldn't settle for Meghalaya (which did not border Burma). We didn't want to join each others' 'tours'.

Leaving the agency we encountered an American, a Californian in the robes of a Tibetan lama. Maybe he would like to go to Manipur? No, he had to be on his way to a Tibetan religious gathering, he told us. But he did give us lamaist reassurance that we should persevere in our quest and would eventually reach our goal. Unfortunately, more discouragement followed, in the form of a fax from Hong Kong. I'd sent a message to my most peripatetic friends there, inviting them along on our splendid Manipur adventure. But one was off to South Africa, another bound for Kazakstan, and the last already booked for Peru. Holly and I sought comfort in more Cold Coffee with Ice Cream.

We decided to try the Foreigners' Regional Registration Office anyway. 'We wish to inquire about Restricted Area Permits for Manipur,' Holly told an officer there.

'If you are wanting to go to Manipur, you must fly to Imphal, the capital, and fly back out within five days.' He handed us permit forms to fill out. We scarcely breathed as we carefully printed our names, addresses, purported purposes, and everything else. But then the officer went to another desk and looked up Manipur in an enormous ledger, the Book of Doom.

'I am sorry,' he told us, 'but you are needing to have four people. It is the Home Ministry regulation. Come back when you have four people. Look, here in this book it tells the tourist attractions where you can go in Manipur: Imphal, Loktak Lake, Der Sanctuary, Indian National Army Memorial, Moirag.'

'What's this one—'Der Sanctuary?''

'It is the deers. Only Manipur has the brow-antlered deers. Please come back with your four people, it will take just five minutes to get the permits when you have enough tourists with you.'

Holly and I went to dinner at the home of an Indian abstract painter, and he thought of an architect's son who had a French passport. 'Please call him,' we implored the painter, even though the electricity had just gone out. A lens had fallen out of his glasses and gone missing in the blackout, but the painter gamely tried dialing the number as I illuminated the phone with my flashlight. No answer. 'I think you are just shooting in the dark,' the painter told us, gently trying to disillusion us about the odds of winning one against the Indian Government's vast obdurate bureaucracy.

Still not to be dissuaded, we found our way to the residence of the architect's son the next day. He couldn't go to Manipur. Then we visited a photographer, but she had an Indian passport and didn't know anybody up for Manipur. She happened to live very near Holly's friend Tom, an American textile dealer. We already knew that Tom's schedule did not have room for Manipur, but we went over to his place to bring him some Almond Delight herbal tea because he was in bed with a cold.

Tom, thermometer in mouth, was absurdly grateful for the small gift of tea. He remembered to tell us that Vikram Seth's brother had called, looking for us. He knew someone else who was desperate to go to Manipur. I felt the Californian lama blessing us. I felt like the herbal tea was a magic spell. We got Meneka Van Parren's phone number and the next morning Holly and I appeared at her house with take-out tandoori chicken. Miles Davis' 'Sketches of Spain' was ringing out from Meneka's stereo. Tall, with straight black hair and very fair skin, Meneka was a half Dutch, half Indian (Dutch passport) journalist who could speak about a dozen European and Asian languages. Meneka told us she was writing a book about the spread of AIDS through Asia. The book project was in collaboration with a European journalist who was presently in Japan. Manipur was a must for their research.

The only snag was Meneka's co-writer. He wouldn't be back in Delhi for several days. We decided to get his passport particulars and bring them to the Foreigners' Regional Registration Office. We'd get the permits and he could meet us in Calcutta, the jumping off place for flights to India's Northeast. Having filled out a permit form for him, Meneka, Holly and I presented ourselves at the Foreigners' Regional Registration Office and after a long wait, we met the same officer who had explained it all to us before. This time the process stopped short when he realized that our fourth tour member was not exactly physically present.

'This won't do. You are only three tourists here,' the officer said, after counting heads.

'But our fourth group member will meet us in Calcutta, and we will go together from there,' Meneka protested.

'It will be no problem for you, then. Just go to the Foreigners' Regional Registration Office in Calcutta and they immediately shall give your permit there.'

We dressed nicely in *salwar kameez* and paid a last visit to Mr Bala. Holly showed him pictures of her sculptures, which seemed to melt some of the ice. In the course of our visits to Holly's New Delhi friends we had heard that Mr Bala was a legendary gate keeper, under no circumstances giving out any Restricted Area Permits, no matter how heartfelt the pleas for them, how worthy the visitors. All we asked from him now was assurance that we could get our Restricted Area Permit in Calcutta. 'Of course you can get it there. You may have them contact me, if there is any trouble. But there will not be any trouble.' Those words made us feel much better.

Next, Meneka's book partner backed out of the tour group. He wanted to go to Uganda for epidemic comparison purposes, instead. Holly and I decided that we'd have better luck recruiting our fourth person in Calcutta, since it was much nearer to Manipur, so the two of us left for Calcutta by train. When we arrived two days later, our travel agency friend Pema was in town and she had news from Meneka: she would be arriving with tourist #4 the next day. He turned out to be a youthful curly-haired reporter from Barcelona named Javier Manrriquez—soon known as Java Man in our group. Fresh from covering the Olympics in his home town, he'd arrived in India intent on visiting Kashmir and the Punjab, infamous hotbeds of unrest. Meneka promised him the scoop on a less-known, equally violent adjunct of India, the tribal Northeast.

Holly, Meneka, Java Man and I went to Calcutta's Foreigners' Regional Registration Office, located in a turmeric yellow Art Deco building, at opening time. The man behind the front desk immediately denied that we could possibly get an Restricted Area Permit for Manipur there. 'No. Only in Delhi. Only at the Home Ministry.' We marched upstairs to the office of his boss. Seated in our four chairs in front of the massive hardwood desk of the superior, we invoked the name of Mr Bala. We smiled, we schmoozed, we supplicated. The man from downstairs appeared with some new rigmarole about us needing a tour guide to be a tour group, he had it in his Book of Doom, but I pointed out that it was only a regulation for entering India on group visas, nothing to do with getting an Restricted Area Permit. We pleaded with the desk officer to call Mr Bala. He refused but he did say that a letter from the Government of India Tourism office attesting that we were a 'bona fide tour group' might just do the trick. For now, the Foreigners' Regional Registration Office was closing for the day after an hour or two of business. We decided to throw ourselves on the mercy of the Tourism office in the morning.

The four of us went to dinner that night at a delightfully sinister Chinese restaurant with Pema and a pal of hers, a burnt-out flight attendant who came from Imphal, Manipur's capital. 'Why the hell you want to go there?' the flight attendant asked with a sneer. 'It is totally boring! Nothing to do. Nothing to eat except rice. It's backward. It's nowhere.' Her negative opinions somehow only strengthened our conviction that Manipur was the only place to be that fall.

Everyone awoke with colds, our coughing made all the worse by Calcutta's disgraceful air pollution. Anticipating a crucial day of bureaucratic encounters we hired a taxi to take us from office to office. It sat in front of the Government of India Tourism office on Shakespeare Road while an obliging clerk heard our case. Posters enticing tourists to enjoy the natural beauty and tribal cultures of Manipur and Mizoram decorated the walls. 'See, you want us to go there, don't you?' said Holly, pointing at the glossy advertisements. The clerk replied that he did indeed, but the person needed to sign our letter would be out until noon, we should return then. We tried calling Manipur House, a kind of embassy for the state in Calcutta, but they said it would be inconvenient for them to grant us a permit because there had been some apparent British mercenaries arrested recently in another strife-torn Northeast Indian state. It wasn't a good time to bring foreigners to the region.

We returned to the Tourism office and the authorizer was out having lunch. While we waited for him, Meneka sat down at one of the computers to help the Tourism clerk compose our affidavit. Holly was appointed Group Tour Leader, as the only one in the group without any hidden political/ medical agenda. After two hours, the letter was ready and photocopied. The proper person showed up to sign and rubber stamp it. We piled into our taxi and it crawled the traffic-jammed blocks to the Foreigners' Regional Registration Office. The desk officer was already gone for the day. The office would be closed the next day, we were told, because a general strike was to take place throughout Calcutta. Holly and I had made plane reservations, Calcutta to Imphal, for our group of four, but the reservations were lapsing the day of the strike and now we learned that we needed the tickets to get our Restricted Area Permit. Java Man was not amused. He was tired of wasting his valuable India time in stupid offices as a participant in our preposterous scheming. He gave us a deadline. If we weren't on our way to Manipur within two days after the strike he was going to ditch us.

Our colds and the sweltering climate of Calcutta had given our activities something of the mad hot gleam of a tropical fever. I welcomed the general strike as a respite from bureaucracy. The work stoppage was an impotent though high-solidarity protest against a hike in petrol prices. The city was dead quiet, and I slept off my cold for most of the day. We all rested up for the next bout of permit begging.

As the Foreigners' Regional Registration Office stirred to a semblance of life in the morning, we were there, without Java Man but with his passport. I had accused him of 'jeopardizing the mission' by not coming with us and he'd said he didn't care, he was going to see Mother Theresa instead. We countered the Foreigners' Regional Registration Office's initial knee-jerk refusals with much brandishing of the official Government of India Tourism letter and chants of 'Mr Bala! Mr Bala!' until the clerks relented and we were each given a fresh form to fill out plus one for Java Man. When I put 'cultural tourism' down as my purpose of visit I was told to cross it out, it implied we would be 'singing and dancing' in Manipur. We offered to sing and dance if it would get us there. Finally the permit was handed over to us, one sheet of paper for the group of four. Our leader Holly put in a plastic file folder with our Government of India Tourism letter and our Manipur tourism handouts. The brochures featured winsome photos of the brow-antlered deer.

Meneka went off to meet with an AIDS-treatment physician, who told her how to contact a colleague of his at a hospital in Manipur. Holly and I resurrected the Calcutta to Imphal plane reservations, changing them to the next morning's flight, in an airline office where, amazingly, nobody told us 'no'.

At 4:30 the four of us woke up, ready to go. We took a taxi to the airport, where Holly (perky even at that hour) had our tickets in hand and played Group Leader at the check-in counter. In the boarding lounge a signboard for travelers' checks proclaimed 'Travel Without Tension!' Our Manipur tour group was the very personification of tension as we proceeded to the runway bus. Sitting amongst indigenous Northeasterners and assorted Indians, we sank down in our seats, trying to ignore a frantic lady in a pink Indian Airlines sari who was knocking on the windows. She forced her way onto the bus as it was pulling away towards our plane. Marching straight down the aisle she zeroed in on us and demanded, 'Where are you going?'

'Imphal!' we chorused.

'Oh. I thought you were on the wrong bus...foreigners never go there...very sorry to disturb you.'

Our plane flew over mountains that I was happy to see were still thickly forested. Having been around Asia since the early '80s, I had witnessed so much ecological devastation that any forest surviving into the '90s was a pleasant surprise for me. A rough landing put us down on a small airstrip: Imphal at last. The minute we walked into the modest terminal we were accosted by a plain clothes intelligence operative. He shooed us into a narrow office where two uniformed policemen began noting down the details of our passports and permit. When they finished their paperwork, a tourism official brought us over to an empty tour bus which would take us to the Hotel Imphal. The Chin National Front's Chairman had recommended that I stay there. My CNF Manipur contact was in a town that foreigners weren't permitted to visit, so I was to telephone him and let him know that I was at the hotel so he could meet me in Imphal.

The Hotel Imphal had once been part of a deluxe chain but had been spun off, unable to keep up appearances or income in this remote, touristless place. It was in quite a state of neglect and decay. There seemed to be no staff on duty other than the manager, who showed us to our rooms. Holly and I were room-mates, being compatible travelers with the same habits of unpacking and resting and cut-and-pasting collages of tickets, brochures and local newspaper clippings. Meneka and Java Man each got singles. The rooms were comfortable enough, though undecorated and undusted.

Large expressionist paintings were splashed across the hotel stairwells and lobby, scenes of local dancing and polo players. Manipur claimed to be the birthplace of polo, and Manipuri dance was famous as one of India's most refined blendings of folklore and Hindu classicism. Ritual dance figured in the creation myths of Manipur, and the ancient kings and queens had been dancers. Hindu legends were acted out in flowing gestures by women accompanied by leaping male drummers. Their dance form had nearly died out in the 20th century but it was revived and preserved through the efforts of the great Bengali poet Rabindranath Tagore. Manipuri dance was an expression of gratitude for the riches of nature, the blessings of life in Imphal's verdant, fertile valley.

I checked at the hotel desk, but I had no messages from the Chin National Front, though I had mailed the CNF contact a note alerting him to expect my arrival. I would just have to wait and act like a tourist. The local authorities were ever-vigilant. Plain-clothes officers from an intelligence/security unit arrived to take our passports to their office, where we could collect them later.

Our group of four went for a walk about Imphal. I found the town overwhelmingly reminiscent of Burma. Saronged women ambled Imphal under rainbow parasols. They sold vegetables, fruit and lotus pods in the market. Back in the 1930s, women in Manipur had staged a feminist consumer revolt and won the economic empowerment that was still only a dream for most South Asian women. Uniformed women directed traffic, which was mostly bicycles and bicycle rickshaws with the occasional jeep.

Most people's appearance was more Southeast Asian than Indian—shorter stature, straighter hair, flatter noses, epicanthic eyes—they were from the tribes of Manipur. Graffiti around town, scrawled in Hindi (India's national language), local dialects and English, told the troops of the Indian government to get out and championed Manipur's right to its own culture and even independence. 'Manipur is not Vietnam!' slashes of red paint declared. I took that to mean that the state was not to be subdued by India's military might.

Imphal is not far from Burma. The city is less than forty miles west of the Chin-populated territory of Burma called Sagaing Division. Imphal is sixty miles or so north of Burma's Chin State by thoroughly checkpointed roads. Those border areas were forbidden to us, as were the mountains surrounding the city. A compact 8,721 square miles, Manipur is formed like a soup dish, with the Meitei tribe, mainly Hindu, in Imphal at the center and in adjacent rice-fertile plains. Christian tribes—the Nagas, known in the past as fierce headhunters, and the Kukis, a Chin sub-group—occupied the outer foothills and a rim of mountains. The dish was overflowing with ethnic conflict: tribe against tribe, clan against clan, and all the indigenous people furiously hostile to the Indian Government and its security troops. Every week the smudged four-page newspapers of Manipur carried news of an official or soldier assassinated in Imphal, or word of violence in the hill villages or at roadblocks set up by the ethnic political factions.

Everything appeared peaceful enough that day in Imphal. Our alien presence caused remarkably little stir. Every so often people greeted us in English, but we attracted few stares, no crowds of curious kids, as would happen in other regions where foreigners were not nearly as rare. Perhaps Imphal was blasé due to its own ethnic variety. Or maybe it was not considered polite—or safe—to stare at outsiders.

The air was wonderfully clean and the sun burned down as we walked to the center of town, where we stopped for Thums Up colas in a café full of teenagers. I photographed an AIDS education poster that was pasted on the café wall. Teenaged boys in Manipur were the primary target of such education campaigns, as they had an astounding affinity for intravenous drug abuse. They mostly shot up on dirt-cheap heroin from nearby Burma, although Indian narcotic cough medicine would do in a pinch.

Huge pop art billboards around town decried the dangers of drug abuse and AIDS (schoolboy + syringe = skull) and advertised Indian condoms, as well as an upcoming concert by local heavy metal favorites, The Cannibals. Like urban Burma, Manipur had a bleak hell-bent teen subculture that still worshipped Ozzy and Black Sabbath. But not only the longhaired stoners shot the hard stuff. Clean-cut honor students, Christian choir boys, Bible school girls—they all tied off and jabbed too, enthralled with heroin's deadbeat allure and the sharp hot stream from the needle.

We got our passports back from the intelligence/security unit. Attempting to parlay our charm offensive into a permit extension we dropped by the local office of the Home Ministry for tea. Holly pointed out that our 'five days' in Manipur was really three, since we flew in on the first and out on the fifth. This was met with sympathetic murmurings from the person in charge. We could apply for an extension, he told us, but that would take seven days, and of course we would have to be back in Calcutta before then. To make matters worse, the official smiled and announced, 'You will have a policeman who will enjoy with you.'

Returning to the Hotel Imphal, I tried to telephone my Chin National Front contact. I only got howler monkey sound-effects through the wires. The call would not go through. Meneka had managed to reach Dr Chowdhury, the AIDS specialist at a local hospital, and he'd invited us to meet him that evening. Just as Meneka and I were leaving the hotel for the appointment, we were accosted by a thin-faced older policeman in civilian clothes, who introduced himself as Inspector Abdulla, assigned by the intelligence/security unit as our escort. The Inspector would come with us the next day on an excursion to the Deer Sanctuary, and wanted to accompany us wherever we were now headed, as well. We brushed him off as nicely as possible, saying we were just going out for a walk, no company necessary.

Inspector Abdulla followed us out of the hotel at a not very discrete distance. As a diversion I told Meneka to stop at a pharmacy stall and buy herself a packet of cough drops, which she needed anyway. As soon as we walked on, Inspector Abdulla went up to the stall to ask what she'd bought. While he was thus occupied, we ran around the corner and jumped into a baby taxi. Our espionage maneuver nearly resulted in a clean getaway, but the Inspector caught up and grabbed onto the baby taxi's awning before the driver started it up. We had told the driver to take us to a movie theater (which happened to be near the hospital.) Inspector Abdulla tried to come along, but the driver wouldn't let him sit on the front seat with him. He'd have to squeeze in back with us. A Moslem, the Inspector apparently found that too indecorous, so he gave up. He jotted down his phone number and handed it to the baby taxi driver, instructing him to call and inform him of our destination. Inspector Abdulla did not realize it, but Meneka understood every word he said in Hindi.

When Meneka and I got out at the cinema, it was dark and drizzling. We got lost and took an unintentional detour through the hospital's pediatrics emergency ward before we found Dr Chowdhury waiting for us in his office. A bespectacled young man with a dry laugh, he served us milky tea and biscuits and explained charts he'd drawn up tracking the demographics of HIV/AIDS infection in Manipur.

'It is intravenous drug use that has brought this on,' Dr Chowdhury emphasized. The cheap heroin poured in across the Burma border. Nobody was stopping it. People in the region had long invested a lot of faith in injections and intravenous drips as cures for all ailments. They seemed to lack the kind of squeamishness about needles that Americans grew up with. So the tribes' younger generation departed from traditions of opium smoking into the bigger rush of shooting heroin with great ease. Their terrible susceptibility to the introduced substance resembled the way alcohol destroyed lives for the tribes of North America.

As if addiction sapping the strength of the young wasn't bad enough, AIDS came with the heroin fad. The disease had spread so swiftly through Burma and thence into remote China and India, and the Slorc was so oblivious, so callous, that it was being compared to the smallpox-laden blankets presented by colonists to Native American tribes. An exiled Kachin doctor from Burma had written to Hong Kong's *South China Morning Post,* 'The military dictators, of course, suppress the existence of the "AIDS Route" as it serves their purpose—what better way to eliminate troublesome ethnic minorities without wasting a single bullet! This is tantamount to an extremely cruel and sophisticated genocide.'

At least India's Government was finally paying some attention to the disease, Dr Chowdhury told us. Research projects were starting to get funding at last. Recently, educational efforts had been stepped up in Manipur—all those marvelously lurid billboards. But needles couldn't be legally obtained by the addicts, making needle-sharing ubiquitous and deadly. Blood supplies for transfusions weren't screened for the HIV/AIDS virus, hastening its infiltration of Manipur's population.

Very little help was available for the many addicts who wanted to quit. 'There are a few small drug rehabilitation programs,' Dr Chowdhury said. 'A Twelve Step foundation, plus a Christian effort in another town. But most people have no idea of Twelve Step programs and such for keeping people off drugs.' The doctor gave us directions to the local Twelve Step center. He had a good laugh when we told him about being shadowed by the CID's Inspector Abdulla. 'You may evade him by getting up early. People in town are not such early risers. The two of you must wear your *salwar kameez* to look like Indian women and arise at dawn to "go jogging". You can reach the Twelve Step foundation in the countryside—they will be awake—and get back before your Inspector even arrives to your hotel in the morning.'

I gave copies of *AIDS and Society* to Dr Chowdhury, who made some comments about governments and the drug trade as he turned the pages. We agreed that Burma's junta was up to its eyeballs in it, but he also insisted that 'all US presidents since Eisenhower have been elected with narcotics money.' I couldn't go quite that far, though I had to agree that the so-called 'war on drugs' had been so wrongheaded on so many levels as to give off strong hints of conspiracy. I had been to conferences of anti-drug-war experts who debated whether the US Government had waged the Cold War to disguise its own drug involvement—or if the US Government had gotten involved in the drug trade in order to fund the Cold War. The drug war really looked that bad, if one started examining it closely. I'd seen civil liberties trampled on in the US, and hill tribe fields sprayed with American chemicals in Burma, in the name of narcotics suppression. It never worked. All anybody ended up with was shared dirty needles and crowded jails, it seemed to me. The US and India were both woefully short on the treatment facilities that were really needed, and long on 'zero-tolerance'.

As we left to look for a baby taxi, Dr Chowdhury wished us good luck with our covert research and told us not to worry about the intelligence/ security unit: 'You are not a threat to security, and they are not so intelligent.' Nonetheless, when we returned to the hotel it was apparent that Meneka's room had been searched. Nothing was missing, but the light had been left on and her belongings were ever so slightly disrupted. Somebody, somewhere along the line had to know she was a journalist.

Meneka and I crept out of the hotel at four in the morning, ready to tell anyone that we were going jogging in the early coolness. Nobody was awake to question us. We wore our Indian outfits and both had black hair (mine dyed again) so we didn't attract too much attention from the few people who were out and about in the dim light. Meneka and I walked briskly through a Kuki neighborhood abounding in Christian churches, to the outskirts of town. At the crack of dawn, animals were being fed and goods loaded up for market, by Kukis wrapped in striped hand-woven blankets. We hailed a passing rickshaw to take us down the road toward the rehab center. We rode for several miles, between silky chartreuse rice fields, past a Hindu temple, past an Indian Army camp. When we reached the right village, Meneka got directions to the Twelve Step center by miming the universal Lou Reed spike-in-arm gesture for heroin use.

The Foundation fought its uphill battle in a walled compound with a concrete residential/office bungalow and a well-weeded vegetable garden. Dr Banerjee received us as the dozen rehab residents, all male, began their day with a Twelve Step pledge. The residents looked like any other youths we might see on the streets of Imphal, fit, alert, smiling, dressed in clean T-shirts, shorts, warm-up pants. Dr Banerjee, an enthusiastic young Bengali, was in charge of rehabilitation for The Foundation. 'It has its successes and its failures,' he said. Nobody there got tested for AIDS. 'We presume everybody here has HIV. The odds are their IV use has led to HIV and they have to L-I-V-E with it,' was how the doctor spelled it out for us. Most of the young men were healthy once they got off the heroin, with no AIDS symptoms yet, he told us. The ex-addicts recruited others for treatment, and conducted peer-counseling sessions at the compound and in Imphal town. They would in all likelihood each die quite young, with no costly medicines like AZT available to prolong their present vibrancy. Large placards listing 'The Twelve Steps' to rehabilitation and another 'Twelve Conditions of N.A.' (Narcotics Anonymous) were on display on the back verandah.

Dr Banerjee took us for a walk around the vegetable fields, flower beds and duck pond. A leech fastened onto my sandaled foot and I brushed it off before it drank much of my blood. I wondered for a moment about leeches as possible HIV/AIDS transmitters, the way they spent their days crawling from bloodstream to bloodstream. Unlikely, I decided. The blood flow seemed to go all one way—into their rubbery wormy bodies—with leeches.

Tea and cookies were brought to us on the verandah, which a sign declared a 'NICOTINE FREE Zone'. The Foundation seemed humane, even effective, but it was such a drop in the bucket. Dr Banerjee mentioned that some parents of addicts were so desperate that they had their teenagers arrested on petty charges so they'd detox in Imphal's jail. There, a Dickensian Sikh warden ran his own rehab program, experimenting on the HIV positive inmates with herbal infusions and 'sweat therapy' and claiming to have cured cancer as well as AIDS within his prison walls. Dr Banerjee told us that the warden was going to present his medical 'breakthrough' at the upcoming New Delhi AIDS conference. We'd see Dr Banerjee there too, he promised.

Meneka and I baby taxied back to the hotel, where Inspector Abdulla was already waiting to go with us on our tour. He waited some more as our tourist party ate breakfast in the hotel dining room. The only other 'tourists' there were a pair of bohemian-looking Indian men, one of whom had an oversized camera bag on the chair next to him. Meneka, acute of overhearing, caught them speaking in Bengali about visiting a prison. 'They're not tourists either,' she told us *sotto voce*. 'I think maybe they're some kind of human rights monitors.'

Right off, we tried to get rid of Inspector Abdulla by telling him there wasn't room to bring him with us in the bulky Ambassador taxi we'd hired. But he climbed in front, between the driver and Java Man. As soon as we left town, Holly and Java Man began commanding photo stops. The countryside was lush green, and they had to get pictures of all the ladies planting rice and all the kids fishing in the river. Meneka and I encouraged them to keep it up, in hopes of annoying the Inspector so much that he'd leave us alone for the rest of our stay in Manipur. We stopped at Moirang, the only town outside of Imphal that was open to tourists, and split off in four directions. Holly and Java Man photographed every fruit seller in the market, every heap of chili peppers drying in the sun, nearly every schoolchild. Meanwhile I took pictures of Moirang's anti-drug billboards for my collection.

The Deer Sanctuary was our supposed goal. Inspector Abdulla claimed to know the way, but he got us not only lost but headed into forbidden territory. As he realized that and told the driver to turn back, Meneka spotted an especially choice Meitei graffito in English and read it out loud: 'Misguided Manipur Policemen return to the correct path'. Eventually we did reach the Deer Sanctuary, a barbed wire enclosed hillside reforestation project planted with spindly pine saplings. A visiting schoolmaster told us that 'stags will be available here around two or three o'clock' but then admitted that in all his years of visiting the spot with various groups from his Catholic boys' school he had never actually seen an actual deer. Neither did we.

Our deer-disappointed tour group went off to have tea in a mosquito-infested lodge at Loktak Lake. The view there was celestial, a royal blue sky, creamy clouds, all mirrored in clear water. The light was so glorious that we had to stop the car again near the lake for more pictures: the lake dwellers' reed huts, their laughing children flourishing stalks of pink lotus blossom, the elders robed in white homespun like citizens of Heaven. We made the car stop, and stop again. Pigs, puppies and chickens had to have their photographs taken. A man in a canoe among the lotuses, and a Monet bamboo bridge appeared, and Holly and Java Man still had not run out of film.

On the way back, Inspector Abdulla seemed to be nursing a headache. Meneka played a cassette she'd found in Imphal of an old man moaning Meitei folk tunes. Then we tourists sang Christmas carols. Then we joined in with Holly's hearty rendition of 'Hey Big Spender'. We stopped in Moirang for lunch and more pictures. In front of the Jughead Hotel (Archie comics were inexplicably popular in India) Holly and I posed as Betty and Veronica. It was still weird for me to have jet-black hair and be Veronica.

Rain fell when we got to Imphal. Inspector Abdulla didn't even seem to notice, or at any rate to care, when Meneka and I jumped out of the taxi in town before we got to the hotel. I went straight to a telephone office and placed a call to the Chin National Front representative. This time I got through but a girl who answered the phone there told me that the Chins had all 'gone to Imphal'. I could only hope that meant they were on their way to meet up with me. I left a message with my name and the hotel phone number, anyway. From my experience in Bangladesh I knew that I could expect crossed signals with the CNF, but to come all the way to Imphal without seeing them seemed intolerable to me.

Meneka and I walked around without getting much in the way of second glances from the townspeople. She purchased hanks of knitting wool and we had just enough rupees with us for a rickshaw back to the hotel. Meneka had been feeling ill beyond our usual bronchial cold, but ignoring it. She promised go to the doctor when she got back to New Delhi. Meneka was famously intrepid—she had flown to Bangladesh to cover the aftermath of the cyclone the year before, one arm broken, in a sling, the other carrying her laptop computer; and had flown from there to report on carnage in Kashmir. In Manipur, being sick and having her room searched never fazed her. She would just carry her AIDS book notes around with her all day, and knit herself a sweater when pains kept her up at night.

Holly succeeded in getting a local phone call from the hotel to ring through. She reached a retired Indian Army officer, a Kuki, whose number Pema the travel agent had given her. Holly charmed the Major, her voice so genteel that he assumed she was an elderly English lady, perhaps in town to visit one of the graves in the local World War II Cemetery. He invited Holly, and companions, to attend a Sunday sunrise Baptist church service with him the next morning. Holly subtly brought up the subject of my Chin National Front contact, also a Baptist, and the Major knew him and thought he might be at the church if he was in Imphal. Furthermore, the Major—instead of the intelligence/security unit—would take charge of our remaining sightseeing. We had each received printed invitations to a

'World Tourism Day', and Sunday was also the day for polo and a traditional martial arts tournament. The Major would take us to the events in his own Land Rover.

Dressed for church, we met the Major, a bulky rhino of a man in a knit beret and gray suit, in the hotel lobby. We handed Inspector Abdulla a note telling him that his services would no longer be needed. He looked quite relieved, and we never saw him again. I would think of him months later, though, when Asia's press carried word of anti-Moslem rioting in Manipur. I hoped he wasn't a victim of yet another variation on the theme of ethnic violence, in that case inflicted by resentful tribespeople on Moslem immigrants from Bangladesh.

All was serene among the Kukis at the Baptist church. They wore red-banded blankets over striped sarongs and sweetly sang their hymns. The sermon held references to 'the plague of AIDS'. At one point during the long service, we foreign guests were asked to stand and tell the congregation our names and countries. 'Good,' I thought. 'If my CNF contact is here, he'll be able to find me.' But no one came forth afterwards.

We returned to the hotel for breakfast with the Major, his graceful young wife and their children. Meneka introduced herself to the other two 'tourists' in the dining room and sure enough, they turned out to be reporters from a Calcutta magazine working on an AIDS story. They were going to an off-limits to foreigners town but invited Meneka along, as she looked Indian enough and could speak Hindi to get past police checkpoints. I gave her a note to drop off for my Chin contact on the way.

Holly, Java Man and I toured the city with the Major, and his niece, a judge. We peered through the padlocked gate of Imphal's Orchidarium, where the Judge observed that 'there are no blooming orchids'. The Major drove us in his Land Rover down the runway used in World War II for the air support of Allied attempts to retake Burma from Japanese forces. The Japanese invaders who held Burma had laid siege to Imphal in 1944, attacking along the roads leading into the city. Supplies were then air-lifted in for Imphal's Allied defenders. The Japanese surrounding Imphal went hungry and tens of thousands of them died, but they fought on for months until retreating from the India border.

Imphal had been the high water mark of the Japanese drive to seize the British colonies in Asia. Repelled by Allied troops and their tribal guerrilla supporters as well as a mostly Burman army led by General Aung San (the father of Aung San Suu Kyi) the Japanese were eventually forced all the way out of Burma. But animosity between the frontier tribes and the plains-dwelling Burman ethnic group (which had largely sided with the Japanese at the beginning of the war) was never resolved. So groups like the Chins and Kachins were still fighting the regime, whose *modus operandi* derived directly from World War II's Japanese secret police terror tactics against indigenous civilians. On the frontiers I constantly felt as if I was as much in the 1940s as the 1990s. And never more so than speeding down that Imphal runway, as if about to take off into the deep Japanese-occupied jungle. Even though on the Burma side of that border the only foreigners now would be employees of an American oil company, Amoco, in a petroleum exploration business venture with the Slorc.

Fuming somewhat about the bolted Orchidarium, the Major drove us to the festivities for 'World Tourism Day', where the Judge got miffed when she was mistaken for Japanese, as if she was our fourth tour group member. The celebration's planners were thrilled at having actual tourists, at least three of us, present. We watched children dance, not terribly well. Speeches hailing a new dawn of tourism in Manipur were served up with tea. A program booklet was handed to us, containing this description of Manipur: 'It is in the sub-tropical zone on the north of Tropic of Cancer, featured with exceptional/conjestion of cloudly beautiful.' An Indian television camera crew interviewed Holly and Java Man regarding tourism in Manipur and at the Major's urging they registered a complaint about the Orchidarium.

We left the Tourism Day festivities early to get to the martial arts exhibition, and arrived there just in time to watch the masters: old reformed-headhunter Nagas doing ritual combat with red-wrapped spears, and elderly Meiteis wielding swords in each hand. War-making had been the way of life in the Northeast long before any Japanese or Brit had set foot there. While the Nagas solved disputes in their own villages peacefully through discussion and mediation, disputes with other villages, Naga or any other tribe's, inevitably wound up in head-taking with spears, knives, and eventually guns. Until the British showed up and tried to suppress the binges of decapitation, nobody had the authority to stop it.

Even after the British had vanished, to be replaced by rulers from India, the pattern of violence persisted, often given a political gloss. It crossed over from *ad hoc* vengeance at mid-century when the Naga leaders Jadugang and Gaidiliu (who devised her own sacred secret writing) called for Naga attacks on the Kukis, who were vilified as land-stealers. More recently, Naga rebel groups and Kukis fought each other, and non-combatants, even children, were fair game. The old men with their medieval weapons were no play-actors; they had doubtless shed their share of blood in their time.

The polo grounds resounded with more elaborate antiquated combat, on horseback. The teams played rough, on a battered ground more divot than turf. The black and gray polo ponies were dwarfish and bony and made their riders look oversized to me. The halftime show was another mock swordfight. After several men's *chukkas*, two women's teams took the field, such as it was. The women rode extremely well but played badly. The Major explained that the ball kept getting stuck in the muddy ground and the women did not quite have the arm strength to whack it out with their mallets. Still, they too seemed made of warrior stuff.

A goddess appeared later, as we sat in a café eating our afternoon chowmein under posters promoting the 'mindbending metal' of The Cannibals.

We heard long-drums pound and horns blare so we rushed to the door to watch as a procession filed past. White-turbanned men danced barefoot. Meitei women in red and green velvet blouses trimmed with gold, and stiff white skirts, whirled fiercely—like warrior princesses. Barefoot children in pristine white costumes danced the true classical Manipuri way. A jeep followed them slowly, carrying their Hindu idol, the painted statue of a goddess riding a tiger.

When we met up back at the hotel, Meneka told me she had delivered my message but had been told that the Chins 'were gone out'. With the Calcutta journalists Meneka had visited a Christian drug rehab center where the addicts were chained up by the ankles while they detoxed off heroin. The addicts were read to from the Bible while chained up. The lights were on in Meneka's room at the Hotel Imphal again, tipping us off to another search in her absence. Nobody ever cleaned there, so it wasn't merely a matter of housekeepers letting themselves into her room.

Day Four arrived, without the CNF. Java Man left for Calcutta, having seen enough polo and not enough brow-antlered deers or orchids. Holly and I wandered around Imphal looking for postcards of Manipur, which were not to be found, although the tourism office gave us postcards with scenes of an island far away in the Indian Ocean. I was still hoping for the miraculous arrival of the CNF, but it was looking like a replay of their Bangladesh no-show. Then, walking up the hotel driveway in the afternoon I spotted a jeep parked in front with a *Read the Bible* sticker on it. 'They're here!' I cried out.

My contact was waiting patiently in the hotel dining room with his wife and children. One of the girls was having her birthday that day, so I immediately produced a box of toffees out of my shoulder bag for her. The contact, an intellectual, evangelical Chin in denim, told me he hadn't gotten my letter, and the phone message had been garbled. But the Meneka message had done the trick. With a fine sense of the covert, he said, 'You can call me Mr Smith, Winston Smith.' He had brought me a present, a photocopy of his postgraduate thesis about the political views of his hero, George Orwell. We agreed that Orwell, who had served as a colonial policeman in Burma, had been the prophet of things to come, not only the power mongering and corruption evident in *Burmese Days*, but the Slorc-speak of *1984* and of course the entire *Animal Farm* scenario. Mr Smith groaned when he learned that our Barcelona companion, Java Man, had already left, 'I so would have loved to discuss *Homage to Catalonia* with him!' He asked me to wait at the hotel, saying that he'd be back in an hour with CNF representatives fresh from inside Burma.

An hour passed quickly and I got in the jeep with the Chins, who now included Salai Sang Hlun, a CNF Vice President. A Geography graduate of Rangoon University, Salai Sang Hlun had joined the CNF after the 1988 Slorc crackdown. Next to him in the front seat of the jeep was a CNF underground operative who had just been across the border in Burma's Sagaing Division, where many Chins lived. We drove off to 'the safest place to talk', which turned out to be Imphal's World War II Cemetery. Like the one in Chittagong, it held row after row of Allied graves, neatly planted with flowers. We sat on a marble plinth as Mr Smith's kids played tag among the graves.

I tape recorded the Operative's story. A shy-seeming man in his thirties, he had been jailed in Burma's second largest city, Mandalay. He described how torturers there had buried him in a pit for a week, and then 'they took all the blood samples from us—they say they want to take the blood sample, but they took a half bottle—500 milligrams from each and every one of us, blood. Since, because of the loss of blood, weakness, poor diet also, many collapsed, mainly students. Without any trial they put us behind bars, because, they say, "you are secessionists, you are out to break Burma." They flogged me and beat me and shocked me with electricals and when I could not tolerate any more, I banged my head against the wall so not to feel the pain.'

After being freed by Buddhist monks who had temporarily taken over administration of Mandalay during the ill-fated democracy uprising of '88, the Operative had joined the CNF. Now he slipped in and out of Sagaing Division, gathering news of an ever-increasing Tatmadaw presence. 'They're going to put more here,' he said, pointing straight at the exploration concession of the US oil company Amoco on my Burma map. 'They mobilize here—seven battalions here patrolling, under the pretext of exploring for oil, they are around.' The Chicago-based corporation Amoco's interest in Sagaing Division had, unfortunately for the local Chin and Naga civilians, intensified the Slorc's drive to pacify their remote homeland. I would take the Chins' information and confront Amoco executives with it in Chicago. They would be most surprised that I had gotten anywhere near their Burma concession. Eventually, dry wells and relentless demonstrations by Chicago activists would force Amoco to leave Burma, abandoning their expensive drilling equipment to the jungle. But unfortunately they wouldn't be the last petroleum multinational in league with the Slorc.

The Operative described Slorc forced labor in Sagaing Division and in the Chin State, where civilians were made to grow crops to feed the Tatmadaw soldiers, and build army barracks for troops newly stationed to guard the oil drillers. The Tatmadaw also forced people to cut down teak trees, so the timber could be sold, illegally, in Manipur for more Burmese military profit. 'They made the villagers fell the trees without paying anything. Then they pull them by buffalo to this side of the border and from there Indians get it.' The captive villagers had to hack roads through what was left of their forest. The road crews worked 'chained at the ankles', the Operative said. As we sat among Imphal's war dead, images were revolving in my mind: Slorc blood vampires, chain-ganged Chin slaves, contaminated blood in Manipur, shackled heroin addicts.

Two young men strolled through the cemetery and Mr Smith's wife called the children closer to us. 'I don't want to risk their political kidnapping,' she said. Mist turned to rain and we took shelter in the jeep. We drove into town and as the jeep sat parked on a dark, rainy street I interviewed Salai Sang Hlun, the CNF Vice President, holding my tape recorder up to the front seat to catch his soft voice. He confirmed the Operative's report of stepped-up Tatmadaw activity around the Amoco site and described the very small-scale yet determined activities of the CNF. 'Our situation is not so different from last year when we missed to meet you at Bangladesh. We have 350 soldiers trained, 200 more recruited. For weapons, through ambush we got some Burmese G3s and carbines, old Sten guns, nothing heavy.'

Salai Sang Hlun officially denied links between the CNF and the myriad rebels fighting the Indian Government in the Northeast. He had to. While the Indian government gave verbal support to Burma's democracy movement, it was not happy to have Chin and Burmese student refugees added to its Northeast ethnic mix, and was extremely suspicious about tribal people with guns possibly helping other tribal people with guns. Whatever dealings the Chins might have had with Naga or Kuki rebels needed to stay secret.

'What kind of military engagements have you had going on in the past year?' I asked Salai Sang Hlun, anticipating a description of overall strategy. His answer was utterly honest in its minimalism: 'We seized a knife from the enemy. Five of our boys made a commando raid on a police/Tatmadaw post, killed some there and took their arms. And another such. And in June of this year we got a Tatmadaw man with a mine at their mountain camp. Later we were attacked by the Tatmadaw but they got more casualties from mines we made. Then, July 17, the Tatmadaw attacked a CNF camp and took two of our rifles, killed one CNF boy. Later, our CNF took guns from police in Paletwa town, southern Chin State.'

When he finished his account of their minute corner of Burma's war, the CNF Vice President turned around to look directly at me and said with quiet intensity, 'When we Chins began this revolution, we never, never expected that anyone from the outside world would have come to see us, like you have.' Then I knew that going out of my way for the Chins had always been the right thing to do. It was worth all the Mr Balas in the world.

We drove back to the hotel and I had presents for the Chins: tins of 'gourmet' coffee, a picture book on Washington DC, postcards of the Statue of Liberty. Theirs for me were far better—soft hand-woven Chin blankets from two different clans were wrapped around my shoulders, and a carnelian bead necklace, the kind prized by tribal aristocracy, adorned my neck. They also gave me a rice-wine gourd to give to Holly, 'because she is a sculptor and likes the cultural objects'. Mr Smith told me that every day at noon, CNF supporters said 'a prayer for the revolution', and that he had taught 'the boys' in training at a CNF guerrilla camp to sing 'We Shall Overcome'. Final handshakes, and the Chin rebels got back in their jeep to speed through checkpoints and get home in time for the little girl's birthday party.

Holly had spent the afternoon cutting up the Manipur tourist brochures to collage the images onto the Indian Ocean postcards, creating surreal images of landlocked Manipur's dancers and brow-antlered deer cavorting on the white sand beach. That night Holly, Meneka and I ate dinner at the Major's home, a gated Kuki compound in a Naga neighborhood that did not like Kukis, especially those who had served in the Indian Army. The Major cured our colds for good with brandy and hot water. The next morning, he drove us to the airport in his Land Rover. Within months the Major would be assassinated by gunfire in Imphal as ethnic rivalries grew more bitter than ever. Later, Salai Sang Hlun, the CNF Vice President, would die in Indian Army custody in Mizoram. Sometimes in Manipur the border trade in Burma's teak and heroin would be disrupted by Naga or Meitei or Kuki rioting or roadblocks. But it was too late for the forests and too late for the infected addicts or those they would infect in turn.

Meneka and I had burned, hidden or disguised all of our notes, tapes and film, to deter airport confiscations, but we were allowed to board the Imphal to Calcutta plane without any search or fuss. The photographer from the Calcutta magazine team was on the same flight, white-knuckled in an aisle seat. He was mentally reliving the many airplane crash sites he had photographed for his magazine. Holly and I played with a toy aviator, a World War II Flying Tiger that my friends in Hong Kong had given me as a talisman. I stood the aviator on the windowsill so he could scan the mountains below. The aviator was my World War II self, and he always accomplished his missions unscathed. Across the aisle, the photographer did yoga breathing with his eyes closed. We flew, safer than he believed, over the emerald green, violent Northeast.

5

THE OFF SEASON

Dragon Gold. My Burma border travels again took form at a restaurant in New York City, this time a Chinese place by that name near the United Nations. Burma's government in exile, composed of members of parliament who had not been allowed to take office despite winning seats in the 1990 election, was in New York to lobby for an anti-Slorc resolution at the UN. They arranged for me to meet a visiting Wa representative, a fifty-five-year-old geologist who used the Old Testament name of Benjamin. I had long been intensely intrigued by the Wa people, of eastern Burma's Shan State.

In the British colonial days the Wa tribe had maintained quite a reputation for headhunting. 'Wild Wa' chopped off human heads with a particularly intimidating randomness, while 'Tame Wa' merely purchased heads from their wilder cousins, and with them adorned 'skull avenues' leading to their villages, ensuring healthy crops of rice and opium poppies. In the 1980s, when I haunted the Thailand/Burma border, the Wa were mainly serving as troops, really cannon fodder, for the Burma Communist Party. In 1989 those soldiers had gotten rid of their Communist officers and pronounced themselves an indigenous Wa army. In a quick spate of negotiations the Slorc proffered various inducements—cash, development projects, *laissez-faire* drug trade—and Wa leaders signed a ceasefire agreement with the Slorc.

The mountain lands of the Wa tribe had for decades been the most opium-productive region of Southeast Asia. After the Wa rapprochement with the Slorc, the narcotics business became more efficient and profitable than ever. Heroin refineries multiplied, transport routes were greased and streamlined. Now, in the fall of 1994, the Wa remained well-armed, with some factions in the southern Shan State still fighting against the regime. I was above all curious about how fragile the ceasefire might be. I wanted the Wa back in the fray, in alliance with the Kachin rebels, their neighbors to the northwest.

I was wondering if I might broker an arrangement, perhaps food for arms. The Kachins had their jade money, and were not hurting for rice, but were always short of weapons. The Wa were terribly poor, the civilians and soldiers in bare subsistence mode. But the Wa still had plenty of those old Chinese guns, bullets, shells and rockets from their Communist days. Perhaps if both groups got what they needed they'd unite and unleash their battalions of well-trained, experienced troops on the Slorc, driving the war to the center of Burma, all the way to the Slorc-held strategic city of Mandalay. Perhaps.

I didn't make any secret of my Kachin-Wa liaison agenda to Benjamin as we ate our Dragon Gold lunch. The Wa officers and soldiers I'd met before, on the Thai border years ago, including members of the tribal aristocracy, had been from the small factions which were still resisting any ceasefire deals. Benjamin, however, appeared to represent the United Wa State Army (UWSA), the enormous formerly Communist, now ceasefired force. At least 100,000 strong, the UWSA was ensconced along the China/ Burma border. Benjamin was not full-blooded Wa, he told me, but 'half Wa, half Lahu tribe, half Kachin'. There weren't a lot of educated Wa people anyway, and few could travel as Benjamin had, so he was a *de facto* representative for the whole ethnic group and a link between the UWSA and the outside world, from the UN to the US to Burma's government in exile.

Benjamin and I talked about where I'd been in Burma's frontier regions, and my relationship with the Kachin Independence Organization (KIO). I explained the mysteries of his first ever fortune cookie to him, the hidden message, the auspicious lottery numbers, the symbol of the smiling face. We lingered over jasmine tea and my map of Burma, and then Benjamin blurted out, 'You can visit our Wa land, if you wish.'

A handful of foreigners had managed to cross the border of China's Yunnan Province into the UWSA territory in 1994, including an American Christian ethnobotanist who studied the medicinal plants of Asian hill peoples. The botanist was planning to go back 'just after Christmas,' Benjamin informed me, and might I like to join her on that trip? I already had plans to revisit the Kachin headquarters, Pajau, from Yunnan Province. I promised to change my plane reservations to a post-Christmas departure. Of course I would go to the Wa.

I saw Benjamin again when a group of indigenous leaders from Burma (Karen, Chin, Mon, Wa) assembled in New York City for a seminar. For most it was their first trip to New York. As I walked past Central Park with one of the distinguished guests, an exiled Chin parliamentarian, he enquired of me, 'What is the name of that forest?' After the meetings I took the group to The Museum of the American Indian, a childhood favorite of mine that had recently been moved to lower Manhattan. As we toured the displays of Hopi pottery, beaded moccasins and Crazy Horse's war shirt, I was assured by Benjamin that all systems were go for my journey to the UWSA. I was to telephone him at the botanist's home in Arizona, on the day after Christmas, when everything would be arranged.

Christmas came and went and I called and the ethnobotanist professed to know nothing of a trip to the Wa when she answered the phone. She put Benjamin on the line and he stammered something about things not being quite set up yet. I did what I always did in such cases: I said I was going to Yunnan anyway. I'd be in touch with Benjamin *en route* in hopes that I could still go to his territory. If not, there was still Pajau, the Kachin rebel headquarters.

I left New Jersey for Hong Kong, stopping over in Seattle. In the fall of 1994 I had not only met a UWSA representative, I had met my true love. Destiny put John, who lived in the Pacific Northwest, and I in each other's paths at a garage sale in New Jersey. Slowly our attraction became irresistible. One of Cormac's cowboys, a carpenter, an engineer, a Blake buff, a jazzbo, John was meant to go fly fishing in Borneo and was meant for me. It became more and more obvious in Seattle, as we watched Travolta and Uma dance together in 'Pulp Fiction'. But I was on my way to Yunnan nevertheless. Lightning struck my plane as it took off over the Pacific, and I wrote a note informing John that I loved him and put it in my shoe, as if that would ever be found if the jet plunged to a watery disintegration. We rose safely above the clouds, and then storms rocked the landings in Taiwan and Hong Kong.

Chinese New Year was getting underway. Illegal firecrackers were blasting and ricocheting all over Hong Kong. I got on the phone to my main Kachin contact, the colonel I'd known since 1985, in Thailand and informed him I was ready to head for Pajau. The KIO had followed through on its early-'90s negotiations with the Slorc by signing its very own ceasefire on February 24, 1994. I was quite interested in how the halt in fighting had affected the KIO, and whether they thought it was temporary or really the end of the war. I also had my concept of reactivating the Wa and Kachins in conjunction.

The Kachin Colonel told me that 'it might be too difficult' for me to visit the KIO by crossing the China/Burma border but I assumed that it was just the usual ritual setback to be plowed through. Anyway if it came to that I could see the Kachins in China then cross into Burma with the Wa. But as if sensing that I was working at cross-purposes to the ceasefire, my Kachin contact also strongly advised me not to visit the UWSA.

The Chairman of the Kachin rebels, Brang Seng, who had 'adopted' me on my first visit, had died from a stroke in August '94. Now Gen. Zau Mai, who had been away on the India border when I was at Pajau, was in charge of the KIO and he happened to be in Thailand. 'Our General does not want you to see those Wa,' my colonel friend told me. I was taken aback that the leader of the KIO seemed to be issuing a direct order to me. I had never joined their army, I just been 'adopted' into a Kachin clan in a friendly and practical gesture in 1991. For some reason the Kachins were so leery of the Wa (even though they were both in the same ceasefire boat now) that they didn't even want me acting as a neutral go-between. Maybe they had decided I couldn't be neutral anymore. I left it at my plan to meet with KIO people in the jade-trading Yunnan frontier town of Mangshi, whether or not I could cross over to Pajau. My hair was, again, 'Natural Black', just in case.

I called Benjamin, still pursuing the Wa trip. He told me that the problem was the lack of anyone at the UWSA headquarters who knew enough English to translate for me. I reminded him that I spoke a bit of Chinese, and he said he'd try to arrange for a Chinese-Lahu he knew of to be my guide. That didn't pan out, and when I called again from Hong Kong, Benjamin confessed that he had 'been out of touch with headquarters for five months'. While he was representing the UWSA in the United States, floating proposals for drug eradication programs, he really had no contact with them.

I didn't want to give up the idea of pushing the Wa and Kachins together. So I called Chiangmai, Thailand looking for the one other English-speaking UWSA 'ambassador' I knew of, Sai Pao. My old border pal, Emma, found me Sai Pao's phone number. She told me that as it so happened, Sai Pao was planning to bring two foreigners to the Wa territory, a relief worker and a zoologist, both of whom I knew. Sai Pao was out of town when I called his house, but I dredged up enough long-unused Thai vocabulary to leave a message for him. I went to watch the New Year's fireworks over Hong Kong Harbor, feeling optimistic again.

Sai Pao called me back and I didn't hint around, I just asked straight out if I might go along on his trip, since Benjamin hadn't been able to arrange anything. Sai Pao said he'd be pleased to have me join them. He instructed me to meet his party at the Camellia Hotel in Kunming, the capital of China's Yunnan Province that bordered both Kachin and Wa lands, on a particular day in February. Everything was set. I'd see some KIO people, probably the Kachin Women's Association, in Mangshi, then I'd go visit the Wa. I figured Gen. Zau Mai had no jurisdiction over what I did—the whole method of my Burma work had always been to remain unhampered by factions and organizations, even avoiding funders or foundations. Anyway, I wasn't even going to Pajau, so a trip to the Wa shouldn't make any difference.

I took a two-day train to Kunming. Nearly everyone on the train chain-smoked day and night. Everyone on the train coughed like black lung miners. I immediately caught the Chinese national upper respiratory virus. Everyone on the train threw their used styrofoam ramen bowls out the windows, fouling the landscape forever. The Year of the Pig was underway.

I didn't stay long in Kunming, where in 1993 the finance minister of Burma's democratic government in exile had been stabbed to death by still unapprehended hands. I had my Kachin jade ring with me but I wore it on a neck-chain under my sweater instead of showing on my finger where it seemed like an invitation to theft. On to Mangshi I went, taking a new, worse variation of the 'sleeping bus'. Airline-type reclining seats were arranged in two tiers, three aisles in China's latest contribution to the advancement of claustrophobia in all its forms. The aisles were clogged with boxes and suitcases, plus a few passengers who weren't lucky enough to have a seat of their own.

It wasn't a fast bus, and we got into Mangshi after dark. I found a baby taxi, a recent innovation in China, and asked the driver to take me to the jade traders' hotel. When he pulled up to a very pretentious establishment I argued with him that he had the wrong address—I'd been there in 1991 and it was an unassuming place—no chrome or marble. But, like so much in China, the hotel had been transformed into something gaudy and grandiose in the blink of a Capitalist eye. It was the right place, *karaoke* lounge and all.

Since 1991, Mangshi had taken on some of the Isherwood flavor of its wild frontier neighbor, Ruili. My window looked down on a beauty parlor that was, like many of the hair-care establishments in Yunnan, a not very subtle front for prostitution. Chinese men tended to have terrible haircuts, I'd noticed. The girls in the tight burgundy velvet dresses must have had other skills. They played mah-jong with each other all day and stayed open for business all night.

By pure coincidence, Gen. Zau Mai arrived at the hotel the next afternoon, going back to Pajau after his business in Thailand. The hotel owner, who knew that I knew the KIO, invited me to a corner suite to meet the General. Lu Ra, his wife, with whom I had stayed at Pajau, was there too, chic in slacks. Gen. Zau Mai was a long-faced, high-cheekboned man with a toothy smile. His English was fluent, containing a hint of the BBC. His civilian clothes were toughened up by a black leather shooting vest with many pockets. One wouldn't mistake him for anything but a military person.

Chairman Brang Seng had been a diplomatic type, suited for dealing with Jimmy Carter's peace people. Gen. Zau Mai struck me as quite the opposite. And yet, the ceasefire with Slorc, concocted and signed by Chairman Brang Seng just before his demise, still held, as far as I knew. I assumed that the Kachins were out of the fight because they'd run out of weapons and just couldn't face battling the Tatmadaw with pipe-grenades and punji stakes anymore. I dearly wanted something to work out so the Kachins could trade rice and potatoes to the hungry Wa for AK47s, and they would all beat the hell out of the Tatmadaw.

Gen. Zau Mai didn't want to know about it. 'I do not trust those Wa,' he said. 'The Wa are still so deeply in the drugs trade, and our KIO has done such a good job of opium suppression that even the government of your United States has given praise to our efforts. Those Wa and our KIO are not on common ground at present times.' Smiling, he emphasized that it wouldn't be right for me to go to see the Wa, 'You are not just some ordinary foreigner, you are Kachin.' Smiling, I said 'I'll just have to see how it all works out. My plans are still flexible.'

We managed to change the subject to the misfortunes of the Karens, Burma's other large insurgent group, in their region to the south along the Thai border, far from the opium fields. The Karens had just about been destroyed recently, by a combination of a breakaway faction, Tatmadaw human waves, and their own poor strategy. They'd lost their crucial headquarters, Manerplaw, as well as a string of other bases, to the Burmese forces. Of course it didn't help the Karens that the Kachins and Wa were out of the war, so the Slorc could devote most of its troops to pounding the Karens into submission. The only surprise at that point was that the Karens still wouldn't submit. No surrender for them. Not even a ceasefire.

We left the Zau Mai suite to go out to dinner with the hotel owner and the General's Chinese driver, who bore a strong resemblance to my favorite Hong Kong movie star, Chow Yun-Fat. We had a room to ourselves in a rather plain little restaurant. A wok bubbled with herb-fragrant oil at the center of our table. 'You will not find this cuisine elsewhere,' the General assured me, 'this is local, west Yunnan food.' A black-skinned chicken like a Gothic basilisk was placed in the wok to simmer with medicinal roots and berries. 'This will cure that cold of yours!' Lu Ra told me, as the scent welled up from the wok. Steinlager beer, the Kachin favorite, was set out for us. I drank the beer. I ate the black chicken. When bowls of noodles cooked with the gall bladder fluid of an ox arrived, I ate that too, praising the astringent quinine taste.

I knew what sort of game was being played. I understood that I would be offered a trip across the border to Pajau in order to keep me away from the Wa. Gen. Zau Mai had heard about me but he was testing me, was I the kind of person who eats ox gall bladder soup without flinching? I was. And I was also the kind of person who could make halfway amusing small talk in Chinese with the driver. That did it. 'Since you can speak Chinese with this driver, I will send him back after he brings me to headquarters. Then he shall drive you there.' It was also to be a test for the driver: were his checkpoint running skills good enough to smuggle a green-eyed, pointy-nosed foreigner past every Chinese police and army border post?

Two days later, the Chow Yun-Fat driver showed up in the morning with a dark Chinese luxury sedan. Gam Sang, a young Kachin lawyer who served as a judge in the KIO's own legal system, rode in the back with me. We drove very fast by Yunnan's rice paddies, stopped for lunch at a tiny wayside café where the employees paid me no mind, and headed up into the mountains. Judge Gam Sang commented that he found the driver's Chinese music 'faintly annoying', so I apologized in Chinese to the driver for interrupting it and handed over a Pam Tillis tape to play in the car stereo instead. We took the turns on the road north as she warbled 'Every

Time You Walk Into the Room', a song I now associated with John and Seattle, and '*Mi Vida Loca*' which I associated with my crazy life. 'Don't you have any sweet music? Any soft music?' Judge Gam Sang complained.

Our driver passed through nine Chinese police/army checkpoints with just a honk of the horn and a nod from whoever was in charge. I turned my face away so the guards would see only my black braided hair as we blurred through. The only border post that would have posed a problem (mandatory searches) was closed. That day was the culmination of Chinese New Year festivities. Villagers from miles around were heading to a celebration, their children jacketed and hair-ribboned in holiday crimson and pink. Apparently the police were off being festive to welcome the Year of the Pig as well. We crossed the border like a sword through beancurd and wound up at Pajau late in the afternoon. I valued every leech-bitten mile of my arduous 1991 journey to Pajau, but it was also not bad to zoom over there in sunglasses in a comfortable car with a well-connected driver in one day.

Pajau looked shabbier than ever, its bamboo buildings rain-darkened and swaddled in plastic wrap for the winter. Smoke from pine logs in the wood- stoves drifted up from all the buildings. Gray fog hung over the scene. I'd stay at Lu Ra's old cabin, as in 1991, but she was down the hill with her husband in a newer place. Their children were in boarding school overseas now.

I was welcomed by a KIO official whom I knew and disliked from the old Thai border days. A slick English-speaker, he functioned as one of the KIO's diplomats, journeying to various countries for conferences and negotiations, furnishing information on the Kachins to relief workers and journalists. On a trip from the Karens' late lamented headquarters, Manerplaw, to a Thailand border town back in 1987, the Envoy had tried to set us up in a hotel room as if I were a local prostitute. I had kicked him out; since then I'd heard more than once about him harassing young foreign women working on the Thai/Burma border. Now he was back at KIO headquarters, though he still traveled. He reminisced to me about a trip he had made to the United States: the joys of fast food at Carl's Jr., and those American women, and 'the many Negroes there'.

Some other KIO officials came to greet me and share economic news. They had tried strawberry growing, but the crop turned out worthless, only cold-stunted berries, they informed me. Now they placed their financial hopes in a sugar-cane refining mill that Slorc was supposed to let them run.

I was given a uniform to wear during my stay at Pajau, since all sorts of Chinese people were in and out of the camp those days and I'd be less conspicuous to them if I was dressed like the rest of the troops. Pajau was pervaded by a damp chill, so I wore wool tights, a silk undershirt, and a turtleneck sweater under the olive drab no-insignia shirt and trousers, and a black cardigan and my black wool overcoat on top of them. That night I slept in two layers of clothing under blankets and a Chinese quilt. When I awoke, the morning was clear, the air fresh. Pajau felt like one of those old British colonial hill stations where the climate was considered invigorating, only now it was the dead of winter when nobody visited.

Nam Grawng, a young woman soldier with a pageboy haircut and some English vocabulary, would serve as my *aide de camp*. Mai Mai, who had been my 1991 assistant at Pajau, had been promoted to sergeant in the War Office. Mid-morning, Nam Grawng brought in a big enamel tray crowded with my breakfast dishes: stir-fried vegetables saturated with garlic, soup, fried potatoes, rice. I'd dine that way twice a day, alone, with coffee, tea and cookies always on hand the rest of the time. Ja Seng Kawn was away but would return to Pajau soon, Nam Grawng told me. Friends from '91—Lt. N'Kyaw Tang, Maj. Pan Awng—were down in Laiza for their health, undergoing cures at the new hospital which had been built with contributions from my Hong Kong friends and others. Lt. Hkun Nawng, who had guided me to Pajau the hard way in '91, was now in Myitkyina at an office the Slorc allowed the KIO to maintain in the city under the ceasefire agreement.

I commenced my Pajau meetings by tape recording the KIO health and education ministers at the cabin, with Judge Gam Sang as my translator. Judge Gam Sang still wore the civilian clothes he'd worn in China, with a warm purple parka that was a contrast to everyone else's army green tones. The health official told me that the KIO was trying hard to educate the population about HIV/AIDS, distributing a calendar that illustrated plainly worded information about transmission and prevention with line drawings (a mother beast-feeding, lovers hugging framed in a heart, a syringe hitting a vein, a man having his back tattooed). Despite the ceasefire, the Kachins received no support from the Slorc for their anti-AIDS campaigning. That did not surprise me. I knew that even AIDS education materials in the ethnic-dominant *Burmese* language had not gotten past Slorc censors to the public. Informing the mountain people about the disease, using their own languages, was about the last priority of the regime.

I gave the education minister an environmental encyclopedia for the school children, and he updated me on the KIO's civilian sector. 'Our education department is mainly in need of teacher training, so the KIO may have staff for all the schools. Each and every village wants a school but we have not enough teachers,' he told me. Exiled Kachins living in America and elsewhere helped out by funding several small development projects, but it seemed that major international aid organizations weren't very interested in the Kachins, and their need for social programs was about to increase.

The Chinese authorities wanted all the Kachin refugees to go back to the Burma side of the border soon, since the ceasefire was in effect. The

KIO was expecting the arrival of tens of thousands of returnees, who would need land and schools and clinics and other assistance. I also found out that the All Burma Students Democratic Front (ABSDF) group whose young ranks had been riddled with spies or spy paranoia at the time of my previous visit to Pajau, had been sent packing. The ABSDF, still swearing to overthrow the Slorc by force, was too awkward for the Kachins to shelter under the ceasefire conditions .

The suspension of battle had by no means stopped human rights abuse in the Kachin State. Forced labor was still ubiquitous wherever the Tatmadaw held sway, civilians had to grow rice for the Tatmadaw, and rape by Tatmadaw soldiers was still common near their garrisons, adding to the spread of AIDS, the KIO officials said.

Gen. Zau Mai, in uniform and shooting vest, stopped by to visit me. I had to ask him for permission for whatever I wanted to do at Pajau. 'Can I revisit the village that I walked to from here in 1991, the one with the middle school?'

'Yes, that visit can be arranged for you, it is not any problem,' Gen. Zau Mai nodded.

'And what about the trail I rode by mule from Laiza?'

'For you, going to Laiza is not really possible now. Too, too many Chinese are in Laiza now, you see.'

'Actually I was more interested in the trail itself—the amazing forests along the way. I want to see those again, make sure they can be protected, maybe studied, if they are still there.'

'Oh, your forest still exists in that area. Don't mind about it. But nobody goes that way anymore. To go to Laiza from here in Pajau we just go through China by motorcar. The old trail is not in use, so I don't think you will really need to go there.' He also firmly nixed my traveling north from Pajau, to a region I hadn't visited before. I understood that having an anti-Slorc foreigner travel around asking questions and taking pictures was not considered 'convenient' or appropriate in the new ceasefire atmosphere.

The KIO had always been hierarchal, quite the military government itself. Snappy salutes, deference, and the privileges of officership characterized the Kachins as much as any past outpost of the British colonial empire. With the General in charge of the KIO and in residence at Pajau the weight of protocol was particularly obvious. Anything else I thought of that I wanted to do would have be requested of my old acquaintance the Envoy and relayed to Gen. Zau Mai for approval or disapproval. I felt controlled and isolated, although I was collecting useful information already. I hoped that Ja Seng Hkawn's arrival would improve things.

U Nu, Burma's first Prime Minister after Independence from Britain, had just died in Burma's capital, Rangoon. The dictator Ne Win had seized the government from U Nu in 1962, and the Slorc had held U Nu under house arrest (as it had Aung San Suu Kyi) more recently. Gen. Zau Mai and I speculated on what the reaction of Burma's alternately cowed and restive urban population would be to U Nu's death. Perhaps there would be some disturbance at the funeral, we imagined. Maybe that would be the spark that could again inflame the country. Gen. Zau Mai felt that unless such central Burma political ignition happened, there was no longer any need for frontier people like the Kachins to wage revolution. The KIO was still an opposition group, he insisted, it had not (no matter what the Slorc newspaper said) 'come back to the legal fold'. But it just wasn't worth fighting anymore as long as one could hold onto one's own territory, a safe haven for one's own people.

My meetings over for the day, I sat in a cane-seated chair by the wood-stove and read. The electricity crackled off and Nam Grawng lit a candle for me. I read the tropical teen erotica of Marguerite Duras' *The Lover*. Outside the camp looked misty blue with a few lights flickering, a few voices laughing, young soldiers talking, a guitar. It began to rain during the night.

In the rainy morning, after another solitary splendid breakfast, a soldier showed up to bring me and Nam Grawng to the nearby village that I had toured in 1991. Walking out of Pajau I noticed the same rubbish tip that had disfigured a barracks area four years before. It had spread further down its hillside, a waterfall of plastic bags and bottles, including debris of Pepsi-Cola, which was being boycotted worldwide by Burma activists because of the company's joint venture with a Slorc crony in Rangoon.

The whole headquarters camp seemed so rickety, frail, a kid's sandbox battle model of barracks, a footbridge, a communications tower. It all looked airplane-glued together out of charred matchsticks. The nearby civilian houses belonging to KIO relatives and returned refugees looked similarly Tobacco Road. Hills had just a fuzz of vegetation, no crops grew anywhere, some mules browsed the cold ground in wayside ravines and untilled fields. The weather cleared up as we walked.

On the way we met a young English-speaking Kachin officer who was very cynical and unhappy about the ceasefire. He claimed that others of his generation felt the same way, and that the Kachin Army was already losing its edge through inaction. 'We would rather fight,' the officer said. He thought that the cities of Burma might explode in violence during the burial of U Nu. He hoped so, anyway.

At the village Nam Grawng and I stopped in at a new clinic, staffed by a woman doctor I'd met before in Laiza. A Phoebe Cates poster decorated the wall along with health-advice posters and a Gothic-lettered sign reading 'Respect The Burden'. The tables and countertops were made of bamboo neatly covered with the Kachins' other favorite material, clear plastic sheeting. An antique-looking pendulum clock ticked feebly on a high shelf. The doctor had her lab-coated nurses show me how they sterilized the medical instruments in beakers of boiling water as an AIDS prevention measure. She asked me to find for her a videotape of 'foreign handicapped people competing in sports events', so she could show it to inspire and encourage the wounded soldiers at the rehabilitation center.

I went on to the kindergarten, which was smoky from a fire built for warmth. The children there were stuffed into as many layers of clothing as their older brothers and sisters had been in '91, and they were just as cute, just as immersed in the alphabet and the nursery rhymes. The adjacent middle school had new teachers, young Kachin women who had replaced the ABSDF teachers I'd met there in 1991. Bright-eyed children wrote their Kachin language lessons on a blackboard, the Roman script so familiar to me, the words themselves so unknown. Some of the older kids already wore the olive drab uniform of the Kachin Army. I asked the students what they wanted to be some day—but only one said 'a soldier'. The rest would be nurses, doctors, engineers, or (most popular) 'study theology'. The ceasefire at least held out the chance for rebel-educated young people to attend a Bible school in Myitkyina.

We walked back to Pajau, where a thunderstorm hit at night. The plastic on the cabin roof kept all the water out. The next morning, as the sun emerged, Sgt. Mai Mai stopped in, radiant in camouflage fatigues and pink nailpolish, with a young army boyfriend who spoke some English. Sgt. Mai Mai told me she was now working in the Cipher department. Their visit was interrupted by the arrival of a KIO anti-narcotics program official, who I interviewed. He claimed that the KIO's opium crop prevention program had been very successful, but admitted that crop substitution was less so. Agricultural help from the Chinese Government or overseas organizations had never really materialized. Fields were being left fallow for lack of replacement crops. The KIO had managed to set up a few rehabilitation facilities for opium and heroin addicts, he said, and no more drug dealers had been executed since 1991.

Late in the afternoon, Ja Seng Hkawn arrived from a Chinese border town where she now spent most of her time. My Kachin sister was tanner and of course much thinner than when I'd last seen her, with longer hair. Instead of the one-size-fits-all sarongs she'd always worn when pregnant, she was wearing gray sweats and an old-fashioned tan wool coat. She was now the mother of a lively little girl and a baby boy—not twins after all. She had just had her thirty-second birthday. 'There have been a lot of changes,' she said, rolling her big dark eyes. But we were still drinking tea with our chairs drawn up to the warmth of the wood-stove, as before.

Having failed in the Chinese sweater business, Ja Seng Hkawn had gone on to the jade trade, visiting the Slorc-controlled mining center, Hpakant, every so often, speculating on stones to sell in China. The Kachin Women's Association members I'd met before had dispersed along with their officer husbands to Laiza or to bases up north. The Association's founder, Madame Brang Seng, Ja Seng Hkawn's mother, stayed in China and took care of the two children because 'the baby helpers kept quitting'.

Since the ceasefire, everybody's political activities seemed to be in a downward slump. People were just trying to make a little money now. To cheer Ja Seng Hkawn up, I told her about the Free Burma movement which was growing among exiles and supporters in the United States, and about meeting John. 'I am so happy you have found your life partner!' she said with a delighted smile. As we parted, the night sky was clear, full of pinpoint stars, and a jet, some commercial airline flight, streaked across them high above Pajau. 'I want to travel,' Ja Seng Hkawn said wistfully, 'I want to go overseas.'

A cold spell settled on Pajau and in the morning frost coated the ground with crunchy white crystals. Condensation dripped off the roof plastic of the wood-heated cabins. The Envoy showed up to be interviewed, sitting well away from me with my tape recorder on the tea table in front of him. In 1992, he told me, the KIO 'conducted a referendum, in the towns and villages we collected opinions about talking to the enemy. We asked the leaders, the mature persons what they thought. A majority said that to negotiate with Slorc was not wrong, but we must not abandon the main goals and policy of KIO. We must hold fast to federal autonomy system. No surrender. No "legal fold" as the Slorc like to say about ceasefires. And so we are still not yet to the legal fold. The alliance groups against the Slorc have rejected us now because of our ceasefire, but we do not reject them. I believe later they will understand us.'

The Envoy described how the ceasefire was maintained: 'We have good relationship with the Slorc, they are respectful of us. We have our KIO border with them, if there is a problem with them coming over to it, we can talk about it with them. They watch us in Myitkyina or if we go down to Rangoon for meetings, they have their security of course. Our people can go to their areas in the Kachin State if we are unarmed.'

He also gave me his version of why the Kachins had signed the ceasefire agreement in the first place: that it was due to 'global politics'. Because so many other conflicts in the world were being resolved, negotiated, the KIO felt it was their turn to 'adapt', to evolve away from warfare. They were no longer recruiting soldiers or purchasing weapons, just going along with the ceasefire arrangements that allowed them to keep their territory, keep what arms they had, and venture down to Myitkyina unhindered. The Tatmadaw had already encroached on KIO customs posts for the jade trade, putting a substantial depression in their finances, but Laiza thrived now, and the sugar business looked promising.

After the Envoy left, Ja Seng Hkawn came to my cabin and we went over to her Kachin Women's Association office, in a wooden building at the edge of the base. The office had a television set connected up to receive satellite BBC TV. A hodgepodge of posters was on display—Kachin calendar-girl brides, a dove fluttering above the word PEACE, old Chinese Mao Tse-Tung tableaux—as well as the spotted skin of an endangered jungle cat. Ja Seng Hkawn and I shared some *lapet thoke*, the Burman green tea salad, and made plans for me to interview women in and around Pajau about their lives. I knew that a few Burma activists would be attending an upcoming United Nations conference on women to be held in Beijing, and I would send my Kachin interview report to the conference with them. I had hoped that Ja Seng Hkawn might go to the Beijing conference, but it seemed to be hard to arrange; her China/Burma border travel ID card was usable no farther than Kunming.

My report project would necessitate my skipping the Wa trip. There was no way I could make it back to Kunming and the Camellia Hotel rendezvous with Sai Pao and the other foreigners, if I was going to spend days around Pajau interviewing women. I felt that since I was already with the Kachins, I should make the best of it, and not regret missing a visit to the Wa, much as they had always interested me. It meant that I was going along with Gen. Zau Mai's wishes after all, as if I really did have some loyalty to the KIO.

Ja Seng Hkawn and I walked up to the compound where the badly wounded soldiers lived. Those who were missing legs were still using rough wooden crutches. Information I had sent to Pajau about making artificial limbs had not been used. Probably they needed an experienced advisor or instructor to get such a project going. Most of the resident soldiers whom I had met in 1991 were married now, with young children. They made their living by cooperatively fabricating woven-bamboo walls, working alongside their wives or buddies. A young soldier gathered up bamboo slats while perched on a low bench, his uniform trousers knotted at the right knee where the rest of his leg had been blown off by a landmine. His pretty wife, all in red, squatted down to weave the strands. Her cherry-cheeked baby smiled over her shoulder in a cloth carrier. Together the couple created an intricate tight herringbone house wall.

Ja Seng Hkawn's daughter was with us on our hike, in tears half the time because she wanted to be carried and her mother refused to pick her up. 'She'll have to learn that when we're here in our Kachin land we have to walk,' Ja Seng Hkawn said sternly. She brought me to my first interviewee, Maran Roi Ja, a sad-eyed sixty-four-year-old example of self-sufficiency who was raising fluffy white rabbits in a shed full of wooden cages. The silky-soft rabbit hair would be combed off to be spun into yarn for a Kachin Women's Association sweater knitting project. I turned on my tape recorder: 'In '63 I joined this revolutionary life and after that, not much longer, my husband and I were captured by Burmese troops and we were put together in jail for four years, because he was in the Kachin Army. And in the jail we got two children. When my younger one was three months old, we were separated—I was put in the women's jail and I escaped. And my husband was left in for ten years.'

Maran Roi Ja had defied all hardship and her children and husband survived. 'In my life I got so many blessings from God, I can't count it. I stay by myself only. My husband is in Kachin Army camp, I have no helpers, no runner, but I can do so many works daily and I never got sick. Just the last three months, some skin irritations, just for one month—that's as sick as I've ever been. So I want to give my gratitude to God for blessing and taking care of me in my life.'

I asked Maran Roi Ja about her hopes for the future and she replied, 'In the past I have already tried my best for our Kachin society and our revolutionary life. Now I'm already an old lady and my goal is for my children and grandchildren—my intention is to further educate these second and third generation. I want to support them as much as I can.'

Ja Seng Hkawn and I climbed a nearby hill to the grave of Chairman Brang Seng, her father. His very plain cement tomb stood beneath an open, red-pillared tin roof. Wreaths of red, yellow, blue and white silk flowers were displayed on wooden easels in front of it. A small delegation of Slorc officials had attended the Chairman's funeral at Pajau, and had even been allowed to stay overnight under close guard, Ja Seng Hkawn informed me.

The ceasefire with the Slorc had been something of a shock to many at the KIO headquarters, but trust in the late Chairman had been such that his vision or strategy was accepted. Then, coming so soon after the ceasefire agreement, Chairman Brang Seng's sudden death had devastated Pajau. His widow had become the first woman to serve on the KIO's Central Committee. But Ja Seng Hkawn revealed that her mother was extremely depressed, barely functioning, 'sick with grief'.

Pajau was very cold that night. Sleet pelted the plastic. In the dark the Jazz Hour on the Voice of America played crystalline through my shortwave radio. Old previously lost recordings by Glen Miller had been unearthed. I was in a tangible 1940s time-warp in my bamboo bed, swathed in silk and wool with Glen Miller's 'Moonlight Serenade' swinging as if the war was still on and that war was still America against Japan in those Kachin hills.

The World War II flashback continued when Ja Seng Hkawn and I went to the military hospital in the morning to interview Dr Bawk Lu, a stocky short-haired KIO lieutenant. The doctor wore a China-Burma-India style leather and fleece aviator's jacket. She was a forty-year-old single woman ('it's unusual for Kachins', she grinned). In addition to medical service in the hospital, she raised livestock and sewed clothing for her own income. I asked her about the position of women in her society. 'In this Kachin custom role, we women are very important persons. We are not very educated people, most of the Kachin people are not very educated. So we have to try our best for our Kachin culture.' She continued, 'For a woman, if we can work more, we will progress from our status now.'

I inquired about the illnesses prevalent at the dimly-lit but spacious hospital, which treated soldiers, their families, and civilians from the immediate area. 'Sometimes pneumonia and influenza appear here, and in the rainy season, diarrhea. Men and women are not very different in health conditions here. In this area we don't know that there is AIDS. But one soldier from 11th Battalion was the first diagnosed for sure.' The hospital had posters about HIV/AIDS prevention on display. 'We never can diagnose which people have AIDS, as we never had such AIDS tests in the area,' Dr Nem Ram, another female doctor at the hospital told me. 'There is not much general education about it.'

Dr Nem Ram, a Kachin Army 2nd lieutenant, made her living raising chickens and pigs and running a small village shop. Married at twenty-seven she was now thirty-eight, and had three children. She had joined the Kachin Army on January 1st, 1979, she told me, 'and the reason is that I knew we women must also do this real struggle, ourselves'. She explained that the Kachin Army did not pay salaries, so it was up to the wives of soldiers to support their families. In Kachin Army life, the soldiers were the 'dependents', their wives the breadwinners. If the wives were themselves soldiers, they still got into business on the side, like the poultry market or the little shops that lined roads in and out of Pajau.

I also interviewed Corporal Laphai Hkawn, a vivacious twenty-five-year-old unmarried nurse who wore a 'Made in America' sweatshirt and worked in the surgical ward. She was drafted into the Kachin Army in 1991, but she was a 'half-volunteer', she said—she had been meaning to join anyway, and was now 'intending to do this work until the end'. Her sincerity and dedication were typical of the Kachin women who kept the whole rebel health care system functioning. The women working at the hospital said that they were quite healthy, themselves, except for the occasional cold. In response to my questions, the hospital staff members told me that they knew of no cases of domestic violence in their area, only brutality directed against women by the Tatmadaw in Kachin regions beyond KIO control.

A café now occupied the building above the parade ground where I had secretly watched the anti-drug rally in '91. We dropped off Ja Seng Hkawn's daughter with her dad there, and went on to a village that had grown up just outside the base. We met Dr Chang Lawm (another doctor/entrepreneur) there. Ja Seng Hkawn and I had noodle soup for lunch at the doctor's shop before I interviewed her. We began with her personal history, or *herstory*: She had 'volunteered to this revolution in the jungle' after high school. 'When I got married I was twenty-nine years old and I

bore three children, two boys and one girl, but only the one girl is left, the
two boys died. Now I serve in the military hospital as a doctor. As well, I
serve as Kachin Women's Association leader at this camp level. Also I find
money for my family by selling goods at a shop.' Her bamboo stall had a
one-wok kitchen, a few tables, a front counter and shelves with the typical
goods—bars and boxes of Chinese soap, cans and bottles of Chinese beer
and soda-pop, yarn, thread, matches, flashlights, batteries. I asked her
what woman she most admired and she answered, 'The Kachin women
who can make a life in the jungle.' For the next generation, Dr Chang
Lawm said, 'We hope for peace, as in our leaders' speeches. So I hope the
future can be better.'

Then Ja Seng Hkawn and I walked over to a large new house where the
decor included flowered cotton tablecloths and chair-covers, and plenty of
calendars on the walls (including the ones with AIDS information inside). In
the front room we assembled a few civilian women in their twenties and
thirties for interviews. They were dressed in hummingbird colors to brighten
a winter day, in sarongs layered over sweatpants, with sweaters and scarves.
The women's children, well-insulated in wool blankets, knit hats and bunny
cardigans, played in the room's corners.

I started asking questions and Ja Seng Hkawn translated. Most of the
women had been Kachin Army soldiers, adventurous, independent souls,
who retired from the service after marriage (usually to other soldiers) and
raised children while working, taking in meagre profits from their shops or
the Kachin Women's Association sewing project. As they'd had to complete
their military service before they could marry, their marriage age had been
later, and their family size smaller, than those of village women elsewhere
in the Kachin mountains.

One of the civilian interviewees, asked about women's role in Kachin
culture, said, 'In the past we heard that our women's status is really low if
compared with Kachin men, but these days everything is changing, so we
women can do whatever we have an idea to do. And we can speak freely.'
Although they lived in an isolated region which had been at war for decades,
the role of Kachin women was changing in pace with the more 'modern'
countries of the outside world.

While Kachin men might still refer patronizingly to a person being 'only
a woman', the Kachin women I interviewed seemed to shrug off such affronts
and view a lack of education as their gender's only real obstacle. As one
woman put it, 'We have the chance to work the same as men in our Kachin
culture. But there's a shortage of education for Kachin women, that's why
there's still a little weakness,' and she continued, 'If the woman has the
ability to work more, if she can work the same as the men, we'll have the
same rights.' Personal responsibility was a theme for all of them. They
appeared to find their roles in the revolution, and as family providers,

clearly defined, and to feel that they had the power to change things through their own efforts.

I asked them what women they admired. The name of Madam Brang Seng, the founder of the Kachin Women's Association, came up frequently: 'because she was indeed giving us love and also when in deep troubled times she gave us food and that kind of love, and also she tried to get some food for the villages and help from outsiders. Until now she still works guiding us. As in the Kachin Women's Association. Guiding and leading us.' And 'because she has been a role model for us in everything'. They also mentioned Aung San Suu Kyi, as 'the real symbol of democracy and she struggles for that'. Although she was of the dominant Burman ethnicity herself, Aung San Suu Kyi had gone to the Kachin State back before her house arrest by Slorc. She had posed for photographs in authentic Kachin embroidery and silver, identifying herself with a tribe the regime considered uncivilized, a radical step for a Burman politician. The show of support earned her considerable affection among the Kachins.

As the health workers had indicated, domestic violence appeared to exist outside of the experience of the Kachin civilian women. Perhaps its rarity around Pajau was due to revolutionary discipline, or even female economic empowerment, but more likely it was because the Kachins had a remarkably non-confrontational culture. Even verbal arguments, heated words between relatives or strangers, were very unusual. I had never seen a Kachin child get hit, and the act of raising a fist to a spouse was viewed as a complete absurdity. About rape and other war zone violence against women, a thirty-one-year-old mother/shopkeeper said, 'When I wasn't joined in the Kachin Army, I heard about it happening in other places. My relatives, two girls, teenagers, they were told by Burmese soldiers to carry their loads in the forest, they have been raped by all the Burmese troops. And one girl became paralyzed at the time.'

The interviewees definitely had the sense that they lived in a safe haven, that outside of rebel regions women were the prey of the Tatmadaw: 'I never heard of such things happening within Kachin Army liberated areas. But in Burmese areas I heard that it is likely to happen.' Rape, and other sexual abuse of women and girls continued to be one of the Tatmadaw's most characteristic tactics. The violation of women's sexual integrity was intended to terrorize civilians suspected of rebel connections, or just rebel sympathies, and to dehumanize entire ethnic groups. The Tatmadaw's rape of women in occupied villages, girls taken as military porters, children in farm fields, pregnant mothers, captured women's group leaders, often included the use of sharp instruments like bayonets for further torture and mutilation, and very, very often, ended only in death.

As usual, I asked about AIDS. I had seen a Burmese women's magazine with an ad offering a patent medicine purported to cure the disease, had heard wild tales of 'vampires' in Burma stealing hill children to use their 'clean blood' to concoct AIDS cures, and I knew that the Slorc had taken no national educational steps. But the women near Pajau seemed to have reasonably accurate knowledge of the disease. 'I've never seen in this area which person is getting this AIDS disease,' a thirty-four-year-old participant in the sewing project told me, 'but by reading and seeing pictures, I know it's international and how this disease may come here, and how we can protect against it.' A shopkeeper said, 'Along this area, I did not hear that anyone was having such diseases, but in the world, we heard that so many people are suffering from this AIDS disease. And even in nearby areas like Laiza, there are some symptoms of AIDS, so we can assume that in this area AIDS is beginning.'

With my final questions I kept having a hard time getting the Kachin women to talk about their own goals in life. In neighboring China, a national public opinion poll had just determined that 60 percent of Chinese people considered their purpose in life to be 'to work hard and make lots of money', but it was hard to get the women of the KIO area to focus at all on what they wanted, materially or emotionally, for themselves. The individual and the political were inextricably braided together for them. Only after the KIO's aims of autonomy, federalism, their own 'nation', lasting peace, were achieved, could the cherished vision of safe, happy, well-educated children be realized. For the most part, the Kachin women had faith that the future would be better for their children, and their children's education was their one fond hope for the future. 'Now I am already a married woman, and now I have the three children. I intend for my children to be great learned people, and I shall try for that.'

Education—a child with a textbook, a university graduate with respect and a good job—was the great love of Burma. All over Burma, rebel-held 'liberated' areas like Pajau and its environs had produced utopian communities during the 1970s and '80s. A richer, stronger, relentless Tatmadaw in the 1990s had crushed most of those safe zones, most recently Manerplaw, the Karen headquarters (with its hydro-power, guest house, and cultural programs). While they lasted, though, the rebel utopias were distinguished by their schools and health facilities, which even if only dirt-floored bamboo huts, tried to exemplify the attributes of an ideal society. Indigenous cultural practices were encouraged, literacy rose, city-educated rebels learned skills from mountain folk, rice grew in terraces, rabbits were raised, strawberries were attempted.

It seemed that the over-all intention of the KIO under Gen. Zau Mai was now to develop their own area along utopian lines, keeping troops in uniform but emphasizing economic and social development. The ceasefired Wa were trying for their own special haven too, but only more poverty had met their demands for favors from the Slorc and international donors, and only opium flowed from their fields. At the same time, in the cities of Slorc-controlled Burma, the universities were shut down by the junta for years. Education in Burma really was the disillusionment of a failed revolt, corruption, a child with a gun, a university graduate with a jail sentence instead of a job.

I gave the interviewees postcards of the Statue of Liberty. I took pictures of some of the women smiling from the counters of their bamboo and plastic emporiums. Their pre-school children poked their fuzzy-hatted heads out the doorways, or rode on the proprietresses' backs in baby carriers with warm yellow appliquéd blankets wrapped over them. Female entrepreneurship was common throughout Burma (a nation of lady shopkeepers) and the Kachin women especially relished their business life, though prices were high on the wholesale Chinese goods and retail mark-ups low for a largely impoverished clientele.

Ja Seng Hkawn and I went back to my cabin, where I interviewed two extroverted, sturdy-looking young female soldiers from the War Office, a corporal with cropped hair and a private with a ponytail. Both had volunteered for the Kachin Army after graduating from high school in government-controlled cities. They both agreed that 'women in our Kachin culture are nowadays not very different from men'. The Private told me that her own goal was 'to be a political leader'. The Corporal said that she admired Aung San Suu Kyi, whose speeches she had heard on the tapes that circulated throughout Burma, and whose essays she'd been reading. The Corporal's own goal was 'for the whole country. Because I'm already a Kachin Army woman soldier, so I hope for the country's freedom, because after that I hope there will be more good status for me and for my family and my nation, for my Kachin people.'

After the interviews were done, Ja Seng Hkawn mentioned that the Kachin Women's Association sewing project had tried making Kachin dolls as I had suggested in 1991 (picturing charming embroidered rag ones with sequins sewn on the shoulders for silver discs.) 'But they were no good at all. They were not proper sellable dolls. Nobody would buy such poorly made dolls. Not even you would like one, I believe.' She thought a more promising project might be a kind of feral tea she'd discovered growing around Pajau. It seemed that real tea had once been planted there, long before the war, or wars, and some hardy bushes still survived. When their leaves were dried, the tea was actually drinkable. Maybe the wild tea leaves could be harvested, used, even sold. Our tea discussion was interrupted by the news that the sister of a Kachin Army officer had just died in a car crash in China. Ja Seng Hkawn had to go back over the border to help the victim's family. She promised to return to Pajau and be interviewed for my report before I left.

The next day I was invited over to Gen. Zau Mai's bamboo house. He was engrossed in a game of Hollywood, a gin variation, with the KIO

Central Committee's economics specialist. It was a complex game, hard-fought though no bets were being entertained. I sat down to watch and sip some of the General's stock of Indonesian coffee. He had cut down on drinking alcohol for health reasons and was deep into the caffeine. I got to have *lapet thoke* too. I was thinking of Gen. Zau Mai as a cunning game player, pitting his wits against the Slorc, playing the ceasefire game for whatever the Kachins might get out of it. The General wasn't doing that well at Hollywood, however. The economics specialist was winning the game, with considerable kibitzing on his behalf by Lu Ra. Turning around to me, Gen. Zau Mai announced that he had a question about the English language. 'I have looked for this word in all my dictionaries but I could not find it. I heard it on the radio, in the report on a film. It is some sort of product of the forest. What is the meaning of "Gump?"'

After I had explained the proper name, the General mentioned to me that the Envoy had told him I'd be 'leaving Pajau the day after tomorrow, as the work with Ja Seng Hkawn is finished'. I managed to get my departure pushed back a few more days. The Chow Yun-Fat driver would come up to headquarters and bring me back over the China border. I also received permission to teach a three day martial arts class for the headquarters soldier girls, the way I had taught Mon female soldiers in southern Burma in 1988. I felt more qualified in 1995 than back then, as I'd since earned a black belt in karate (the first female in the history of my *dojo* to do so) and had taught adults and children for a few years in New Jersey. Sgt. Mai Mai had told me that the women soldiers at Pajau hadn't had any unarmed training, so I was glad I'd have the time to go over the basics with a small group of them.

Having nothing else arranged for the afternoon, I went back to my own wood-stove. *The Lover* was done with and I'd started reading my fourteenth Patrick O'Brian novel, *The Nutmeg of Consolation*. Enthralled as O'Brian's heroes sailed off for the Java Sea, I drank more coffee with 'The Nutmeg'. At the end of the day I tabulated my caffeine intake: pre-breakfast coffee, tea with breakfast, coffee on a visit to the Kachin Women's Association office, two more teas, coffee and *lapet thoke* at Gen. Zau Mai's house, coffee before dinner, tea after. It was rivaled only by the generous use of garlic which infused all food at Pajau. One more condensed milk coffee before bed, and I slept well, drifting off as the Glen Miller Orchestra played 'Stormy Weather' on the radio and a high north wind wailed outside.

A jeep arrived for me after breakfast. It was a fine blue-sky day, and my field trip guide was Sergeant-Major Um Tu Lum, a personable young Kachin Army officer who had been a post-1988 refugee in India, where he'd learned computer skills. With Judge Gam Sang, we drove out of Pajau past the derelict ABSDF camp. We hiked up from the jeep trail to a Kachin

Army post, a ring of bunkered shacks on a hilltop. We could see the peak of Padang Hkawn, where I'd inspected punji stakes in '91, and way beyond it, the Tatmadaw's territory, including the Irrawaddy River, a long white worm winding far away to the east. It occurred to me that since this was winter, it was opium harvest season, when growing areas would be obvious: brilliant with red, pink and white poppy blossoms. For miles in every direction, nothing of the kind was visible that clear morning. The earth was dry, bristly with tough weedy grass and thorn plants. Miniature alpine blooms, wild little purple clusters, were the only flowers. The Drug Free Zone existed in plain sight.

I took photos of the mottled brown hills and we got back in the jeep to go on to Pajau's new pride and joy, a small-scale hydroelectric plant built with hired Chinese engineering and labor plus the clunky, durable made-in-China equipment that was perfect for such a low-cost development project. Stone and concrete channeled stream water down a slope, and the turbines already generated enough electricity to keep KIO headquarters' satellite TV and light bulbs running for hours at a time. The hydro plant and stream course were surrounded by the last fringe of forest around Pajau. To preserve the watershed for the hydro plant, the Kachin Army guarded that forest against any logging or bamboo cutting.

I was invited back to Gen. Zau Mai's house, this time for dinner, which was a goat in many dishes: fried goat, roasted goat, goat soup. About ten men sat around the pushed together card and dinner tables. The goat was accompanied by Chivas Regal quaffed by all from brass cups. Even the abstemious General, at the head of the table in a black leather jacket with a furry collar, indulged in the Scotch. He and I chased ours with tea instead of Steinlager beer like the others. KIO Central Committee members told tales of tiger hunting days long past. When the goat was down to its gleaming bones the party broke up, no later than six in the evening.

I went back to my bamboo sanctuary to read another exquisite chapter of 'Nutmeg' and tune in news of more Karen defeats (the loss of another base to the Tatmadaw) on my shortwave. The Kachins had been openly contemptuous of Karen strategy, or lack thereof, over dinner. I could imagine how Karen rebel officers might feel about the Kachins sitting around in the comfort of their ceasefire, chowing down on goat and drinking Chivas and having a big laugh about the historical losing streak of the down but not out Karen revolution. Neither group was any good anymore, they both had neutralized, defeated their own selves, I thought. The Karens had hung onto their Thai border bases in hopes of reviving their smuggling trade in cattle, logs and tin ore, even though those days were gone (the Thais did their business directly with the Slorc now) and the Karen leadership had refused to unleash the mobile guerrilla war of which their troops were really capable. The Karen rebels ended up trapped like rodents in shelled, burning, chemical-bombarded and germ-contaminated forts, their backs to the border, their only future in refugee camps.

Meanwhile, the Kachins at Pajau had given up the fight at the height of their power and then sunk into an economic and moral slumber, losing their jade gates, letting the Tatmadaw do as it wished beyond the lines of the ceasefire. I respected the longing of the Kachin women I'd interviewed for a peaceful life, and understood everyone's battle fatigue. I tried not to romanticize an 'armed struggle' which was so often ineffective or even counter-productive. But I kept thinking that if those who were capable of fighting no longer fought the Tatmadaw, the Slorc would ride roughshod unchecked over most of the land. We might be safe in Pajau, but Shans and Karens and Rohingyas would suffer all the more for our separate Kachin peace.

I needed something more human than a gushing stone hydro plant to renew my faith in the Kachin revolution, so the eight young female soldiers who showed up for my martial arts class gladdened my heart. They gathered eagerly in the camp assembly hall, where mylar fringe printed with MERRY CHRISTMAS still adorned the stage. My idea was not so much to equip the young women for hand-to-hand combat (these were office workers, and the war was finished for now) but to get them inspired to train more and become female self-defense instructors themselves. Burma was infinitely dangerous for women wherever the Tatmadaw roamed. I couldn't teach my martial arts class anything that would work against a Tatmadaw soldier's gun. But I hoped I could start some self-defense skills circulating among Kachin women, so that eventually they might not be considered such automatic victims.

As morning sunlight filtered through the loosely woven bamboo walls, my class lined up and we began. The students wore their black hair in ponytails or pigtails and had dressed in big T-shirts and sweatpants, except for a couple of them who were still in uniform, olive drab shirts worn out over their trousers. The floor was packed dirt so the girls kept their sandals and sneakers on. Judge Gam Sang translated for me, and he was a good interpreter, having tried 'Kachin martial arts' himself some time before he took up the study of law. The eight students were dreadful gigglers, but ever willing and able. They had no trouble bellowing out a *kiai*—a shout that reverberated over the whole camp. We started out stretching and went on to strong punches and kicks.

In the afternoon the girls brought blankets, as I'd requested. They folded them up to hold as punching-blocks. Paired up for those exercises they giggled and talked incessantly. How could you not laugh when you were punching your best pal in the stomach, or watching her do a Hong Kong movie roundhouse kick at the air? I had to lecture them a bit: 'I want you to have a good time, but please remember, this requires your military discipline, your attention. So less talking would help...' They quieted down until I started them out on a *kata*, the formal solo sequence for demonstrating techniques, which caused much hilarity and mock consternation over how to pivot and in which direction. They caught on fast, anyway. It was not unlike parade drill, which Pajau still featured for special occasions on the old parade ground.

Following the second class, I went to a nearby hill to see Judge Gam Sang's newly opened camp library. Its neatly labeled shelves contained mostly frayed old Burmese texts on subjects like agriculture and mining. Male and female soldiers searched the collection for the reading matter they always craved. I shared their passion for the printed word, having been raised in a house that had a library, that veritably was a library, my childhood distinguished by trips to The Library downtown, a destination as glamorous as all the museums and battlefields of America's East Coast. I recalled showing up at Pajau out of the jungle in 1991 and asking for 'something to read'. Relatively recent Burmese novels and magazines were being shared by young soldiers who sat reading in tandem, thirstily turning pages.

Judge Gam Sang lived in a room off the library, with his own private rack of law books in English and boxes of KIO documents. He 'leaked' me a copy of a new Kachin report on 'resettlement and reconstruction programs' for tens of thousands of Kachin refugees returning from China to KIO areas rather than their original homes which were still in the grip of the Slorc. Describing the ceasefire, the report said 'a tentative process of reconciliation is now in motion'. Most of the returnees were expected to settle in the Laiza area, and the KIO had already installed a hydroelectric plant and town water system there. Smaller villages awaiting an influx of refugees needed roads, bridges, schools and clinics. Quite a few improvements had already been made.

I looked at the report's illustrations. One showed, in Laiza, the 'first of its kind immunization programme in KIO administration areas—anticipated to reach 40,000 to 50,000 children under 12 during the next 30 months'. Kachin Army soldiers were pictured doing road improvement work using a Chinese bulldozer donated by overseas Kachins. The report ended with a couple of photos of fruit trees, captioned, 'One of the major crops in the N'Ba Pa area, in eastern Kachin State, is the growing of persimmons. However, a viable market needs to be found for this prodigious crop in order to make it a profitable enterprise.'

The resettlement report presented a picture of hope, of self-help in a new climate of peace, vaccinations and persimmon jam. In contrast, another document I obtained, also Kachin-prepared, titled 'January to May 1994 Survey of AIDS, Opium, Heroin in Burma', was the prophecy of auto-genocide. 'Recently, a fatal disease known as AIDS has raised its ugly and deadly head,' the report began. 'It is shocking to discover how much headway this fatal disease has made into the lives of the Kachin people, especially among the youth... It is found that the rapid spread of AIDS is directly linked to the use of notorious drug heroin.'

The introduction was followed by a thirty page grotesque litany of the pervasiveness of the heroin trade in towns and villages on the China/Burma border. The cross-border drug traffic was described in detail, as was the free movement of everything from carrying-baskets of opium to truckloads of heroin within Burma. A soldier from Matu Naw's Kachin militia, which had gone over to the Slorc long before the KIO ceasefire, was quoted about his outfit's actions: 'If they do not transport heroin like this in these times, when will they do it?'

'There is wholesale heroin trafficking in Mangshi,' as well as in many other Yunnan, China frontier towns, especially Ruili, the report asserted. The drugs often came from the Wa region of Burma's Shan State. On the Burma side no official law enforcement agency exerted any restraint over the traders. Describing a Kachin border village the report said, 'There have been many deaths among the youth. There is an army [Tatmadaw] outpost in this village. The officer in charge is a Major: soldiers and policemen like to be on duty in this village because they can get money from those who sell opium and heroin.' In another town, 'the police themselves are selling heroin'.

The KIO's anti-drug program, which I had seen swing into action in 1991, had for a while put an actual dent in opium production, according to United States Government reports, and heroin addiction had decreased in some KIO-controlled areas. But the narcotics trade throughout northern Burma just kept increasing, accompanied by prostitution in a surefire recipe for AIDS. Mung Gu was described: 'This town produces the largest amount of heroin. There are about 10,000 houses. Every house has a fencing which is about 12 feet to 18 feet high. The houses are securely fenced off. There are four houses of prostitution. In the heart of the town there is a gambling den opened by the Ko Kank (ex-communist)... There is a large hill on the north side of the football field in Mung Gu. This hill has many names, Mung Gu hill, Hpan Jung, Man Kang, Hpaw Mar and Kang Dap are some of the names. Every water pool on this hill side is a heroin refinery. Water that flows from these pools has an opium smell.'

Hpakant, the Kachin State's notorious jade mining center, merited a lengthy depiction. 'The place is always full of people and cars. As there is a cease-fire at present, between Slorc and KIO, there are all kinds of people with all kinds of habits. All kinds of people are trying their luck there and all kinds of methods are adopted. Among these is the age-old women's profession of prostitution. Although there are roughly about 87 brothels in Hpakant, it is said that there are others right up to the place where jade digging is done and this brings it up to about 100 brothels... Nearly all these girls have venereal diseases. Without blood test no one can say whether they have AIDS or not. If they can get their blood tested many men and women will be [found to be] carriers of HIV. This can be so because after working in Hpakant girls who go back to their homes become thin and disfigured and eventually die of AIDS.'

The grim scenario of heroin boom-towns was matched by dwindling villages in the process of being obliterated by addiction. In one of them, Pang Sak, 'there are about 20 families. From 1989 to 1992 the village lost all its men folks to heroin addiction and the village has now become a village of widows. The only surviving men are 2 old men and a village elder.' Names of people who as the report put it, died 'of heroin shock caused by an injection' in small villages were listed, along with the comment, 'In every village between Bhamo and Momauk there was buying and selling of heroin and a large number of addicts. Due to havoc played by heroin there was heartaches and poverty in all the villages between Bhamo and Momauk.'

Burma's supposed law enforcement agencies and several ceasefire groups (including the Wa but not the KIO) were condemned in the report for their involvement in the drug trade. The document ended with a plea for outside assistance with medical care, rehabilitation, and suppression of opium cultivation. 'We appeal very earnestly to generous well-wishers to sincerely concerned and committed extend the helping hands to a race of simple people who are in danger of near extermination. We are gong to have to fight for our very survival and we sincerely hope that the rest of the world is not going to look on with hands folded while we perish.' I felt like the pages were burning my fingers. I could send Judge Gam Sang's resettlement development document around to various do-good groups. But this drug/AIDS report had to go to the US Government's own narcotics czars and czarinas. Not that they would necessarily do anything about it—American drug policy was always too confused, inept and compromised to be effective—but they had to know. 'Soon all our informations shall be as they say on-line,' Judge Gam Sang predicted. 'Let us go see our friend at his data station.'

We went further uphill to see Sgt.-Maj. Um Tu Lum at work in his computer office. A photographic-looking poster of Jesus and one of a blonde pop singer in serious décolletage (the only blonde pin-up I'd ever seen in Cates-crazed Burma) looked benignly down on the two personal computers from the front of a locked cabinet. Each terminal had its own moth-eaten red Hudson's Bay type wool blanket, 'to keep humidity off'. Creeping mold was always a problem for such equipment at Pajau, as were power fade-outs or surges. Sgt.-Maj. Um Tu Lum wasn't connected up to the Internet, though he wished he was. Burma information had started to flow around the world by e-mail, faster than news had ever been smuggled and distributed before. But Pajau was left out because the KIO radio-telephone system only worked within the camp. The KIO couldn't run lines across the border to link up to the Chinese phone system. The best they could do was to send and receive faxes from machines over in Yunnan Province.

Sgt.-Maj. Um Tu Lum's wife carried their two year old son into the office. I happened to have in my shoulder bag a fuchsia monster-dinosaur from Seattle's Archie McPhee novelty shop. John and I had been playing with the little plastic beast over lunch and lattes the last day I was there. It had been a token of our as yet unspoken love, walking between us down counter and table. Forgetting about Kachin children's amazing freedom from toys, I gave the monster to Sgt.-Maj. Um Tu Lum's son. The child promptly burst into terrified tears: 'No! No! I don't want it!' His father, laughing, hid it away. Probably it would end up decorating one of the terminals. What was a computer without a plastic space toy looming over the screen, after all...

That night a Kachin Catholic youth group, traveling around, gave a stage show in the assembly hall. From my cabin, I could hear the folk-rock groovy hymns, but I wasn't invited to go see it. Nam Grawng kept me company as I read. She perused a newsletter from a women's group based on the Burma/Thailand border. Another soldier came by to practice his English. I asked him about baseball. A Japanese journalist had brought my baseball gear to Pajau, but with Maj. Pan Awng in the KIO equivalent of the Betty Ford Clinic I didn't know if anyone had actually attempted to use it. The soldier did seem to remember some baseball games played on the parade ground in better weather. I couldn't tell how many other foreign visitors Pajau had seen since my previous visit. I knew that a woman from the Morse missionary family had stayed quite a while, and a Thai reporter or two had crossed from Yunnan. But the headquarters guest book I had made in '91 seemed to have been misplaced.

The martial arts class began its second day. One girl, who had missed the first two classes because she was operating the headquarters radio-telephone system, was especially good. She was so well-motivated and attentive that she quickly caught up with the rest of the group. The more they did it, the more enthusiastic the girls were about the sparring. As they blocked each other's punches and kicks, they were still giddy, still giggling, but undeniably a group of powerful young women. They were all more coordinated than any of my American beginners had been, and learned much faster. A couple of them were even managing a confident, smooth *kata*.

After class a few girls still practiced their kicks or *kata*, their Xena shouts ringing from the women's barracks yards. I watched Sgt. Mai Mai, who was not in the class, play similarly fierce barefoot badminton against male soldiers in back of the assembly hall. The dirt court was demarcated with Steinlager bottles buried neck-down in straight green lines. Pajau looked so cold and forlorn in the winter gray late afternoon. It resembled some Appalachian holler, smoke curling from the stovepipes of the plastic-patched tar-paper roof cabins, some dirt road dirt poor coal miners' village, those hills inhabited by Asian rebel soldiers. The Kachins were as dogged, as inured to punishment, brave, as any West Virginia miners, any moonshine runners. I had even at one point suggested to the KIO education minister that they copy the Foxfire idea from the American mountains, students interviewing their elders about the old skills and crafts, learning old ways and preserving them. The Kachins were true hill people, and their Baptist hymns rose to their heavenly Jesus from the poverty of the backwoods. Dirt and punji stakes, piney logs and deer antler wine and dirt. Still, tall Sgt. Mai Mai was joyful in badminton victory, and in such a place joy was just as contagious as despair or any other disease.

My last night at Pajau, pine logs coated with lichen burned particularly sweet in the stove. Nam Grawng was knitting a pink scarf for me but it wasn't nearly finished so it would go to a soldier friend instead. Heavy rain and wind flapped the roof plastic, the electricity fizzled out but came back. I dreamed a zoo dream. I dreamed of tapirs climbing out of their pool, escaping their zoo pool.

My morning class had a male soldier, himself a martial arts expert, as a demonstration model for self defense 'weapons'—umbrellas, ammo clips, a flashlight, held in fists and driven home. We also used him to practice breaking a man's grip, and pretend-practice smashing his facial bones, windpipe or kneecaps. He was a good sport, of course, and it looked like he might continue as a teacher for the War Office women. 'Our headquarters men soldiers are now asking for this 'unarmed struggle' training such as you are doing now, as well. And all the officers are most impressed by the very ferocious girls as they hear their *kiai*,' Judge Gam Sang told me.

When the morning class was finished, Ja Seng Hkawn appeared, and I recorded my last report interview, with her, my Kachin sister. I learned new things about her: that she had been a school teacher in Myitkyina for two years after university, before joining her parents' revolution, and that she had risen through the ranks at the War Office to sergeant-major, before retirement and marriage.

She also revealed that human rights information was still being obtained by the Kachins: 'We collect the stories and our Reverend keeps such lists.' The KIO had, before the ceasefire, constantly distributed meticulously documented accounts of abuse of Kachin civilians at the hands of the Tatmadaw. But after the ceasefire that information source had dried up completely. I felt sure that in the parts of Kachin State not in KIO control and even in some of their own territory, violations of human rights continued—forced labor, rape. I heard about it from other sources from time to time. But the KIO apparently considered it too inflammatory, too embarrassing to their Slorc ceasefire counterparts to publicize such incidents. So their human rights 'lists' didn't reach the outside world anymore, and the narcotics report implicating the Slorc was leaked out very quietly.

On the gender issue, Ja Seng Hkawn felt that Kachin women still had to prove themselves 'because the Kachin men, they are thinking of the women that they are still at the low stage'. Like everyone else I'd interviewed for the report, she felt sure that diligence would overcome prejudice and that education would eventually produce social equality. In good revolutionary form she linked the personal with political goals: 'Because we are still—we haven't yet got our country's self-rule, it must be combined with our self-goal and our national goal. If we do not get our national goal, if we never get peace, then we, personally never can do many things.'

The other women I'd interviewed had waxed optimistic about the future for the 'next generation', anticipating both peace and political freedom in their children's lifetime. Ja Seng Hkawn was a bit more negative or ambivalent in her outlook. She was caught between her father's quest to give peace a chance and the Kachin Army officers of her own age who were champing at the ceasefire bit, wanting to get back in the fight. She wanted something better than Pajau, with or without a revolution, but she wasn't sure what it might be. Like a politician, or a mother, she spoke in plurals. 'Until now, we cannot say that things will be changed to good or to bad, or worse—we don't know. But we are still trying to change to the better stage. But about this Burmese regime, we don't know, because their sins—we can simply say they are very wicked. That's why we are trying for the better side, but we don't know if it will happen to the worse or to the better situation. But anyway we are forever trying for the best for our children.' So finishing her interview, Ja Seng Hkawn hugged me goodbye and left with her son, driven back to China in a black-windowed car.

At noon I hosted the '*lapet thoke* lecture' in my cabin. Judge Gam Sang, Dr Bawk Lu, and a handful of young English-speaking Kachin Army officers showed up to munch green tea, drink black tea from Chinese cups enamelled with camels, and hear me tell them the story of the gas pipeline slicing through southern Burma. We put our chairs in a circle. I took out my ragged old map of Burma to show where I had crossed the Tenasserim, the narrow coastal region of southern Burma (bordering Thailand) with the Mon Liberation Army in 1988. The Tenasserim was the region being cut through by the pipeline being built by Total, a French petroleum giant, and Unocal, an amoral oil company from my own country.

The officers took notes, some tape recorded it. I spoke slowly and pronounced my words carefully. 'To build this pipeline from the sea to Thailand, the oil companies got the Tatmadaw to secure the land. The

Tatmadaw pushed the Karen and Mon people from their villages, which then were burned. They used the people to build roads and a railway line. The forest is torn apart. Ten new battalions of the Tatmadaw stay in the area. The money from the gas will go to make the Slorc richer than ever. The Slorc stays in power waiting to get their millions of dollars in gas money.'

One of the KIO officers suggested 'armor-piercing bullets' as the way to deal with the pipeline, something the Karens—who had at one point vowed to turn it into a 'snake of fire'—had already thought of on their own. I said that I was telling the Kachins the story of the pipeline as a lesson for the KIO not to trust the huge foreign companies that were in league with the Slorc. Letting them in produced only ruined land and manufactured only refugees, profiting only the Tatmadaw's endlessly greedy top echelons. Foreign mining companies (some of the nastiest ones in a business not known for its kindness to indigenous people or the environment) were already entering into Slorc ventures to extract the minerals of the Kachin State.

After the lecture, it was time for the last martial arts class. Everyone, including me, did solo *katas*. We reviewed all the moves that had warmed us up or made us stronger. I handed out prizes, for sparring, *kata*, and improvement: three T-shirts from the New Jersey *dojo* where I'd learned it all. I had cans of *Jian Li Bai* sports pop and chocolate cookies for everybody. The prizes and party were a surprise for the karate girls, as well as my goodbye to Pajau. I returned to my cabin and for good luck Sgt. Mai Mai put my hair in French braids for the trip across the border, as she had in '91.

It was a year to the day since the KIO/Slorc ceasefire had been signed. I stopped in for a last conversation with Gen. Zau Mai before I left. We talked about Aung San Suu Kyi, who was still being held incommunicado by the Slorc, under arrest in her Rangoon home. 'Our KIO position is that she must be released and then the tripartite negotiations must take place,' Gen. Zau Mai said. 'That is, talks between her democracy party, and the Slorc, and our ethnic nationality group forces. Then we may produce the way to democracy, we may negotiate our way to it. But only if all three elements are invited to talk. We are calling for this.'

I agreed with the General that such tripartite negotiations were an idea worth promoting by the KIO. I also mentioned that if such negotiations didn't happen, I would welcome the return of the Kachins to battle. Then I put in a word for improving the environment at Pajau itself by getting the soldiers to clean up the 'plastic waterfall' dumpsite that had flowed downhill from the barracks since at least 1991, and especially to get rid of those plastic Pepsi bottles.

I had always felt I had to do something for the Kachins, not just visit and come out with information about them, their lives, their war or lack of war. The martial arts course, the pipeline lecture, were intended in that spirit.

So was baseball and so was the dump clean-up. Gen. Zau Mai told me he'd have the 'waterfall' disappear right away, and I believed him. I told him how the jade ring given to me by the KIO Central Committee in 1991 had brought me back to the land of the Kachins, and that it would again, and I think he believed me.

Night fell and I got in the sedan of 'Chow Yun-Fat' with Judge Gam Sang and four Kachin women. One of the women wore glasses, and she was my decoy. 'If the Chinese have word that a foreign lady with black hair and spec's crosses their border tonight, they will see her and think, there is no such foreigner, it is only her, this Kachin,' Judge Gam Sang explained.

As in 1991, I had to exit the car to evade one bad checkpoint. I followed a young boy into a maze of dark Chinese streets. A pair of village patrolmen shined flashlights on us, but they perceived nothing unusual, nothing criminal, nothing alien. We walked on silently. Another flashlight man gave us the beam, no problem. The guide boy and I cut down an alley, then we waded through a rubbish pit full of plastic bags and ramen bowl styrofoam, and emerged at the roadside. The boy left me there to go look for my car.

I waited a few minutes, standing there alone in the night, in shadow, in China. Whenever people walked nearby, I would cough elaborately in Chinese into my handkerchief, thus covering my face and dissuading awkward conversation. Horse carts passed by, jingling, creaking. I waited there in an unholy endorphin bliss from being on the edge of a Chinese village, alone, illegal, alive in the world but like a ghost, violating the border.

The car cruised past me and stopped for me a few yards up ahead. The boy and I walked up to it, he shook my hand, and turned back to the village. We zoomed away. 'Chow Yun-Fat' was driving even faster than when he had run me to Pajau, driving by night through Yunnan this time, no brakes for any checkpoints, snaking the road east away from the border.

The other passengers got out to eat in one of the border towns during the night. I stayed locked in the secure sedan because Chinese police were around. The Kachin women left the car along the way. The other traffic on the road was all logging trucks, convoys of them, heavily laden with the teak of Burma. The biggest-circumfrence teak logs I'd ever seen, cross cut in sections, were chained on one of the flatbeds. 'Old, old tree. From the Laiza area,' Judge Gam Sang sighed. 'All teak will be gone in two to three years.'

The night moved by as we passed logging trucks, more logging trucks, and the occasional red glow of an all-night barber shop, beauty parlor, or outright *karaoke* whorehouse. We got to the jade traders' hotel in Mangshi when it was still dark, and a room attendant handed out keys to Judge Gam Sang, the driver and me. When I opened the door to my room and walked in, a drowsy groan emanated from the bed. Somebody already had occupied it, and I was just lucky he hadn't the reflexes to greet a pre-dawn room invasion with gunfire to guard his jade cache.

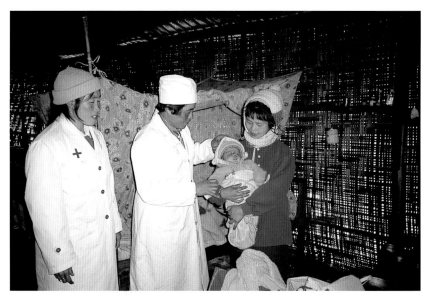

9. Female Kachin doctors, Pajau hospital, 1995.

10. Amputee Kachin soldier and his wife, weaving bamboo house wall, 1995.

11. The salt truck on the way to the Mekong River, Laos, 1995.

12. Mekong River speedboat; Laos to port, Burma to starboard.

I got my own room, and I got a plane ticket out of Mangshi to Kunming. I caught up on news. No disturbances had happened in Burma in connection with former Prime Minister U Nu's funeral. I heard that my friends who went off to see the Wa with Sai Pao as guide hadn't made it past the Chinese border police. Their trip never happened, although Sai Pao had given it a good try. Three years later Sai Pao would end up murdered. Somebody gunned him down as he left a Wa wedding in Chiangmai, Thailand.

In 1991 I had been careful not to fly from Mangshi to avoid the possibility of my notes and film getting taken away by Chinese security inspectors at the airport. This time I had decided that risk was preferable to yet another demented bus ride on the Burma Road. When I got to the airport it turned out to be so full of jade merchants from all over Asia that I, just a green-eyed traveller with no business, occupation: artist, was of no interest at all to customs or security. The Mangshi airport police had enough on their hands keeping track of duct-taped boxes of rocks and steamer trunks lined with heroin. The Kachin revolution did not matter much to anybody anymore, so I waited calmly in transit among the jade men, twisting my Kachin ring around on its neck-chain.

6

SALT

The discussion was about vice, about deadly sins—anger, brutality, addiction.

'Oh, everybody has something of that sort,' I commented dismissively.

'Really—what would yours be, then?' I was challenged.

I had to think for a moment. I had a pretty pared down existence.

'*Burma*,' I replied. It was far more to me than a name on a map (sometimes replaced with Ne Win's numerologically enhanced 'Myanmar'.) Burma was the people I had known over the years, and it was their cause, my cause. It dominated my life like any worthwhile vice, and was as inescapable for me as the deadliest sin. Usually I just spent my waking hours and considerable dream time obsessed with the political liberation of Burma from military domination. Then, sometimes I longed for the physical reality of Burma, a drink of it, a breath of it, a look at it.

In April 1995, about a month after I got back to Hong Kong from the Kachin State, I went to Laos. Travel restrictions had recently been eased in Laos, so I thought the time had come to investigate another border of Burma. Northwest Laos nudged up against Burma's Shan State, with the Mekong River flowing in between. From Laos' pleasantly sleepy capital, Vientiane, I flew to the old royal city of Luang Prabang. Laos had been Communist since 1975, and its Royal Family was mostly exiled or dead, but Luang Prabang's palace and a multitude of Buddhist monasteries remained in all their mosaic-encrusted glory. Few foreigners explored them.

Laos was a very poor country, a landlocked enclave the size of Oregon with four and a half million people. The French had ruled Laos, then war had battered and cratered the countryside. After some years of dreary Communism, Laos in the '90s was 'opening up' to the new world of economic reform inspired by Gorbachev, and neighboring Thailand and China were ready to exploit the country for all it was worth. Tourism hadn't quite reached Luang Prabang, but it probably would, sooner rather than later.

I hung around Luang Prabang for a few days with a couple of American human rights lawyers who were on vacation from their work in Cambodia. We went to an authentic regional restaurant and ate *jaew bong*, the buffalo skin condiment on dried river-weed, pronouncing it delicious. In fact, one of the lawyers, Evan, became so obsessed with that delicacy that I initiated the '*jaew bong* limerick contest', which was won hands-down by the other lawyer, Jim, with:

There was a young lady from Luang Prabang
Who was always dropping her sarong.
She did it for Evan,
Who thought it was Heaven,
*But said he'd much rather have...*jaew bong.

We also went to a spooky French restaurant where we ordered '*le cerf*' (the deer) and savored that too. At the French restaurant I got recognized by a Burma activist who was visiting from Thailand. I lied to him about my next destination. Back to Cambodia with the lawyers, I said. My security consciousness was taking the form of a healthy paranoia as usual. I didn't want anyone involved in Burma to know I was on my way to the border, unless they had to. People talked all the time, and my Thailand arrests had taught me to be wary. My Burma contacts back in the US hadn't even known I was going to Asia. Before I left I had told them that John and I were going to Idaho to climb frozen waterfalls.

Someone who did know everything was Emma, my Shan/English friend who ran a relief project in Chiangmai, Thailand for refugees from Burma. I hadn't seen her since I'd been deported and banned from Thailand in 1988. Northwest Laos was not only next to Burma, it was close to Chiangmai. So Emma came to meet me in Luang Prabang. The day after the lawyers left for Cambodia, Emma arrived by river 'speedboat'—a jolting ride which she did not enjoy, being three months pregnant with her second child. We roomed in a small Chinese hotel and had a couple of days to meander around the Buddhist temples.

Emma was quite the same as when I'd first met her in the Thai/Burma border town of Mae Hong Son in 1983. She still dressed like a lovely Thai hippie and spoke like Oxford University. Luang Prabang, with its Buddhist pagoda atop a hill at the center and picturesque shops selling embroidered cloth and old silver, reminded us both very much of Mae Hong Son. Emma and I had no trouble communicating with people, with her fluent Thai and my long-dormant functional Thai. The Laotian vocabulary was very similar to Thai. Even though I had hardly spoken the language since getting kicked out of Thailand in '88, after a few days in Laos I was able to look at objects and instantly recall their names in Thai. Obscure words for things like 'owl' and 'seasickness' and 'ashtray' came floating up from the recesses of my brain like answers in the Magic 8 Ball.

I got an update on the whole Burma/Thailand border situation, and particularly the Shan State, from Emma as we ate our breakfast. Laotian towns were graced by bakers of French-style baguettes, perfect with a condensed milk coffee in the morning. The other ubiquitous French remnant was Laughing Cow cheese, probably the perfect dairy product for a rather lactose-intolerant nation which didn't especially like cheese but needed to keep some kind of nostalgic tie to the long-gone colonial power. It was equivalent to the Burmese taste for British Horlick's drink mix, vestigial comfort food.

We tore off pieces of our baguettes to dunk in the coffee, so thick like Mekong River sludge. 'Karens are still trying to fight,' Emma said. 'Regrouping. They say they'll take up mobile warfare after losing Manerplaw and all their border bases. The Tatmadaw and Karen factions they sponsor come over the Thai border from Burma and rampage through the refugee camps, burning and killing, the Thais don't stop them.' Emma still never braided or bunched or scrunched her long hair as I did mine, to keep it out of the way. Her hair was a dark curtain around her face. She fiddled with a strand and she laughed, the way we always had in the midst of the madness of the border lands. 'As for the Shan State, now Khun Sa is fighting the Tatmadaw, and he's doing it rather well, it appears.'

'Yes, he is,' I agreed. 'I saw film of the battle on CNN in Hong Kong. Leave it to Khun Sa to attack the Slorc at Tachilek and make the TV news.'

The old Shan State-based drug warlord Khun Sa, whom I'd met in 1987, had been amassing troops and arms for years, and would fight the Wa from time to time, but never the regime's army, the Tatmadaw. Conflict over some ruby mines seemed to have inspired him to use his guns against the Tatmadaw at last. A battle had flared up for a few days in late March, right in the town of Tachilek, a Burma/Thailand border town mostly known as a transit point for 'underage' prostitutes from Burma to Thailand and for the sale of skins of Burma's tigers and other endangered species. 'Everyone else fights the dictatorship for decades and gets just about zero press coverage, but Khun Sa finally gets around to it and he manages to do it right in sight of the camera crews just across the border in Thailand.'

'The Tatmadaw chased Khun Sa's people out of Tachilek, though, and now they are absolutely "ethnic cleansing" the southern Shan State in every direction,' Emma elucidated, 'Of course they don't go near the Wa, it's still ceasefire hands-off them. But the tribes in the south, the Lahu, the Akha, are being driven out, and so are Shan people from the towns. The Tatmadaw even shot a Thai the other day, some poor retarded fellow, shot him in the back, for sport, I suppose. Not that the Thai Government will make much of a fuss. They're doing too much business with the Slorc to let any incursions to refugee camps on their soil, or even any actual Thai citizens murdered by Slorc troops, ruffle their feathers at all.'

The Laotian New Year, a water festival, was being celebrated. 1995 was the year of three New Years for me: the January one in New Jersey, the lunar Chinese one in February, and now the Buddhist one. As was the custom in April in Burma and Thailand as well, statues of the Buddha were being bathed in flower-scented showers. Pedestrians like Emma and me were being 'bathed' by children armed with water-buckets and sacks of scented baby powder. In accordance with Laos' laid-back nature, the water-throwing was not very aggressive, not rowdy, and our clothes actually dried out between dowsings. It all culminated in a gathering on Luang Prabang's Mekong River shore, where people built shoulder-high Hershey's Kiss shaped pagodas of wet sand, decorating them with marigold petals and paper pennants.

Emma needed to return to her daughter and her relief work after only a brief stay in Luang Prabang. She decided to fly back to Chiangmai instead of suffering through another boat ride. I went to the airport too, taking another step towards the Burma border. I'd have to hopscotch from place to place, with little information on transport. My only known destination was a small town called Muong Sing. The journalists Bertil and Hseng Noung Lintner had gotten there a couple of months before, then headed off toward the Laos/China border to cover a curiously booming trade in luxury sedan cars. The cars were driven from Thailand through Laos on terrible roads to be smuggled—rather openly smuggled—into China for purchase by the *nouveaux riches* of Yunnan. From Muong Sing I'd try to reach Burma's border, the Mekong River, although most maps showed no road going there.

My Lao Aviation flight was to take me north to the main town of Udomxai Province and the flight was late. When the airplane finally appeared, it was very small, a sixteen-seater. We had no flight attendant, no safety talk, so I took on the role by trying to convince the men across the aisle to fasten their seatbelts for takeoff. 'No problem,' they replied in Chinese, leaving the belts undone. We lurched into the sky and flew over forest/clearcut/forest/clearcut. The timber companies were already having their way with Laos.

Udomxai's township was described in the only Laos guidebook as 'a strip of dirt'. Which it was, although an ever-widening strip of dirt due to the presence of Chinese road-crews. The roads in northern Laos had been built as a Chinese aid project in the 1960s, and now they were being improved and expanded, again by the Chinese. Not only were foreign tourists now allowed to roam around the hinterlands of Laos, but Chinese workers could come down and get employment in what was known as Infrastructure Development work. That kind of thing, road building, bridges, maybe a railroad at last, might work out to Laos' advantage. The disadvantage would be when Thai and Chinese business interests managed to devastate the environment and establish yet another tacky *karaoke* schlock-fest in yet another corner of Southeast Asia. Laos was no democracy. While the Communist government of Laos wasn't one of the more brutal regimes in the region, freedom of expression was non-existent. Laotians couldn't exactly organize their own environmental protest groups to fight off logging or protect endangered species. It was left up to the government alone to decide if it wanted to bother to control growth or preserve a fragile tropical forest environment, and only the government decided the rights of the indigenous people to their lands. The Laotian government got some decent input from foreign aid consultants, but also plenty of harmful development plans, and a great deal of corruption oozed into Laos from foreign exploiters.

The main Laotian travel restriction with which I needed to deal was a 'pass' that was supposed to be stamped by the police whenever I moved from district to district. On landing in Udomxai Province the stamping was conveniently done by an inspector at a shack adjacent to the runway. Then I got in the back of a truck functioning as a taxi, and went to a Chinese-run café in a new cement building. Guest rooms were available above the restaurant, so I checked into one. My room had construction dust and new furniture including a rust velvet couch, and a balcony. I looked down from the balcony as a New Year's procession marched up the widening road in no particular formation. A cluster of orange-robed young monks led the way and young girls in sarongs followed, the girls holding silver bowls of orchids and jasmine as temple offerings.

Speaking Chinese, I asked the waiter in the candle-lit café (the electricity was out) about passenger-carrying trucks to Luang Namtha, the next destination on my determined course northwest towards the Burma border.

'No trucks are going there.'

'No trucks at all?'

'No trucks go there tomorrow, it is the New Year. Many days, no trucks go to Luang Namtha.'

I went hypothetical—if there was a truck, where would it leave from— and got directions to the passenger-truck stop in the center of Udomxai township. The next morning one of the café workers brought me there on his motorbike.

Plenty of trucks kept pulling into the dirt lot and picking up passengers, so that was encouraging; the New Year's festival hadn't halted all transport in the north of Laos. None of the trucks were going to Luang Namtha, though. I sat on my pack, with nothing to do but wait around in the dirt all day. I talked to other people waiting there, in Thai and Chinese, even in English to a pair of Dutch development workers on holiday. Nobody was very optimistic about my chances of getting all the way to Luang Namtha. I kept asking the truck drivers as they appeared, *'Ja bai nai? Bai Luang Namtha, mai?'* to no avail. The onlookers shook their heads sympathetically. They told me the roads were no good; they told me I could not get there from Udomxai.

Hours later, I was vindicated in my stubbornness. A truck appeared, its driver looking for passengers to bring to Luang Namtha. Then I had to pretend I didn't really want to get there all that desperately after all, in order to bargain a reasonable fare. I got in back along with a couple of Chinese people bound for villages on the way. The roof over the passenger seats in the back was loaded up with cartons of Laotian beer and with kapok-padded red and pink Phoenix brand Chinese mattresses. I wondered why the mattresses were going back north, towards China. A few of them, rolled up, were stuffed into the passenger compartment as well, making the ride along bumpy roads more comfortable than it might have been.

The mountain landscape showed the scars of traditional slash and burn agriculture. It was not necessarily a bad thing to clear some forest by cutting trees and then burning the brush to fertilize the fields. But as tribal farming populations increased or were confined to smaller regions, the practice could seriously damage the land in conjunction with ever more efficient logging operations. The Laotian government tended to blame forest damage on that kind of farming, and off and on tried to relocate mountain people to flat rice-growing land. That seemed aimed as much at controlling politically suspect groups like the H'mong tribe as at preserving the ecosystems.

Although some hillsides were charred bare, most of what I saw from the winding road was still green and wild land. Our truck made a detour to stop off at a Buddhist temple fundraising picnic by the side of a lake. The driver and passengers donated small sums of money and we each got a red and green paper rosette pinned on us in return.

Late in the afternoon, the truck pulled up to the market in Luang Namtha, and I got directions to a hotel a couple of blocks away. Luang Namtha had been something back in the CIA war in Laos days, the scene in 1962 of 'the Luang Namtha Incident' (a factional battle that was trumped up into a supposed North Vietnamese invasion to justify heightened US intervention). Now it was nothing, just another strip of dirt. That war, which Noam Chomsky once described as 'surely one of the most grotesque episodes of modern history', had involved the super-powers of the time playing three Laotian factions off against each other. Royalist/rightists, the Communists called the Pathet Lao, and a neutralist force contended to lead Laos. America, the USSR, and China plus North Vietnam all made the conflict their business. Diplomats forced easily-skirted agreements between the various parties and set 'rules of engagement' for their fight, while the military minds conspired to keep the warfare going on year after year.

Banned by an attempt at a peace accord from sending in actual ground troops or setting up bases in Laos, the United States Government figured out ways to covertly back the Royalist/rightist faction. A pretend civilian air-cargo line, Air America, staffed by unconventional Americans in mufti, flew the rightist clients their arms, ammunition and other supplies. A descendant of World War II's Flying Tigers outfit, Air America was sponsored by the CIA, itself derived from the Office of Strategic Services which had run covert operations in Southeast Asia during World War II.

In the 1970s, US pilots flew surveillance missions over Laos out of Thai air bases. Thai troops were hired to help out the Laotian rightists as trainers and special forces. A 'secret army' of H'mong tribal guerrillas was raised, supported and sent into vicious battles against the Communist Pathet Lao. Large numbers of H'mongs and other indigenous peoples of the mountains fought hard against Communist domination, although many others decided to take up the Pathet Lao's cause. Opium produced by H'mong farmers was flown around on Thai and American planes, and ended up refined into heroin for sale to US troops then fighting in Vietnam. Laos was the scene of a true proxy war: a civil war exploited for the global aims of containing Marxism/Leninism, or expanding it.

Laos borders Vietnam on the east, and part of the Ho Chi Minh Trail, a vital supply route from Communist North Vietnam to war-torn South Vietnam ran through Laos. The United States was not constrained from using its air power over Laos, and began heavy bombing of the Ho Chi Minh Trail. The bombing escalated and expanded to include saturation bombing of villages and towns in Laos, in order to deny the Pathet Lao civilian support. Over two million tons of American bombs ended up being dropped just on Laos in the 1960s and early '70s, about the amount of bombing that was done in the whole of World War II.

The carnage in Laos went largely unremarked, out of the media spotlight trained so relentlessly on the Vietnam War next door. It ended in 1975 with the Pathet Lao victorious. The H'mongs and others who had fought the Pathet Lao fled to wretched refugee camps in Thailand. Laos lost some ten percent of its population that way. When I lived in Thailand in the early 80's, there were plenty of 'secret war' veterans around. A friend of mine who had led Lahu guerrillas in Laos for the CIA still had visitors calling at his house from the Laotian underground anti-Communist resistance, which conducted low-level raiding for quite a few years, and was even more factionalized than the most divided Burma rebellions. But by the time I got to Laos in 1995, just about all that remained was lingering bitterness, and Luang Namtha was devoid of incident.

The hotel in Luang Namtha was an old wooden barracks sort of place, painted cobalt blue. My drab room had holes in the walls, holes in the floor, and holes in the mosquito net. I fixed the net holes with tape, peered through the wall holes at empty rooms, and managed not to fall into the floor holes. I went out to see if I could get my permit stamped, but the police station was closed for the night and would be shut the next day too, for the official national New Year's holiday. I ate good noodles with chili sauce, sitting on a bench by the roadside, and watched kids playing soccer in the dirt. Some Laotians from out of town joined me with their noodle bowls as I ate. One of them squeezed the plastic *nam pla* bottle too hard, spraying the fermented fish sauce on the rest of us. In the easygoing Laotian way everyone laughed instead of being angry and insisted it was 'no problem' as we scrubbed the acrid brown spots off our clothes with rags.

I got up at 6:30 and went to the market to investigate transport to Muong Sing. One and all assured me that there was nothing, there would be no trucks because of the New Year, because of the road being so bad, there would never be any such trucks. Often Southeast Asians, with their innate courtesy, tell foreigners what they think they want to hear ('Sure, of course the museum is up that road') whether it's quite accurate or not. In Laos it seemed the opposite. I guessed that maybe all those negative reactions were because most people really didn't go from place to place very much. They couldn't afford it. A truck trip to another town was as inconceivable as taking a plane to Cambodia or America.

I sat down at a market stall for a glass of condensed milk coffee and a hunk of French bread. After the continental breakfast I went back to pestering the truck drivers. I kept getting no for an answer. But then the Muong Sing truck, a black Toyota pickup with seats in the back, showed up.

I got to ride in front with the driver. We picked up a few Chinese passengers in town, then drove off on mountain roads. Small villages of thatched-roofed bamboo houses on stilts were visible from the road, surrounded by yellow-green banana plants and farm fields cleared by the slash and burn method. As we went higher in elevation, the air grew cooler, and forests were more intact. I even noticed a few stately teak trees still standing, inexplicably unmolested by loggers. The driver bought red-bellied squirrels for his wok from some boys of the Akha tribe who'd been out hunting.

Our truck blew a tire on the mountain road, shivering to a lopsided stop by a H'mong village. The driver set to work changing the tire. A little girl who had been picked up as a passenger down the mountain with her luggage of rice sacks, happened to live there. Her sisters and brothers (with their pet bird, an exotic red-beaked pigeon) gathered around to welcome her home and watch the tire get changed.

An old man from the village noticed me standing at the roadside with the truck passengers. Dressed in black homespun trousers and jacket, leading heavily on a bamboo staff, he hobbled over and beckoned me to his humble family house. It had one room, no stilts. He was just rich enough to own some fat white chickens in dome cages of cane. A fire warmed the center of the room. The old man handed me an enamel mug of hot boiled water to drink.

'Father, how old are you?' I asked him in Thai.

'I am eighty-six,' he grinned, and asked, 'What country do you come from?'

'I come from America.'

'Oh—America! *Chai dee!*' He was saying that Americans had good hearts. Then he made flying motions with his hands, which did not refer to the dead bat that was being smoked over the fire. He was describing American airplanes. He told me that he approved of the Americans for bombing the Pathet Lao back in the 1970s. He actually thanked the Americans for doing that. It turned out that he was from the Tai Dam ethnic group. Shan-related, the Tai Dam people were originally from North Vietnam. Their culture and Communism were really not compatible, it seemed, and many Tai Dam people had fled to Laos, only to keep running when the Pathet Lao took over the border area next to Vietnam, and then the whole country. Thousands had ended up in refugee camps and eventually overseas. Some who stayed in Laos ended up living in villages of H'mongs who shared their distaste for the Pathet Lao.

It was all a classic example of indigenous people fighting for a big-power cause and getting left behind, forgotten, when their usefulness was finished, without the autonomy or independence or even respect they'd dreamed of, just like in Burma after World War II. The Tai Dam wanderers and the H'mongs either ended up exiled in some cold spot like Minnesota or kept fending for themselves in Laos.

The truck was ready to go. The little passenger girl, who was so self-sufficient, travelling by herself, was the Tai Dam man's granddaughter. I noticed that she wore star-on-a-chain earrings, so I took off my necklace and put it around her neck. It was a double chain of nondescript metal with tiny stars dangling from it. My Aunt Molly in California had sent it to me when I was a teenager. I had worn it without ever taking it off for over twenty years. I hoped it would bring the Tai Dam girl some luck. I hoped it would be an amulet to keep her safe when walking through danger. It had served that purpose for me. With the mountain road truck rides, and the shells and bombs (countless of them still unexploded) that my fellow Americans had left all over the place in Laos, and whatever the Thais and Chinese had in store for the area, I was sure she could use a talisman of stars. Without my necklace, I felt a bit naked, yet still secure, as the truck descended to the flat terrain of rice paddies and reached Muong Sing.

With its teakwood buildings, multi-gabled Buddhist temples and clean, quiet streets, Muong Sing reminded me greatly of Shan towns in Burma and Thailand. Shan-related people did live there, along with some Chinese a long time out of Yunnan. One main street led past a large high-roofed marketplace where tribespeople who came down from the hills traded their goods in the mornings. Further along, I found a hotel. It had two stories— restaurant below, rooms above—and a wooden balcony along the front, plastic flowerpots nailed to the balcony railing. The tattooed owner didn't have much to say to me in Thai or Chinese. His mother was friendly, though. Dressed all in blue, her white wispy hair escaping from a blue towel turban, she provided me with a perfect lunch of fried pork and sticky rice, special New Year's sesame cakes and watermelon.

I made inquiries about getting to the Mekong River, the Burma border. A village called Muong Long was midway from Muong Sing to the river, according to a photocopy I carried of a detailed old Vietnamese map of northern Laos. Maybe, maybe, some young men in the restaurant said, there might be a truck that would go to Muong Long. That got my hopes up. From Muong Long, I imagined, I could hike to a village called Xieng Kok right on the river, the border. I'd find out the true truck situation in the morning at the market.

I walked around Muong Sing, past many houses on stilts, a few new brick buildings. Some fine old wooden buildings had the kind of tin gingerbread trim I'd always liked in Burma's Shan State, of which Muong Sing has once been part. Dominion over Muong Sing had been contested by the British who were ruling Burma and the French who had colonized Laos, until the late nineteenth century, when the French won.

I took pictures of three small boys in shorts and patchwork shirts, who posed in a group hug in front of a Buddhist monastery known as the Temple of the Wind. New Year's drums pounded a heartbeat all through the town, and people sang New Year's songs, gathering in friends' houses, getting drunk in the hot, dry afternoon. Turkeys, chickens, geese and pigs scrounged around yards and pathways. A few Laotian soldiers lounged around in front of their post near the market. When I pointed my camera at them they told me 'No photos' in Chinese.

Back at the hotel the owner's mother was in her favorite spot, a low rattan chair by the doorway, looking out at the main road. 'Perhaps you can get a truck to Muong Long,' she told me reassuringly. Then she grimaced as only a septuagenarian with a mouth full of betelnut juice can, and added, 'It will be a very bad truck ride indeed. If there are roads to Muong Long they are very bad roads indeed! But this is the dry season, so maybe you will have your truck. You can only try for it at the morning market.'

I talked to more restaurant patrons about getting to the Mekong River (maybe, maybe) and about Burma. 'A dangerous place, that Burma,' a young businessman said. 'Better to trade with China, you get out alive and with a profit. China is just as close, much more convenient, so much business.' Drunken New Year's water-throwing was going on outside, boys driving by on 'iron horse' tractor carts with buckets of water, bottles of white whiskey. The restaurant customers were intent on getting New Year's soused, too. Having garnered as much information as I was going to, I went up to my room. I realized that the hotel owner was up on the balcony peering in my window, and I slammed the wooden shutters closed and bolted them.

A 6:00 AM blast of Thai fake reggae music awoke me from downstairs, and I headed off to the market as the sun rose. Scores of black Chinese bicycles stood parked in front, and under the tin roof the bazaar was crowded with shoppers pushing slowly along the narrow aisles between sellers of vegetables, poultry, mushrooms, the carcasses of barking deer, Chinese hardware, Chinese baby clothes and blankets. I began asking the truck drivers out front about getting to Muong Long. 'No truck goes to Muong Long,' I was told. 'No truck goes there.'

At last I found a cargo truck that was going to a village called Muong Nang, which was actually on the way to Muong Long. It was an enormous truck, dark dirty blue, made in China, licensed in Laos. I offered the driver, a skinny old man called Ai Nok, payment in Thai money if he'd let me be a passenger. The weak national currency of Laos, the *kip*, was universally disdained. In Laos it was the fourth choice, after Thai *baht*, US dollars, or Chinese money. I carried quite a bit of *baht*, with dollars as backup, and a memo pad full of scribbled arithmetic: exchange rates, negotiations, transactions. I bargained a fare of exactly one thousand *baht* (about $40.00 at the time) for the driver to take me not only to Muong Nang, but beyond it all the way to Muong Long.

For that ridiculously exorbitant amount of money I had the privilege of sitting up front in the cab with Ai Nok and an associate of his who chattered incessantly, in Thai for my benefit. Before leaving Muong Sing, we drove around town for an hour or so, acquiring other passengers to ride in the back. Circling back to the market, we were flagged down by six lucky H'mongs who were also going towards Muong Long. Then we stopped at a store where our cargo was waiting. I got out and watched as seventy large bags of salt were loaded in back. I knew it was salt because I tasted some; I knew it was seventy bags because I counted them.

At last we left Muong Sing. Ai Nok drove slowly. The truck was exceedingly noisy, grinding gears as we went creeping up into the mountains. The truck was bucking, heaving, crunching, bumping along dry but deeply rutted dirt roads. It fouled the pure, clean mountain forest air with a grimy plume of diesel exhaust. We crawled up through scraggly dried-out secondary growth forest, the kind of forest that sort of comes back after major logging. Sometimes the road went down and then back up, and the truck's gears protested with ancient moans. Farm fields were burned out of much of what was left of the forest, but green thickets of bamboo and wild banana plants flourished. Lofty stands of teak still survived here and there.

In clearings reddish logs were being sliced into boards by small two-person pit saws. That at least was an improvement over the commercial logging of most of Southeast Asia, in which all sizes of logs were carried out on big trucks on wide logging roads to be processed elsewhere. If logging in Laos could be kept small scale, with the wood processed and used locally, all the remaining trees might not be clearcut and the other plants, the wildlife habitat, might not be destroyed. Laos' watershed and climate might not be thoroughly ravaged. But more likely, Laos would follow the usual Southeast Asian route into semi-desert. One could bomb a tropical country 'back to the Stone Age' (as America had done to Laos) and still not manage to do the lasting, irreparable environmental damage the sale of some logging concessions would inflict.

Smoke drifted over the road from new farm fields, and the day got hotter and hotter as noon approached. Little fires licked up hillsides. Flies died on our windshield. We had no radio in the cab, no tape deck, which was probably a good thing, considering the type of schmaltzy Thai pop music that had captured the airways of Laos in the '90s.

We stopped in Muong Nang for a couple of hours at midday. Ai Nok and his garrulous pal went off to lunch with friends. I waited around in a shop with the H'mong passengers and drank lukewarm bottled orangeade. I looked illiterately at Laotian newspapers and examined the shop goods for things of Burmese origin, finding none. Everything was Chinese or Thai. Many bags of the cargo salt were offloaded on the outskirts of Muong Nang. Then we got going again, leaving Ai Nok's companion behind.

The mountains became higher and more forested. In the truck cab it was oven-hot while we passed smoldering fields and sweaty-hot when we drove through intact jungle. Akha people walked along the roadside, backing into the bushes and staring as our snorting dark blue behemoth passed them by, horn blaring—as if they wouldn't have noticed us without it.

The Akha people lived in Yunnan Province of China, in Burma's Shan State, and in Thailand as well as Laos. Peace-loving Animists for the most part, the Akhas' traditional way of life was trashed by Slorc 'ethnic cleansing' in Burma and commercial exploitation (including the captivity of Akha girls in the sex industry) in Thailand. Laos seemed to pretty much leave the Akhas alone, at least in comparison to the neighbors' preying on them. The Akha women wore their customary headdresses of old silver coins and strands of glass beads. Their short embroidered skirts showed their leathery-tan knees and thighs, and if they noticed me in the truck, they'd squint—is that a... foreigner?—and smile with mouths stained red by betelnut juice. Akha children in rags and beads pulled water buffaloes out of the way of the truck.

In the late 1980s I had visited extraordinary Akha villages in the Shan State, while investigating the US Government's donation of 2,4-D herbicide, an Agent Orange ingredient, to the regime of Burma. Done by then with its war in Vietnam, Cambodia and (secretly) Laos, the US Government had decided to wage the War on Drugs in its place, in another corner of Southeast Asia, Burma's Shan State. Opium and food crops alike were chemically ruined by saturation 2,4-D spraying from American-provided airplanes and helicopters. The Akha farmers, who had never made much money from their opium crops, just subsistence, were outraged, helpless, defiant. In 1988 the spraying program ('counterproductive' according to at least one government agency) finally got cancelled by the United States.

The reprieve for Burma's Akhas was brief. The Slorc in the 1990s depopulated their region, burning village after village, raping, killing, enslaving anyone who did not escape. Refugees fled to Thailand, where they were met with a culture-shocking mélange of education, Christianity, tourist cameras and HIV infection. Perhaps some Akhas had made it out of Burma to this part of Laos, to stay in the villages of relatives, I supposed. Maybe they were growing opium poppies in those hills, maybe they were just growing sesame and corn and rice and trying to survive the way they always had.

We forded a few brooks, riding high over the hot season trickles of water. The H'mongs got dropped off within sight of their hillside village. Then the truck got stuck in a creek that must have been a torrent the rest of the year. A tangle of greenery drooped over the creek. As the truck sat there a sheen of oil appeared on the water's surface and spread like something out of 'The Wages of Fear'. Ai Nok jumped out and splashed water up over the engine. I sat in the cab, staring at the iridescent skin of the water and listening to the bugs of the jungle and thinking, this is all because I have to get to Burma, just to look at Burma. It was as if I had a compass magnet needle embedded in my heart that made me have to go through places like this with such grim, weird determination. It pulled me onto jungle roads, through stream, creek, river.

Ai Nok got back behind the wheel and the truck somehow lumbered up out of the creek. Ai Nok decided to make conversation, in Thai: 'In Muong Long, there is no hotel, and no trucks leave from there.'

'Really...' I murmured, hardly surprised.

We descended to rice plains again and reached the spread-out village of Muong Long. Most of its low tin-roofed wooden buildings looked brand new. Ai Nok delivered almost all of the remaining salt to one small shop. I waited on a bench in front as the bags were unloaded. Children bicycled by, their handlebars decorated with real and plastic flowers. A novice monk biked up and I took his photo next to the salt truck.

The shop owner came outside and announced to me, 'We have people of our family living in your country.' She showed me an address in Utica, New York (a terribly cold place for someone from Laos). 'This village, Muong Long is now building a hotel,' she said, 'It will be very neat, made of brick. It will have the shower and toilet too. But it is only just started. We are sorry it is not ready for you. If you wish, you can stay at our shop.' Just then, Ai Nok decided that for another thousand *baht* he would chauffeur me right to Xieng Kok on the Mekong River, that very afternoon. I only managed to bargain him down a token ten *baht* or so—he knew when he had an obsessed fare. We set off again, picking up a few passengers of opportunity, including a monk dressed in a combination of the red robes worn in Burma and the orange worn by monks in Laos.

More broiling deafening hours followed, a tedious struggle up the worsening roads in worsening light, always accompanied by the industrial clatter of our rather horrible vehicle. Late in the afternoon we stopped by the approach to an Akha village, where people were relaxing after their work day, under a leaf-roofed open shelter. Round-faced, wide-eyed children wandered up to gawk at the truck and I photo-ambushed them, causing a commotion of mixed tears and giggles. Ai Nok sold off the last sacks of salt. The villagers were delighted. A truck, a foreigner, and even salt. What wondrous things would appear if you waited by a dirt road in the jungle long enough. They gave us glasses of that Laotian mountain treat, hot boiled water. Then they passed a beautiful blue and white porcelain cup, like a Ming Dynasty tea thimble, to me. It contained white lightning rice liquor of their own design. It welcomed me to their jungle world. 'Obsession is its own reward,' I thought. I drank the moonshine and handed the cup back, and they poured a wee dram into it for Ai Nok. It occurred to me that he might never have driven beyond Muong Long before.

In indigo twilight we found our way to Xieng Kok. Ai Nok stopped the truck at a café where the road ended and a web of narrow dirt paths began. We walked through a deserted marketplace with a child who guided us to the bluff overlooking the Mekong River. Darkness had fallen so that I could not see the river, but I could tell it was there, and right across it was Burma. A mountain horizon was barely discernible over in Burma, and a light, held in someone's hand, moved there. The child showed me to a new-looking bamboo cabin on stilts, my own accommodations. It had a porch facing the river. A line of others like it stood empty along the bluff, apparently waiting for Tourism to appear in that corner of Laos. I gave Ai Nok his payment, which just happened to amount to all the *baht* I had with me. He gallantly offered to stay in my cabin if I was afraid of ghosts. But I had anti-ghost Shan tattoos, which I supposed would work in Xieng Kok right across from the Shan State if they'd work anywhere, so I declined the offer and he vanished, probably back to the café where the truck waited.

The child guide fetched a key and unlocked my cabin for me. It had one little room and no furniture at all. I gave him a dollar with which to buy me candles and soda-pop, and asked in Thai where the toilet might be. '*Arai godai*,' he replied, meaning, 'anywhere you want'. Xieng Kok was not quite ready for Tourism. I located some appropriate shrubbery. Walking back to the cabin I startled a few village piglets. I fixed up my home for the night. I made a bed with a rain poncho under me and a spare sarong over me, an O'Brian book wrapped in a towel for a pillow. I lit a candle and stuck it onto a soda can, and set a burning mosquito coil on its tin stand. I was traveling light, but not so light that I was without my radio, and I tuned in the BBC, to hear 'Sixty-two people hacked to death in Liberia.' The badness in the world was as far away as Africa, or as near as Burma. I turned off the radio, blew out the candle and slept. But not for long.

A generator just past the market revved up and New Year's party music started, raucous, pop, Thai and irritating. It went reverberating right through the flimsy bamboo walls of my cabin. I could sleep through nearly anything but I couldn't sleep through that. At about midnight I walked out onto the porch in the dark and something stung me hard right on the throat, as unerring as the jugular leech in the Kachin State. The sting throbbed, and I wondered if it had been a scorpion falling out of the thatched roof. Whatever it was had made a buzzing sound, though, so I guessed it to be some kind of pissed-off wasp that couldn't sleep either. The wound began to swell, and I dabbed on antibiotic and *Yunnan Bai Yao*, the Chinese anti-bleeding powder, for lack of anything more suitable.

I went back to my floor-bed. It occurred to me that if my throat started swelling up and choking me, nobody would hear me call for help, particularly with the music still blaring. My thoughts turned to John, back in the United States. Under normal circumstances I would have thought it would be appropriate for me to die of a mysterious bug bite right on the border of Burma. It was the kind of thing I just about sought for myself. But now I had a lover whom I would never get to know better if that happened. I didn't really want to die without going farther into the future with John. Such morbid musings lulled me to sleep even before the party generator conked out for the night. I dreamed about misplacing my necklace of stars and searching for it.

I woke at 5:30 to beautiful quiet, only the sound of the river, and slept again. It was still quiet at 6:30. No market was held that day, all New Year's celebrations were completely done with, the villagers were sleeping off rice whiskey hangovers. I went down to the Mekong River to wash. The river flowed low, brown and wide. A long sand-bar stretched exposed just off the Laotian beach. No boats were setting off or going by. Burma looked soft in the morning mist, a green fuzz of vegetation on its hills. I walked back up over the sand and rocks. Xieng Kok's houses were small, though not as small as my river-front cabin, and shaggy with palm thatch. I went to a café near the row of cabins for coffee and breakfast noodles (since I was beyond the French bread zone). As the village woke up, people filtered into the café. Ai Nok appeared, with a couple of truck passengers heading

13 (right, top). A Baum elder with longbow, Bangladesh, 1998.
14 (right, bottom). Baum children do the bamboo dance, Bandarban hill Tracts.

15. Jade traders, Ruuili, China, 1991.

16. Old growth log from Burma, Yunnan Province, China, 2002.

back towards Muong Sing. They ate and left. He didn't even bother to ask me if I wanted to return that way.

My scheme now was to head down the Mekong River by boat, all the way past the place where the Burma border met the Thai border, as far as a town called Huay Xai. Then, from Huay Xai I could catch a flight to Vientiane and leave Laos before the expiration of my non-extendable visa, which had just a few days left on it. That was if I could get a boat. If I couldn't I would just have to wait around in Xieng Kok for a while, maybe go back the Muong Sing way eventually. I'd let my visa run out, pay a fine in Vientiane, leave when I could.

After lingering over coffee and talking with village ladies, I left the café and took a walk around the village. A police post stood on the hill above the market, with nobody up and about yet. Workers were finishing construction on a new tin-roofed Buddhist temple. I walked back down to the river bank, where some kids were playing with matches in the sand. I returned to my porch to gaze across at Burma, which I might have been content to do forever. Three small huts were visible over there, in a clearing up on a wooded hillside, surrounded by vine-draped rocks like the overgrown battlements of a ruined castle.

A young Laotian named Vinay, who was acting as caretaker of the tourist cabins, came by and we drank soda-pops on the porch and talked in English about Burma. 'People come over from the Burma side to trade us vegetables sometimes, for Chinese things, but they do not have much and do not stay long,' Vinay said, 'But we do not like to go there. The Burma Army has a place on their side up the river from here. They don't want any foreigners like you at their place. Now the Burma Army is fighting Khun Sa.' Across the river from us, according to what Emma had told me, was territory that could well be pulled into the current conflict between Khun Sa and the Tatmadaw. 'Laos is better than Burma,' Vinay stated firmly, 'because we have peace here now, and we have few bandits here. Burma is full of bandits and bad soldiers who will take people away to kill them without telling why.'

Vinay also informed me that the river had no boats. 'It is too low. In China, where this river begins, they have done something to make this water so short. So, at present, our motor launches cannot travel along it. You have to wait for another truck to come along the bad road from Muong Long, if you need to leave this place.' I would have been amazed had I been told right off that I could easily catch a boat down to Huay Xai. It would have been too absurdly different from all the other pessimism of travel in Laos. I was happy enough to wait around on my porch, which had a limp brown orchid in a hanging tube of bamboo and wasp nests in the rafters. 'You cannot take a boat on the river to go away from here, but if you like to go across the river just to take a photo in Burma and

come back, I think one of our small village boats can take you across,'
Vinay told me.

Some friends of Vinay's showed up to while away the morning on the
porch. They were boat-drivers put out of work by the river drop, which
turned out to be thanks to a new hydroelectric power dam up in Yunnan,
China. As if wrecking the watershed through deforestation wasn't enough,
the countries in the region were always building giant dams that played
further havoc with the environment and the land rights of indigenous
peoples. Thailand kept foisting off such dams on Laos, so that Laos could
provide Thailand with more electricity. Thailand wanted to do the same to
Burma. The course of Burma's Salween River, as well as the Mekong, was
threatened because of Thai electrical greed, the same greed that was
ramming the gas pipeline across southern Burma.

One of the boatmen, tattooed with cobras, told me he had relatives in
Oakland, California. The young villagers reminisced about US airplanes,
Air America supply runs, that they had seen when they were children. I
showed them copies of a Shan rebel newspaper from Burma's underground,
that Emma had given me. They couldn't read the Shan writing any more
than I could, but examined the photos and drawings. They commented
that over in Burma, 'soldiers could come and burn your house down', and
people 'could get taken away and never seen again by their family'. The
cobra-tattooed man left, and after a while we saw him on the boulders that
led down to the river, grabbing a very long, acid-green poisonous 'Hanuman'
snake and smashing its head on a rock. He threw the dead snake body
down into a ravine. 'That kind of snake is no good to eat,' one of the other
boatmen remarked to me.

The temperature was cooler in Xieng Kok than anywhere else I'd been
in Laos, but it was still lazy hot. By noon my guests had left and I was
deciding between putting on a sarong for a bath in the Mekong or just
taking a nap. Then I heard the insistent hum of 'speedboats'—the long
skiffs equipped with truck motors that provided the fastest transport on
the river. Two of the boats came into view from downstream and pulled
up on the shore. Vinay came up to my steps and announced, 'Boats are
here and they will go back soon. Do you want to go to Huay Xai today?'
I knew it might be my only chance. Apparently the river was still just high
enough for the boats to make it as far as Xieng Kok and return to a town
downriver. I could catch another boat to Huay Xai from there. 'I guess I
should go,' I thought. Not that I would have minded a longer stay in
Xieng Kok (maybe some barbecued bat noodles in the evening) but the
Mekong boat trip offered me a look at much of the Burma/Laos border.
'I'll take the boat,' I said.

Vinay warned me that if I was traveling by river I should have my papers
in order, as sometimes speedboat passengers got checked by Laotian police

en route. So I went over to the police post, to get a provincial stamp on my travel pass. I had to wake up one of the slumbering guards who were occupying the post, and he sulkily told me I'd have to wait for an officer to get back at 1:30. I waited around with the boatmen, who needed their landing permits stamped. We sat silently wilting in the heat and I used my passport as a fan.

It occurred to me that not one checkpoint had marked the road from Muong Sing, or for that matter, from Udomxai Province. If my truck had carried, say, acetate anhydrate, the necessary precursor chemical for processing opium into heroin, it would have made it into the hills just as smoothly as the bags of salt. If the Akhas were growing opium, if Khun Sa's people or the Wa or the Tatmadaw were trucking heroin through Laos, if Shan refugees were melting into the villages on this side of the Mekong, it could all go on without disturbing a somnolent border post like this one.

Finally the officer appeared. He entered my first name (I spelled it for him in Thai) into his big book of permissions, which cost me 200 *baht*. It could have been more like 2,000, since I had gotten no official stamps since Udomxai's airport, but he managed not to be excessively disturbed by my too-blank travel pass. I paid Vinay a butane lighter and a few US dollars for the cabin plus the police permission and he handed over the 200 *baht* to the officer for me. The boatmen received their permissions too, and we boarded their brilliantly painted made-in-Thailand crafts. I had my own boat and the other one carried a few passengers returning downstream. 'Goodbye to you! Have the good trip!' shouted Vinay and then he walked back uphill from the shore. His cabins couldn't expect any more visitors for quite a while, with Xieng Kok inaccessible by road in the wet season and by boat in the dry season.

The boats skimmed atop the Mekong, the great 3,000 mile river that began as a dribble somewhere around Tibet and gathered force (and lately, lost it) through Yunnan, formed a border between Burma and Laos, then Thailand and Laos, cut through Laos, flowed into Cambodia, then became Vietnam's delta and met the sea. At other times, I had boated on the Mekong in China, watched its log barges in Cambodia. Now the river would carry me south, alongside Burma.

My boatman obligingly pulled over to the Burma side of the river, just beyond the three huts. I waded onto the Shan State shore, wearing the orange life-vest and crash helmet required of all speedboat passengers by the Laotian Government. I took off my helmet and posed for a couple of pictures snapped by the boatman with my autofocus camera. The sand beneath my sandaled feet was sparkly with mica flecks. Far uphill two people, barely visible, stood motionless, watching us. I waved to them. They did not respond. I put a pebble in my pocket and waded back to the boat, leaving my footprints in Burma's sand.

We zipped along at a comfortable pace, cooled by a fine spray of water. Secondary forest, all picked over by loggers, forest in which tall ferns were the greenest plant, lined both sides of the Mekong. A small group of people stooping down to pan for gold or perhaps sapphires, were the only humans I saw on the Burma side for many miles, and they might have gone over there for the day from Laos. Our companion boat had a breakdown, and my boat's driver waded over to a much larger Burmese boat which seemed to have gone aground on the Burma shore and been abandoned. He cannibalized it for a part which our drivers used to get the companion boat running again. We passed by a knocked-over Buddha statue on the Burma shore and I wondered if it was the remnant of a New Year's ritual, or some kind of desecration.

My boat obtained a few more passengers on the Laotian side, as the shoreline changed from rounded boulders to high crags suitable for perches of the Rhine maidens. Jagged rocks protruded from the river, to be carefully threaded around. Spongy jellyfish floated on the water's surface. We passed people in Burma again, a group of Shans doing a late New Year's dance on the beach with a couple of Buddhist monks present. Soon some dwellings appeared over there, hovels really, which turned out to be for construction workers employed on two huge four-story peaked-roofed buildings. Bamboo scaffolding outlined the concrete structures and one of the roofs had already been tiled with bright ceramic. The complex was the Golden Triangle Paradise Resort and Casino—a Thai venture in Burma that, like the gas pipeline far to the south, had 'scam' written all over it.

The Slorc had been remorselessly promoting tourism to Burma, as a way to earn more hard currency for its enormous arms purchases while it waited for the gas money to come pouring in. The Slorc had decreed 1996 'Visit Myanmar Year', using its official name for the country, derived from old manuscripts by Ne Win's wizards. All sorts of Southeast Asian business interests, especially the drug gangsters seeking a niche for money laundering, were ripping down Burma's architectural heritage and throwing up concrete firetrap 'international' hotels with various *karaoke* teenaged whorehouse amenities, in Rangoon and Mandalay. The regime instituted ham-fisted 'beautification' projects (paint your house a nice bright color or it will be confiscated), and set up zoos of hill tribe people in costume, and forced political prisoners to dig out a palace moat, all to give the tourists what they supposedly wanted. A retro-Raj boat cruise on the Irrawaddy was launched, with well stuffed and insulated tourists floating by Burmese surreality.

The Golden Triangle Paradise Resort and Casino that I was cruising past in my stripe-tailed Laotian speedboat was one of Slorc tourism's crowning touches. Still nowhere near finished, it was a Thai conglomerate's sleazy idea. Some day, after all the step-by-step bribes to the Slorc cleared, the complex was intended to provide every luxury: high-stress golf, loaded dice, unsafe sex and dam-draining air-conditioning. I supposed that once the smoke and cordite died down from Khun Sa's battles with the Tatmadaw a few miles away, the Casino site would again crawl with workers, well paid, poorly paid or unpaid.

Burma ended just past the Casino and then the Mekong River was flowing between Laos and Thailand. We passed Sop Ruak, the Thai site of the much-vaunted Golden Triangle. That term used to describe the whole big opium growing region of Burma's Shan State, northern Laos, and northern Thailand (before crop-substitution took hold in Thailand). The area was really 'golden' only for the more talented drug traffickers and their hired heroin chemists. 'The Golden Triangle' had also come to specifically mean the point at which the borders of Laos, Burma and Thailand met, always an intriguing spot for the golden hordes of tourists who thronged Thailand. I had bicycled to Sop Ruak on a dusty trail in 1981, when it was a backwater village.

Now, in 1995, the Laotian passengers gasped in awe as they beheld Thailand at its most theme parkish. Vacation condos jostled for space on the river bank. Gigantic bloated replicas of traditional Thai architecture housed and fed the tour groups arriving on fancy air-conditioned riverboats made to look like airplane fuselages and in shiny convoys of buses. The Laotians were particularly impressed by the buses, being from a nation that still mostly rode around in the backs of pickup trucks or rickshaws.

Our speedboats continued past Thailand, which was deforested even of secondary growth, its river shores covered with flower gardens or painted cement, or plastic bag dumps. I recollected attempting to apply for a visa to Laos back in the '80s when I lived in Thailand, only to be told that American visitors were not allowed in Laos. Now I was *persona non grata* in Thailand, able only to gawk at it from afar, but I could roam Laos at will.

We Huay Xai bound passengers switched to other boats, and further downriver we changed boats once again. Darkness was gathering when we got to Huay Xai. The town had long been an infamous wholesale opium/ heroin distribution hub. Way back in the 1960s some Shan and Chinese forces had fought a bloody battle there, right in the town (like Khun Sa's recent Tachilek surprise.) The clash had erupted over a major opium shipment, which had ended up confiscated by the corrupt Laotian military leader of the time for his own purposes.

Huay Xai may have still been thriving on drugs in 1995, but as a river port across from Thailand it was also bursting with legal trade in consumer goods. It even had baby taxis, and I took one from the river shore to the center of town and checked into the Manirat Hotel. From the scufflings in the wallboards, I realized that it could as well be called the 'Many Rat Hotel'. I showered but still some of the glittering sand of Burma stayed on my legs and between my toes. I was told that there would be no plane out of Huay Xai and that I could not get an airplane ticket, but there was, and I did.

7

THE VIEW OF THE CEMETERY

'Don't get typhoid,' advised Maleah, my husband's younger daughter, as I was about to leave for Bangladesh. 'Don't get lost,' counseled Becca, his elder daughter. Ordinarily I despise and reject pre-travel admonitions, the worst being the loathsome 'Be careful'. But the girls came up with such idiosyncratic caveats that I decided for once to take the words to heart. I had already taken several doses of oral typhoid vaccine, so I didn't imagine that part would be a problem, at least.

John and I had gone to the share-cottage where Becca, in college, was living. It was the week before Halloween, 1998. We brought the girls a spider-webbed cheesecake, and they admired my freshly dyed hair as 'very Goth'. It was a shade called 'Dark Brown' which had turned out shockingly ink-black. I intended to be somewhat inconspicuous in Asia again.

Three years had gone by since I had last gone raven-tressed into a Burma border zone in 1995. In the interim, I had been to a Burma conference in India (where I'd spent time with Chin refugees), and I had gone to Malaysia's capital, Kuala Lumpur to try and undermine Burma pipeline-related ventures based there. I had flown to Brussels to testify on forced labor in Burma to the European Trade Commission, and to Geneva to do the same before the International Labor Organization. Those trips, plus many shuttles to Los Angeles to choreograph press-worthy demonstrations at the big oil companies, ARCO (which left Burma) and Unocal (which did not), racked up six figures in frequent-flyer miles for me. More than enough mileage to get me to Hong Kong, on the way to Bangladesh. My travel expense money was earned the hard way, with months of wrist-straining work throwing magazines and Christmas catalogs into conveyor-belt bar-code sorting machines for the overtime-crazed US Postal Service.

The Chins were drawing me back to Bangladesh. They had been so elusive during my first time there, in 1991, the cyclone year, although I had managed to meet them in India and elsewhere later on. The Chin National Front (CNF) Chairman whom I had met back in 1991 in Calcutta had been dismissed for corruption, and other young leaders had guided the group since. In July 1998, two Chin National Front representatives came to North America. Christian rebels, they used the names Stephen (a CNF Vice Chairman) and Dr S.K. (the group's foreign secretary). I flew to Berkeley, California, to see them, and we had a long talk over cranberry juice in a student lounge. I had a special affinity for the CNF, because I had gone much farther out of my way than Berkeley to meet them in the past, and because they were still fighting the good fight. One of the last of Burma's ethnic groups to enter into insurgency, it seemed as if the Chins might be the last to quit it under the regime's pressure.

During our discussion in the lounge, Stephen wore a raincoat despite the summer heat, and socks, no shoes. He had glasses and a very wispy Ho Chi Minh sort of beard. Dr S.K. was more urbane looking, in a diagonally striped warm-up suit. Both appeared young, in their late twenties or early thirties. At one point, Stephen mentioned a town called Bandarban in the Hill Tracts of Bangladesh, near the Burma border. I knew from my 1991 visit to Bangladesh that the CNF operated around Bandarban, and that it was off-limits to foreigners. 'If you could go to Bandarban, you might see us there,' Stephen said.

That caught my interest, so later that summer, when I was again in Berkeley, in a coffee shop with a Buddhist peace activist who had been in Bangladesh's Hill Tracts, I asked about Bandarban. 'Now that the Bangladesh government has signed a peace accord with the Chakma hill tribe guerrillas who were fighting it, the Hill Tracts are really opening up. I think maybe you can get a permit to go to Bandarban now,' the activist told me.

When India had become independent from Britain in 1947, the Bandarban area had at first been allocated to Burma, and the rest of the Hill Tracts to the north of it were 'Indian'. But the Partition of the Indian subcontinent which produced Pakistan placed both sections of the Hill Tracts in East Pakistan. Then the Liberation War of 1971 made East Pakistan into Bangladesh.

Tribal people of the Hill Tracts, especially the mainly Buddhist Chakmas, rebelled against Bangladesh in response to the flooding of much of their land by a massive hydroelectric project and Bengali settlers migrating in to farm what land was left. Indian agents backed the Hill Tracts rebellion to some extent, as a proxy war intended to harass Bangladesh. The tribal rebels attacked Bengali settlers, and the Bangladesh military and the settlers committed large-scale human rights violations against Chakmas and other indigenous civilians throughout the Hill Tracts.

Finally in 1998 a tenuous peace accord was reached between the Bangladesh Government and tribal leaders. Much remained to be resolved, especially land rights, migration and environmental protection issues, but the Hill Tracts people were looking forward to local autonomy and demilitarization of the area. Although Bangladesh was still below the tourist radar, the Hill Tracts leaders were eager for at least a few visitors with dollars, so I had a good chance of getting in there.

I checked further, e-mailing Brother Francisco, a Catholic peace advocate in Bangladesh. I had corresponded with him back in 1991, at the time of the Rohingya refugee outpouring from Burma to Bangladesh. Brother Francisco e-mailed right back, informing me that permits for Bandarban were indeed available from the Home Affairs Ministry in Bangladesh's capital, Dhaka, and he didn't think the application process should take very long.

By the time I established communications with the CNF again and made my plane reservations through the frequent flyer program, it was October. I'd fly to Hong Kong, then Dhaka, then proceed to Chittagong to see the Rohingya groups' leaders, and then head into Bandarban's hills for the Chins. I knew that off in Asia by myself for a month or so, I would miss John, and I would miss our second wedding anniversary. Since we'd been together, John had gone away a couple of times on his own Asian journeys, working on sustainable technology projects in Borneo. It was something we just had to get used to.

We could get though it because our love was very strong and portable, like a nomad's sheltering felt-walled yurt. Anyway, we both understood that I unquestionably needed to go to Bangladesh, that the word 'Bandarban' had taken hold of me like 'Manipur' and 'Pajau' and 'Muong Sing' had before, enticing me irresistibly to the frontier.

On a drizzly Hong Kong evening in late October, I waited in a gray passenger bay for my Bangladesh Biman flight to begin boarding. Hong Kong Immigration police frog-marched four young Bengali men up to the gate. Having been run out of Thailand twice in much the same fashion, I recognized that the Bengalis were being deported. One of the deportees sat next to me on the plane, in the aisle seat. He wore a brown suit and a baseball cap, and kept thumbing through his passport as we waited to take off. The waiting stretched into abnormality, and the pilot got on the public address system and mumbled something about 'mechanical problems'. An hour passed on the runway, immobile, with a sari-clad flight attendant handing out cups of pineapple juice and apologies every so often. The air-conditioning seemed to be off. Some passengers picked fights, arguing in Bengali with a portly male steward. I groused inwardly: 'It's hot, it's crowded, tempers are frayed—this is like already being in Bangladesh.'

Two hours inched by on the plane before we were let off for a cafeteria meal. Then everyone hung around in the sterile gray new terminal for another four hours until the mechanical problem was deemed solved, we reboarded, and took off. The seat next to me was vacant then. The deportees had apparently taken advantage of the delay to fade back into the depths of Hong Kong.

When a Bangladesh Customs officer waved me through at Dhaka's airport, it was after two in the morning. I bargained a fare into Dhanmondi, a Dhaka neighborhood, with a baby taxi driver. After stopping at a petrol station for a slug of kerosene, the baby taxi varoomed down dark roads I'd last traveled seven years before. Guards at a nearby Indian Embassy facility directed the baby taxi driver to the Ambrosia Guest House, which was discretely unmarked behind high garden walls. An Ambrosia night-watchman showed me to the room I had reserved. The next day, foreign guests there expressed dismay that I had risked my life by taking a baby taxi in the middle of the night. Dhaka had changed, they cautioned me, now there was crime.

Dhaka did seem different. The traffic was frenetic. Herds of baby taxis spiralled madly around traffic circles, competing for road space with rusty buses and new chauffeured sport utility vehicles. Flocks of antiquated bicycle rickshaws wobbled unsteadily into the seething cauldron of carbon monoxide miasma at every intersection. In 1991, when I'd last been there, I had appreciated Dhaka's quietness, the dominance of gently urgent rickshaw bells, the lack of exhaust fumes. Now in 1998, rough-hewn Dhaka was known as a 'Mega-City'. Dhaka's population must have multiplied again and again since 1991, with its vehicles keeping pace.

Before, I had sailed around town in rickshaws, but now I contributed to the two-stroke engine smog by opting for the speed of the ferret-like baby taxis for my errands. On my first day back in Dhaka, I caught a baby taxi to the Home Affairs Ministry, a security-walled compound of several buildings. I was allowed to walk right in, and I made inquiries about getting a permit for Bandarban. Loitering men who seemed to know what they were talking about informed me that I was too late to apply for a permit that day, but should come back at ten the next morning. When I did so, full police security was in effect. I was told to wait in an office near the main gate, a room full of dusty desks with green glass paperweights and shelves disgorging rolls of old documents. Eventually a policeman whom all the other cops saluted walked me over to another building, and we took the elevator to the Deputy Secretary's office.

'I would like to apply for the permit for travel to Bandarban,' I told the desk-bound assistants in the anteroom.

'No need!' the Deputy Secretary's staff chorused.

I tried again: 'I've been told that this is where I can get the permit required for a foreigner like me to be allowed to go to the Hill Tracts, to Bandarban.'

'Madam, we can assure you that there is *no need* any longer for such permits to Bandarban. The time of needing permits is over. Now you may proceed freely, as you wish, to the Bandarban Hill Tracts. Just check in with the District Commissioner on your arrival there.'

I had expected the permit business to be a siege, a long drawn-out waiting game like Mr Bala and the Manipur affair. Instead I had time free in Dhaka, which I spent tagging along with an anthropology professor who was documenting the local rickshaw paintings. Flamboyant artwork still graced the tin panels of Bangladesh's rickshaws, and the baby taxis too. Movie gangsters scowled, turquoise and pink birds spread their wings, the Concorde flew past the Tower of London, sultry women cast come-hither looks into the traffic, and pious little boys clasped hands in prayer, all in endless motion on the streets of Dhaka. I went to the cramped atelier of one of the best-known rickshaw painters, Ahmed Artist, with the anthropologist. I commissioned a tin panel to bring home. 'Something with Bengal tigers,' I requested. 'A jungle scene,' he agreed, and I was promised that it would be waiting at the Ambrosia when I got back from points south.

The anthropologist and I went down to Dhaka's Buriganga River, so she could digitally videotape the boats scudding back and forth along it, a Canaletto scene of Venice's Grand Canal come to life. At the jetty, I tripped and stopped my fall with my left hand. A grain of soil was embedded in my palm, and I hoped it would stay there, a corner of Bangladesh forever held in my hand.

I met Brother Francisco in his small, dark office, and he told me about Bandarban. 'Typhoid, they have so much typhoid there. And malaria as well. It is a very humid place. Disease and climate are the main problems. Bandits are outside of town; they won't bother you.' Bandarban was the seat of one of the three hereditary Rajas of Bangladesh's Hill Tracts. That very week, Brother Francisco told me, a new Raja had been confirmed to take Bandarban's throne, which had been left vacant since the death of the previous Raja. But a succession controversy was continuing among rival heirs. The situation reminded me of research I had done that summer while writing an encyclopedia article about Indonesian history. The Indonesian islands of Java and Sumatra had suffered one succession crisis after another during the Middle Ages. How intriguing it was, I thought, that such pages from history should still be taken seriously in Bandarban. It had to be a special place. Tourist-bereft Bangladesh kept optimistically publishing travel brochures, and one of them showed scenes of Bandarban: hill tribe girls in short striped sarongs, green mountains all around. I was typhoid-proof, and I would get extra anti-malarial doxycycline and go off to see the Raja's palace and the green mountains of Bandarban.

Now Bangladesh had big air-conditioned inter-city buses. The one I rode to Chittagong carried just five passengers. The fare was not expensive for me, but it put me near the top of Bangladesh's transportation class-structure pyramid. My plush, cool, sealed bus was only out-classed by the private cars that carried the country's absolute elite around in luxury. Most people suffered through travel in tightly-packed open-windowed buses with bright slashes of paint disguising corrosion and some veneer of authority hiding the drivers' suicidal psychoses.

One other foreigner was on board the Chittagong air-con coach. He was a virologist from Peru, a diarrhea buff. When we got to Chittagong we talked disease over a dinner of fried pomfret at a restaurant I knew from

1991. He treated me to the sight of a leishmonaisis sore he had on his calf, a gunshot-wound-like flesh cavity from a deliberate immunizing dose of the infection. I told him nothing of what I was really up to in Bangladesh, and got him to inspect the doxycycline capsules I purchased in a bazaar stall. They looked good, he said, guessing they were probably filched from some foreign aid project. That antibiotic was the only thing that warded off malaria anymore. The parasite had grown immune to all the other pills.

I checked into the Hotel Golden Inn, a moderately posh new place on the road leading past Chittagong's railway station. It was just a few blocks from the Hotel Mishka, where I'd stayed in 1991, and it looked a lot better. The first night, my window faced another building, and I could see one sewing machine of a sweatshop across the way, a floor below. A woman's arm with red bangles on it, all I could see of her, pushed cloth under the needle.

In the morning I moved to the other side of the hotel, to a superior room. It had very clean cream-colored walls, curved Bengali Deco teak furniture, and cable TV, on which I watched astronaut emeritus John Glenn get launched on a US space shuttle flight. My new room was just large enough for its single bed, its collection of cabinets and chairs, and a path to the green tiled bathroom. A rumbling air-conditioner jutted outside from below the one window.

I opened the curtains and looked out on what I at first thought was a park of some kind, but soon realized was a block-long Moslem cemetery. A gray concrete archway on Station Road opened to a small courtyard and a shrine. Beyond the courtyard, shrubbery and flowering plants bordered each of the hundreds of mounded-earth graves. I chalked it up to Islamic rationality, having the nerve to site a hotel next to a cemetary. Innkeepers of any other belief system would have taken the ghost factor into account and built elsewhere.

A room boy brought me a curl of shiny paper, a fax from John. He would soon be off to an artists' colony on Washington State's Olympic Peninsula. A creative woodworker, he would be devising boxes for a friend's artwork called 'The Book of Within'. I used the Golden Inn's fax machine to get my meetings in gear, sending a message to the Chins in Bandarban. I was prepared to wait patiently for communication from the CNF, filling the time by renewing my old Rohingya friendships.

A phone call to Anwar Hussein, the Rohingya businessman who had been of great assistance to me in 1991, produced him at my door, along with Uncle Jilani, the white-bearded brother-in-law of a Rohingya exile I knew in the United States. Uncle Jilani had been one of the democracy activists elected to Burma's parliament in 1990s national election. Like the rest, he was never allowed to take office. Now he and much of his family lived in uncertain exile, scattered around at least three different countries. Through his brother-in-law, I had also become friends with Anwar Hussein's son, another stateside refugee.

Anwar Hussein and Uncle Jilani and I caught a baby taxi in front of my hotel. It darted down clamorous streets to a quieter neighborhood where Uncle Jilani lived in a fourth-floor walk-up. We talked over the Rohingyas' state of existence. The two main groups, Arakan Rohingya Islamic Front (ARIF) and Rohingya Solidarity Organization (RSO), were set to merge, Anwar Hussein told me. Old personal, factional differences were being set aside and I could meet both leaders together in Chittagong. Uncle Jilani telephoned the RSO leader, Dr Mohammed Yunus, and we made an appointment for two days later. Though I had been to RSO headquarters in 1991, Dr Yunus had been out of town then, so I had not met him before.

Back at the Golden Inn, I got a phone call from the CNF Vice Chairman, Stephen, who was in Bandarban. He would come down to Chittagong to see me the next evening. I passed the day reading *A Civil Action*, about a skein of litigation arising from deadly polluted wells in New England. I watched a funeral procession wind into the cemetery below my window. Soon thereafter, a line of gypsy-like pavement dwellers assembled in the cemetery courtyard to be given alms by the bereaved relatives in tribute to the deceased.

At around five the next afternoon, Stephen appeared, beardless and with a book for me. It had been published in Dhaka, about the Baum people. 'Baum' was the name for the Chins living in Bangladesh's Hill Tracts. The ethnic group as a whole would properly be called the Zo; I was used to calling them all 'Chin' because that was how they were known in Burma, and—politically correct or not—the main rebel group, the Chin National Front, went by that designation. But Chins were a type of Zo, as were Baums, and the Kukis up in Manipur. They were all relatives, but fractured into hundreds of clans and dialects.

Photos in the back of the Baum paperback book showed bamboo houses decorated with the skulls of cattle called *mithuns*, wild boar roasting over coals, girls dancing solemnly in their handwoven mini-sarongs. The old Animist Chin culture had centered on feasts of sacrificed *mithun* meat and ceremonial rice beer drinking bouts, a 'Steak and Brew' religion. Christianity, introduced to the Chins of Burma a hundred years ago by American Baptists, had gained immense popularity with its hymns, literacy and educational opportunities. It had not united the clans, though, and Chins were still prone to disparaging comments about other Chins from a different mountain ridge or valley. Additionally, just about every known sect of Christianity, and a few brand new ones, had gained a foothold amongst the Chins, adding to rivalries. There was even a Jewish 'Lost Tribe of Israel' group of Chins, some of whom had managed to obtain asylum in Israel itself when they fled Burma.

A lot of Chins took the Bible awfully literally. Not just in the fundamentalist interpretation way, but in the carrying crosses around and having 'I *am* Jesus' delusions way. The first Chin I'd ever been in touch with, around 1987, was an exiled dissident in Europe who had a severe Christ complex and used to send intricately collaged hate-mail to Pope John Paul II and Queen Elizabeth denouncing them as imposters. I had gained a certain amount of respect for his claims of divinity when he accurately predicted not only the democracy uprising of 1988, but the time and manner of its bloodbath suppression by Ne Win's Slorc.

The Chin Christians adored evangelizing. Spreading the translated Bible and their tambourine-banging hymns from place to place had become the Chins' peaceful way of raiding other villages. They hunted for souls to bring to their denominations. Nothing the Slorc did got the Chins as angry as the suppression of their Christian religion, which the Tatmadaw liked to persecute in both large and petty ways—taking Chin children away to be reared in Rangoon's Buddhist monasteries, or tearing the wooden crosses down from the hilltops and forcing people to build Buddhist pagodas in their place.

'I am not so good at my English as Dr S.K., our Foreign Secretary,' said Stephen as we drank room service coffee. 'Dr S.K. is still north in India, but we expect him very soon. Then he can arrange everything for you, Mirante.'

'Do you think it will be OK for me to go up to Bandarban then?' I asked.

'You may go to Bandarban, but it is better for you to meet us CNF here, in Chittagong. The security, you see. In Bandarban the police can see us. So let us meet here.'

'But then I can go to Bandarban for a look around on my own?'

'Our Foreign Secretary will arrange for you, sure.'

Stephen had sad news about an acquaintance of mine from my 1991 visit to Bangladesh. Comrade Thaw Da of the Red Flag Communist Party, whose letter appealing for help I had dutifully mailed to President Bush back then, had fallen ill in Bandarban and died.

We talked about Burma's horrible state of suspended animation, with an economy running on empty, the reviled military regime teetering on the edge of destruction, but no movement inside the country strong enough to seize the moment, to push the junta over the edge. Although Aung San Suu Kyi had finally been freed from her house arrest in the summer of 1995, her movements were completely constrained by the Slorc and her party members were constantly jailed, threatened and harassed. She continued to bravely defy the regime, but there was little question that the whip-hand was still the upper hand in Burma.

After a hotel room boy walked in without knocking to collect the coffee cups, I raised the scenario of an invasion of Burma by Bangladesh.

'Something coming out of a border clash,' I said, having visualized it on the bus from Dhaka, 'Remember, it almost happened in '91—Bangladesh went on full war alert when some border posts got destroyed by the Tatmadaw. So often when there is a really hard-core dictator, like Somoza or Idi Amin or Mobutu, they get brought down not by the superpowers, but by an insignificant neighbor who just gets fed up with them.'

Stephen smiled, 'This would be good. But we ourselves have no influence with the Bangladesh Government. We are only quietly in this country. Maybe you can ask your Rohingya friends, perhaps they are having more connection to this Bangladesh Government.'

After we had racked our brains for a solution to Burma's impasse for a while longer, Stephen placed the Pacific Northwest photo calendar I had brought for the CNF office into his embroidered Chin shoulder bag. He left promising that Dr S.K., with his superior English, would be calling me soon. I still had plenty of time to get the Bandarban trip together. The next day was only Halloween, a day when spotted goats and white-faced cows roamed among the graves below my window. At breakfast I opened a card which John had tucked in my shoulder bag to be opened that day. It was printed with a picture of an ox that, according to John, was meant to be one of the giant cattle of Asia that interested me, like Burma's humongous *gaur*, the *mithun* whose sacrificed skull was part of the CNF insignia, or the probably extinct *kouprey* of Cambodia. Up in my room, the beast on the hoof was a thumb-sized cockroach, so I had a hotel worker spray aerosol insecticide behind the furniture before my next meeting.

The Rohingya leaders arrived together, both wearing white shirts and gray slacks, and in a genial, jovial mood. Nurul Islam, the lawyer who was leader of ARIF, looked well, his beard a bit grayer than when I'd last seen him. Dr Yunus, the older and shorter of the two, the leader of RSO, had a full white beard striped with grey, and a kind smile. Nurul Islam led off with apologies for not sending me a wedding card two years before because he had lost my new address. 'But I did, as per your request in the announcement, invite some Rohingya refugees for a meal—we wished you and your husband well at our marriage dinner!' I had asked my friends in the Burma border zones to donate meals to refugees as their wedding gift to us.

Both leaders were in high spirits about their organizations' merger. It would be formalized soon, with a new statement. I hoped that the announcement would use language as expressive as the old ARIF manifesto, with its flamboyant legalese and phrases such as 'the regime totally jackboot the fundamental rights and freedoms of Rohingyas.'

We talked foreign policy, the futility of hopes that the United States would ever send the Marines to liberate Arakan, the utter vulnerability of the Rohingyas in Bangladesh. 'We are at the mercy of the government here,' Nurul Islam said. A Website would help, the two leaders thought.

Such cyber-strategies were without borders, were beyond the reach of security bureaus. The Rohingya leaders promised to come back and be interviewed so that I could post their words on the Internet's thriving Burma e-mail listserves, and they left with their Pacific Northwest calendars.

On this visit to Bangladesh I would only be meeting with the Chins and Rohingyas; not the Rakhines, their Buddhist neighbors from Arakan. As always, many Rakhines continued to struggle for freedom, in jungle squads or as defiant non-violent activists in Burma's cities, and I admired their undaunted spirit very much, but my Rakhine contacts were not as they had been in 1991. My great Rakhine contact and companion of the first visit, U Kyaw Hlaing, had died of a sudden illness a few years later.

In Arakan, the Slorc's resettlement of Rakhines onto confiscated Rohingya farmland had fanned resentment terribly. Tensions ran high between the two ethnic groups, and the Rakhines tended to identify me with Rohingya interests. When I had met with Rakhine politicians and political monks in India in 1996, they mentioned other Rakhines' suspicions about my 1991 appearance on the Bangladesh/Burma border. Since my showing up there out of the blue had been followed by my local newspaper story (in an Islamic fundamentalist publication) on the Moslem refugees, and that was followed by an enormous flood of those refugees, the Rakhines put two and two together and figured me for some sort of secret agent. 'It is thought you were FBI,' a Rakhine activist had told me, to which I reacted by saying that the Rakhines in India were watching 'The X-Files' on satellite TV too much.

Not only had I lost trusted or trusting Rakhine contacts in Bangladesh, but a newer Rakhine group which I would have wanted to meet, the Arakan Army, had recently been virtually wiped out. The best officers of the Arakan Army, an insurgent unit that had appeared on the scene since 1991, were ambushed and assassinated by a crooked Indian Army officer during a con-game arms transaction code-named Operation Leech, on an isolated island beach. Before their demise, those Arakan Army officers had gotten along well with the Rohingyas. Their island murder had deprived the Rohingyas of the only good relations they'd had with a Rakhine group since the death of U Kyaw Hlaing.

The next day was Sunday, and I had nothing to do but wait for Dr S.K. to get back to Bangladesh. I took a walk, dodging rickshaws and baby taxis, to a riverside neighborhood where Chittagong's Portuguese community had once lived. I began reading another litigation epic, Gaddis' *A Frolic of His Own*. The room boys came in to replace the old beige cotton curtains with white polyester satin ones. I pushed the satin aside to watch graves being dug and two funerals, one small and one with at least a hundred mourners, all male. The sun set and crows wheeled *en masse* above the cemetery grounds. A fungus-colored cow and a tan goat trotted into the dark together. The snowy, scratchy CNN my set pulled in showed off the experimental cockroaches on John Glenn's space shuttle. Another CNN space shuttle story reported that a Chagas' disease expert was on board, making some connection between zero gravity crystallization and a possible cure (from the Costa Rican rainforest) for that blood parasite.

I slept, dreaming of being buried alive, although not in a bad way, just temporarily. Then I dreamed that I had to write the buried alive dream down on a ribbon of red paper to put in the 'The Book of Within'. In the morning I turned on CNN and watched a piece on controversial revived Native American whale hunts on the Olympic Peninsula, a few miles from where John was staying. I spent the rest of the day as a sporadic funeral voyeur. A little white ambulance pulled up to the arched gate. Wiry gravediggers bore a dead body in its blood-soaked shroud far into the cemetery, beyond my line of sight. Then they came back to the courtyard to wash themselves at the cemetery water tank.

Later, another corpse was dropped off on the sidewalk. I watched it being carried in on a board. It was wrapped in dingy burlap. One arm, a thin woman's arm with red bangles on it, hung down exposed. A couple of poor women, wraiths in cotton saris, accompanied it into the cemetary and were given a charity shroud, a decent white one, for their friend. They threw the old burlap shroud over the cemetery wall onto the sidewalk, where not five minutes later, it was seized upon by a strolling rag-picker who happily added it to the bundle of cloth atop his head.

In the evening, Nurul Islam and Dr Yunus came by for their interviewing. This time they both wore safari suits in subdued colors. Salim, another Rohingya activist, accompanied them and took pictures with my camera and his. The Rohingyas spoke the most mellifluous English. They took my questions and transformed them into stirring answer-paragraphs without a moment's hesitation. Perhaps they kept the language up by reading Bangladesh's English language press, but their phraseology was better than anything in those misprint-laden newspapers. Maybe it came from years of listening to the BBC for glimmers of democracy and sifting through British colonial records for intimations of autonomy.

Things were as bad as ever in Arakan, the Rohingya leaders told me. Relentless forced labor had rendered agriculture unproductive. The rice markets of Teknaf on the Bangladesh side of the border no longer sold grain from Arakan; a surplus to smuggle no longer existed. What little got harvested often ended up confiscated for Tatmadaw rations, so famine always loomed. Under pressure from the United Nations and the Bangladesh Government, most of the refugees had gone back to Arakan from the Bangladesh camps. In Arakan they faced the same old array of abuses by Burma's military. Usually their land, houses and livelihood were gone. Often the returnees were called by the Tatmadaw for extra forced labor to make up for the time they'd missed while stewing in the squalid refugee camps near Cox's Bazar.

'What kind of forced labor is there?' I asked Nurul Islam.

'Mainly they use people for portering,' he replied, 'to carry military supplies to the border area. Construction of military barracks, and roads, they are constructing roads there, and also sometimes there are a lot of shrimp culturing dams there. This has been actually confiscated from the Moslems. Now the government is taking care of that, and they engage people there, because every year the saline water enters and it has to be mended. So the people are used there as forced labor.' He smiled ruefully, adding, 'and they force people to collect this and that, that they put into the golf courses, for the army.' Burma's military penchant for golf was well-known, and emanated from General Ne Win himself, who was widely said to have beaten a rival nearly to death with a golf club, on the links once, decades ago.

I asked Dr Yunus about the Rohingyas' role in Burma's future. He veered back and forth between hope, personified by Aung San Suu Kyi (for whom he used a Burmese honorific meaning 'Aunt'); and eternal gloom. 'We believe the present democratic struggle led by Daw Suu Kyi, will be in a better position to evaluate and analyze the whole situation,' the doctor said. 'Taking care of the sentiments and the aspirations of different people. And if these things are really given importance, only then we can hope for the future. But if the state of things now presently going on, if the same things are harbored by those people, we don't see that Burma will have a very good future. We are optimistic in any way, by demonstrating ourselves as a positive force, and we are reiterating that we would like to be part and parcel of the democratic struggle here. With the condition that we want to have our rights ensured. Not compromising on our rights. So those who are struggling for the establishment of truth in Burma, cannot ignore us. They should also have this broadmindedness. Because Burma is a multiracial, multicultural, multilingual country. It does not belong just to the Burmese and the Buddhists.'

When I awoke the next morning, CNN was carrying news of at least 7,000 people dead in floods from a hurricane that had swept across Nicaragua and Honduras. It gave me the eerie sense that this disaster a world away had somehow just missed Bangladesh, as if every catastrophe was really meant for Bangladesh and sometimes they just happened to end up elsewhere.

Even without a major storm, Bangladesh was keeping its calamity zone status all too active. Just a couple of months before my return visit, flood waters had risen far more than usual all over the land north of Chittagong, including Dhaka. Over a thousand Bangladeshis had died; homes and valuable farmland were ruined. Mud traces still remained in Dhanmondi, where I'd stayed in Dhaka. The next awful thing, again avoiding Chittagong but causing heartbreak just about everywhere else in Bangladesh, was arsenic contamination. Tests were revealing that for years, a nationwide system of tube wells meant to bring clean, healthy drinking water to all the citizenry had instead been giving them daily slow-acting cancerous doses of arsenic. Like those wells in *A Civil Action*, Bangladesh's village drinking water supplies were the source of a gradual, insidious mass poisoning.

Waiting for a call or appearance from the Chins, I whiled away hours at the window. Midday, I saw a very tiny corpse in a stained white shroud arrive by ambulance. It was whisked away quickly, without mourners. Later a political march, all well-dressed men carrying two long red banners written in Bengali, moved briskly down Station Road. Trouble between the Awami League (in power) and the Bangladesh National Party, BNP (maneuvering) seemed to be heating up.

In 1991, at the time of the cyclone, when I'd last been in Bangladesh, Prime Minister Begum Kaleda Zia of the BNP had held office. Then by means of strikes and other civil unrest, Begum Zia's arch-rival, another female pro-democracy leader, the Awami League's Sheikh Hasina, had forced new elections and replaced her. Under Sheikh Hasina, Bangladesh had considerable freedom of expression and an improving economy. But overcrowding, crime, and class divisions made for a dearth of stability. The two parties, the two leaders, continued their power struggle, often seemingly at the expense of national progress.

Several political killings from the period immediately after Bangladesh broke off from Pakistan had gone unresolved. One of those was the assassination of Prime Minister Sheikh Mujibar Rahman, with most of his family, in 1975. Now, the present Prime Minister, Sheikh Hasina, had just gotten several people tried, convicted and sentenced to death for that bloodbath, of which she, a kind of Asian Anastasia, was one of the only surviving family members. Sheikh Hasina's opponents voiced the opinion, often and loudly, that she was wasting the country's time and resources on personal revenge; and they spent their own energy plotting revenge against her for pushing them out of office. They wanted to create enough pressure to compel her to call new elections, even if it meant forcibly grinding the economy to a halt over and over again.

Another day went by mostly in my room, and Stephen stopped by with CNF publications and the news that Dr S.K. was still in India, but was certain to be back in Bangladesh 'quite soon'. I called the Rohingyas to see about making a trip to the two remaining Rohingya refugee camps near Cox's Bazar. Only about 25,000 of the 250,000 official Rohingya refugees from the early 1990s remained in those camps, though more Rohingyas were always sneaking across the border from Arakan and taking shelter elsewhere. With Anwar Hussein as translator, I might be able to get some information from the refugees about conditions back in Arakan. We made plans to go, but then word came of the death of a brother-in-law of Anwar Hussein. The Rohingyas would be busy with preparations for the funeral (not at 'my' cemetery) so our trip south to the camps was called off.

I kept reading Gaddis and watching Hindi musicals on TV. Each morning I had tea and toast and mango juice in the red-curtained Bedouin-tent-effect restaurant downstairs in the Golden Inn. I hardly ever saw women there, just business-men. The hotel's foreign guests were mostly Indians, occasionally Africans or Koreans.

Uncle Jilani brought me an installment of his manuscript on Rohingya history to edit and proofread. It was a fascinating, well-researched chronicle of the ethnic group's medieval Golden Age and subsequent persecution. But Uncle Jilani had trouble with the English plurals, so I went through his manuscript painstakingly adding and subtracting the letter 's' where it had gone awry.

When I wasn't working on the manuscript, sometimes I took a walk, or went on a baby taxi excursion on some errand across town. I developed a cold, the nasal drip kind, and kept blowing my nose on airline cocktail napkins I'd saved. Every evening I had the Bengali concept of Chinese food (prawn chowmein, chicken rice soup) from room service. I came to recognize the King of the crows that staged their aerial ballet over the cemetery each dusk.

One morning the cooks and waiters came charging out of the kitchen after something that ran under the rug of the restaurant and hid there successfully. Carpenters hammered in the next room all day, a small boy flew a striped plastic bag kite from a graveless reach of the cemetery, a man in India displayed his collection of bars of soap on TV, another roach scuttled across my jute carpeted floor. I took codeine-tylenol, that most innocuous of opiates, to stop my coughing at night.

The Golden Inn staff never asked me about my purpose there, my Asiatic and bearded visitors, my length of stay. My hair was getting lighter every time I washed it. When I went outside I was covered up in one of my two *salwar kameez* outfits, with a scarf over my hair. I was becoming self-conscious, looking in the mirror a lot, discovering an ear piercing I could see daylight through, and gum recession from an incisor. A rotten molar reminded me of its long-delayed root canal requirements. I breathed in extra-hot Tiger Balm, which seemed to help my cold by making my eyes tear up.

On Friday, the Moslem prayer day, men and boys went to visit their family graves, and I watched them in the thousands there, standing barefoot, reciting prayers with their eyes closed, their palms turned up to heaven. Later a rickshaw brought a baby bundle in clean white cloth to rest on a scrap of reed mat in the cemetery courtyard. A man who must have been the father stood by it awkwardly, while a baby-sized grave was dug. The rickshaw driver stayed with him. I saw a man in a silk tunic give the father money. The rickshaw driver tried to park his rig inside the courtyard for safekeeping, but a caretaker scolded him and he meekly pushed it out onto the sidewalk instead.

Saturday came, and Uncle Jilani fetched me by baby taxi, for a feast of *biryani*, fragrant spiced rice with chicken, cooked by his wife at their flat. Uncle Jilani found out my Irish-Italian background and said he'd been wondering if I was 'related to the Kennedys'. I was not, I told him, but just as good, my Irish ancestors had been involved in anti-colonial sedition and labor rights agitation.

Anwar Hussein and Nurul Islam joined us for the *biryani*. Nurul Islam told me stories of his rejection by the pro-democracy set at Manerplaw, the old resistance headquarters on the Thai border. He had gone there to petition for ARIF's membership in an alliance of rebel organizations, but Rakhine groups had vetoed that. Nurul Islam had felt humiliated and unsafe there, among those democracy fighters. It was apparent that the Rohingyas had a long way to go for getting their civil rights recognized even within the anti-Slorc movement.

We also talked about deforestation in Arakan, and I suggested that the Rohingyas put an environmental paragraph in their new merger manifesto. Nurul Islam asked me for other text suggestions for the document. I came up with the idea of a clause pledging support for the 'economic empowerment, health and education', of Rohingya women and girls. The Tatmadaw abused them horribly and I suspected that even in peaceful times their lot might be somewhat like that of the cloistered Bengali females. Maybe in the future there would be a chance for Rohingya women to join the men in enjoying new-found freedom on a more equal basis.

Leaving, I mentioned that I'd seen another protest march on Station Road that morning. 'They are all paid,' said Nurul Islam cynically. 'In this Bangladesh, if they are not paid for, they shall not march.' We discussed a nationwide general strike that the BNP opposition politicians had called for two days, starting on Monday morning. Uncle Jilani gave me several more chapters of his manuscript to occupy my time, as I'd be stuck in the hotel during the strike. Transportation, aside from rickshaws and perhaps a few trains, would be shut down for forty-eight hours.

'The Golden Inn will be in full function, do not worry,' Anwar Hussein assured me. 'It is owned by a Member of Parliament, in fact.'

'Which party?' I asked.

'Oh, he is from the Awami League, the government party in power.'

When Nurul Islam's van dropped me off back at the hotel, I noticed that a half-dozen policemen had been stationed at the front entrance along with the usual pair of security guards. The good part about the Golden Inn being owned by a member of the government was that stepped-up level of security. The bad part was that I was residing in a prime target for opposition mobs. I called Bandarban and talked to Stephen, commiserating over Dr S.K. now being stuck just a day away to the north because of the strike. We resolved that I would somehow head for Bandarban as soon as it was over with.

That night I alternated reading Gaddis with reading Rohingya history. I was starting to see a resemblance between Gaddis' hero Oscar, with his scholarly, complex play about the American Civil War, and Uncle Jilani with his endless supply of manuscript chapters. As the night wore on I began speculating about escape routes in the event of a mob invasion and/or firebombing of the Golden Inn. I inspected the anti-theft steel window bars, a hated fire-trap feature of Asian hotels. The bars did not open, unlock or unscrew from the inside. They were welded on. 'Next time I come to Asia I am packing a hacksaw,' I swore. The bathroom window had those bars too. The best I could do for an escape would involve kicking out the air-conditioner and rappelling out of the hole into the familiar terrain of the cemetery.

I went into harbinger of doom mode. Anwar Hussein's offhanded revelation of the Golden Inn's ownership reminded me strongly of a similarly casual 'just the lead-in to this cyclone we're supposed to have...' in Cox's Bazar seven years before. Was this strike going to be another cataclysm, I wondered, was my very presence a portent of chaos in this apparently cursed nation? Then I recalled an article in the English-language *Bangladesh Observer*, the paper slipped under my door every morning by the Golden Inn. It was an essay about the abuse of women in Bangladesh. Not only were Bengali women constrained by a still evident *purdah* mentality—I saw so few out and about in cities or villages, men seemed to have a monopoly on everything except having babies and being Head of State— but they seemed to be increasingly victimized by violent crime. Beatings, rape, murder, and acid-throwing were not uncommonly inflicted on women in Bangladesh.

The male Moslem scholar who wrote the *Observer* article debunked one motive for such violence, which was that superstitious husbands blamed their wives for downturns in the family fortunes. If a man was unemployed, broke, in debt, it was because he had married an unlucky woman, a bad omen in the flesh. That was nonsense, insisted the *Observer* writer; such thinking affronts Islam. The Prophet Mohammed himself, Blessed be His Name, had assured us all that there are no bad omens. If you want to believe in favorable portents, OK, but there are no *bad* omens, the *Observer* writer's argument went. On that pre-strike night in Chittagong, I decided, after all my years of acute sensitivity to the inauspicious, that I would take the Prophet's philosophy to heart on at least this one thing. And so I willed myself to quit believing in bad omens, bad ju-ju, bad joss. Four floors above the graveyard's silence, my windows barred, I slept in peace.

At breakfast I opened the Anniversary card John had given me, because it was that day. I rubbed gold on my fingertips from its Klimt print. My husband had signed it, 'in rampant, ferocious, inspired love'. Back in my room I kept switching between the window and the television. The Indian TV news carried a piece on deodar trees in the Himalayas turning yellow and dying from 'a fungal pathogen'. A deodar stood majestically over our house back in the United States, a landmark, a rain shelter.

In the cemetery courtyard, a street woman smoked a cigarette and unwound her faded yellow sari to bathe in slip and blouse at the water tank tap. She chased away the men who objected to her using the water facilities that were meant for their ritual clean-up before prayer. The cemetery caretaker was always losing his half-hearted battle to keep the pavement dwellers from making off with jugs of that water for their own cooking and drinking needs.

As I watched returned space shuttle astronauts hold their press conference on CNN later that day, a racket from the courtyard brought me back to the window, where I saw men with sticks driving another skinny pavement gypsy woman from the courtyard. They used the sticks to threaten, not to hit. That was typical in Bangladesh—many hands, many fists, were raised in anger, although less actually seemed to make contact. Public arguments were frequent and strident, but brief.

Monday, strike day, I slept a deep codeine-tylenol sleep until my alarm clock went off, instead of being awakened by morning traffic on Station Road as usual. Only pedestrians and rickshaws and police trucks traveled the road. A large funeral took place early in the day, the dead body borne in elegantly on a blue litter with a green embroidered covering.

The English-language newspaper was slipped under my door, like any other morning. I telephoned the Rohingyas, who were already bored with being cooped up in their flats, and the Chins, who were expecting Dr S.K. in Bandarban as soon as the strike would end, Tuesday night. I could go to Bandarban on Wednesday.

After 1:00, a group of boys on Station Road began to harass the rickshaws. Led by a couple of teenagers (probably on the payroll of the BNP) little kids would run up and hit the rickshaws' front fenders and night-lamps with sticks. Leadership and provocation were very apparent from my observation post. The rickshaw vandalism was a microcosm of the ways in which bad people are able to instigate ordinary people, especially children, to commit acts of wilfull cruelty. Nobody intervened on Station Road, even though the rickshaw-bashers were just street children, urchins. The passengers would get out and walk, and the rickshaw drivers would humbly wheel their damaged rigs back the way they came.

It looked like a mean way to run a political campaign—the rickshaw drivers were on such a thin margin of survival. They might be approaching middle class status compared to flooded-out farmers or beggar women, but they really only earned enough off their leased vehicles to buy the food that gave them the energy to pedal all day. The rickshaw drivers were supposed to be exempt. They weren't strike-breakers, they were strike-broken. Now the whole country was shut down in a power struggle, but not in the kind of popular general strike I hoped would happen in Burma, with the masses defiantly, passively resisting oppression. In Bangladesh, people simply didn't want their windshields and shop windows busted, so they stayed home for the day—or days.

The barefoot boys in the street below got wilder. When rickshaws tried to race through their gauntlet, to get to the station where a few trains were still running, the boys would seize the rickshaws and overturn them. They'd jump on the awnings and the wheels to crack pieces off. I went to the front hallway window on my floor and watched the scene with a room boy who distracted us from the action below by reflecting on the fortunes of 'Cleen-ton' and 'Lee-ween-sky'. The police detailed to protect the Golden Inn showed no interest in the rickshaw trap just up the road.

At about 2:00 in the afternoon a mob of boys began chasing one teenager who was clutching a fistful of papers, perhaps Awami League flyers. Some of the boys caught hold of him, kicked at him, hit at him, then he broke loose. The mob changed its focus to a rickshaw which ended up right in front of the hotel, where the police finally got involved. They forced the boys to retreat in an unruly way, chanting something insulting at the cops. Two little girls in grungy frocks were among the boys. One, in yellow, looked up and saw me, a foreigner, in the hall window. She pointed up at me and tried to tell the older boys, but they ignored her. I stepped back out of view before she could convince anyone she had really spotted me. In such a turbulent scene, anything unusual could become a target, I supposed, including a foreigner (FBI agent) in an Awami-owned hotel. I decided to confine my observation to the more discrete side window of my own room after that. Nobody had ever noticed me staring out at them from that vantage point.

Station Road quieted down again, and then three rickshaws headed right for the bashing point, just past the cemetery gate. The first rickshaw was attacked by a few little boys with sticks, but then the passengers, well-dressed young men, jumped out and grabbed the sticks away. The passengers—Awami league 'activists'? undercover cops?—chased the kids up the road and then turned and walked calmly back towards the hotel and its uniformed, carbine-toting policemen. Instantly a boy mob even bigger than the previous one, perhaps two hundred children and teenagers, assembled and chased after them. The boys started grabbing up the chunks of paving stone used by the street gypsies to anchor their lean-to tents on the sidewalk. They smashed the chunks on the street and hurled the pieces in the direction of the police. Since the police were in front of the Golden Inn, large shards of stone began pelting the hotel. It occurred to me that it was like being in some US Embassy being stoned in the 1960s Third World. I began to imagine this riot breaching security and entering the hallways of the Golden Inn, but two truckloads of police reinforcements soon pulled up, and the riot boys dispersed, jeering but subdued. No bullets or tear gas, and after ten minutes even the shouting was over. The gypsies began to retrieve what they could of their tent stones.

Just down Station Road past the cemetery gate, the rickshaw harassment continued all afternoon, boys stopping, tipping over, smashing rickshaws. The little girl in the yellow dress and a half-naked younger brother got an extortion racket going, warning rickshaw drivers that they were approaching the gauntlet and demanding a tip for their help. Two other little girls in pigtails and ragged ruffles proved quite talented at sneaking up behind rickshaws and letting the air out of their back tires while their stick-wielding brother swiped at the front wheels. In the evening, a crowd of thousands of men exiting a rally at the center of town moved past the hotel. The marchers stopped suddenly. Sensing more violence about to erupt, bystanders ran into the cemetery courtyard for shelter. But then the procession moved onward. As Chittagong darkened into a night without truck, bus or baby taxi noise, I turned on the BBC radio to hear, 'and there have been violent clashes in Dhaka...'

It seemed to me that Bangladesh was addicted to adrenaline. If a natural disaster wasn't making mayhem, the excitement void had to be filled with a trumped-up political crisis. During much of the time I'd been there, Bangladesh's true collective attention had been taken up with an international cricket tournament being held with great fanfare in a Dhaka stadium. Men all over the country were glued to the cricket matches being played out on TV screens. I couldn't get into it. The game seemed like slow-pitch softball on valium to me. But I decided it was just perfect that cricket had turned out to be the national sport of Bangladesh. Let other countries have their catharsis through symbolic warfare on their playing fields, their body-slams, body-checks, scrums, tackles, hooligans rioting at the thrill of a goal. For Bangladesh there would be cricket's manicured-lawn vision of polite society, its languid perfectionism, the bowler, the batting, oh dear the sticky wickets. Real life was damned cathartic enough in a land of floods and riots; give us peace, give us cricket.

In the morning, with something between a groan and a laugh, the front desk clerk informed me, 'This strike is not finishing today. They are extending it for one additional day, to the evening of tomorrow, as well.'

Unable to get an international phone call through to John, who would be home from the art colony, I tried sending a fax from the hotel office. I gave him the Golden Inn phone number, which he hadn't had, and promised that I would certainly be there for the next two days. When I went back upstairs, the phone rang and I got John's voice, next-room clear. Instead of endearments I cut straight to a gripe about the strike: 'I'm stuck here waiting for the Chins like in '91, and this country is so fucked up politically...' and the phone went dead.

The air-conditioner and the lamp went off at the same moment, so I knew I wasn't being censored. A room boy summoned me down to the lobby, where the desk clerk told me that John would call back 'in five minutes'. I sat there on a mauve velour banquette with stranded Indian businessmen. They were also expecting callbacks from their truncated conversations, on the hotel's one functioning phone line. John never got through again, and within an hour the electricity went back on so I returned to my room and the TV. CNN ran a story (showing only a map of Bangladesh, no film) on strike-related violence in Dhaka, and that day's newspaper listed a few political party clashes resulting in killings in Chittagong. It was quiet on the road below, no marches, no vandals, the only conflict a savage battle between a pair of hawks and a gang of crows in the air above the cemetery. I chased a cockroach with a sandal until it ran away under my door, and I watched it scurry across the corridor and into another, perhaps more hospitable, room.

On the third day of the strike I went out for a walk, exploring the narrow, filthy alley behind the cemetery, which led to a market where fanned dried fish, baskets of multicolored chilis, and caged live chickens were all on display and for sale, strike or no strike. No women were out walking, and bored guys stared at me as I passed by, scuffing through rubbish in my sandals. The mayor of Chittagong had threatened to empty the town's garbage trucks in front of the headquarters of any political party that blocked their trash pick-ups during the strike, and I'd seen the trucks go down Station Road unimpeded, but they seemed to have avoided the back streets.

Back on Station Road, at another gate to the cemetery, I saw a tattered group of people gathered about a small thin corpse which rested on the sidewalk under a grimy shroud. A few coins, which were nearly worthless, lay on the edge of the cloth. The relatives were soliciting contributions from passersby for the burial. I remembered seeing the same scene by the roadside on the way to Cox's Bazar seven years before. A gaunt woman, perhaps my age, approached me and I pressed some paper money in her hand, maybe enough to make the burial fee.

By 5:30, with the strike officially due to end at 6:00 PM, the motor vehicles were off and running. Uncle Jilani came by with an elderly Rohingya barrister who practiced law in the High Court of Chittagong. The hotel elevators were out of commission, so they'd trudged upstairs to my floor. Uncle Jilani was used to that from his own staricase, but I felt sorry for the barrister. Over coffee we discussed human rights law, and he told me how a British officer had given a relative of his a letter promising to make him a Raja in Arakan for services rendered during World War II, when peace came. But then the British had left, wartime pledges were discarded, and the Rohingyas remained at the mercy of ever more hostile overlords.

After my Rohingya guests departed, Stephen telephoned, with news that my Bandarban trip was all arranged for the next morning. Then, collecting my dinner dishes, the room boy handed me a fax from John, another very welcome communication. Which was followed by a phone call from Dr S.K., the CNF foreign secretary, who had just arrived in Bandarban at last.

Down below an upper class funeral, perhaps somewhat delayed by the strike, had just taken place and the neighborhood poor people were massing in the courtyard for a big-time rice and *dhal* feed. Lining up, they got their plates or plastic bags filled and then were shooed away. Eventually the courtyard, illuminated only by the lamps of the shrine, became quiet again. At around 10:00 that night someone in the hotel decided to play with a laser pointer, aiming its red dot down into the courtyard. An old gravedigger danced alone, following the bright dot as it moved over the cement.

When it was finally time to go to Bandarban, things moved very fast. A rumored twelve-hour extension of the strike did not materialize, supposedly because Bangladesh's labor unions begged the BNP not to wreck the economy any further. I was itching to get out of Chittagong. I craved the Hill Tracts.

My role in Burma's ongoing revolution had been, for some seventeen years, that of information collector. I went to places few other foreigners bothered with, and found out what was going on there. I investigated, researched, alerted. But now I realized I was in search of something besides information. Reams of Burma facts and figures, documentation, news stories, human rights data, came flowing over the Internet every day.

I had such huge files of human rights documentation from so many sources that I had already compiled two full length reports on war crimes in Burma by cross-referencing the documents for citations of specific Tatmadaw units and officers by name. Even the Chins, so obscure, had been the subject of two reports in the previous year, one a compendium of documents that I'd assembled, another by Thailand-based Burma organizations. Hundreds of overseas Burma freedom groups were plugged into the info supply, and they demonstrated and wrote letters. With considerable effect, the groups boycotted the companies collaborating with the Slorc (which, hopelessly Orwellian, had lately changed its name to the State Peace and Development Council.) The Burma movement was hailed as a 'cyber-revolution' in popular American magazines. Burma information was in overload.

I went to Bandarban in search of something else. I was in search of the experience. I wanted to go where Chins lived, so I would not only know them as refugees and lists of Human Rights Violations on paper or computer screens. I wanted to go to Bandarban to drink glasses of tea with Chins in their bamboo houses, as I had with Kachins, Rakhines, Mons, and so many others. I needed that to give my data perspective, the view from the jungle, the view of the Chin Hills out there just beyond the Hill Tracts.

Early Thursday morning Dr S.K. called me from the hotel lobby, and came up to my room with two silent young men whom I guessed were CNF soldiers in civilian blue jeans. We went down to a passenger van hired for the trip to Bandarban. Dr S.K. got dropped off *en route*, and we acquired a bespectacled gentleman named Mr Ezekiel. He was a Baum elder who would serve as my guide. A Gordian knot of post-strike traffic snarled Chittagong. The CNF soldiers laughed as rickshaws got caught on baby taxi fenders and a van driver got in a face-slapping match with a rickshaw driver.

When we finally got out of the city, our van took off on a pitted highway and then turned sharply east for the Hill Tracts. Then the first substantial uncultivated countryside I'd seen in weeks appeared, brush-covered green hills. Soon we drove by bamboo houses high on hills, and a Buddhist pagoda. No doubt about it, we were in the Hill Tracts. Convoys of military trucks passed us on their way down from a Bangladesh Army cantonment that occupied the edge of Bandarban. As we drove into the town, we picked up Mr Lemuel, a tall Baum who spoke English, Bengali and several tribal languages. We drove through the bazaar area, past Bengali mosques, a hospital, homes and shops interspersed with palms and fruit trees. Following my Home Affairs Ministry instructions we stopped at the District Commissioner's office first.

Mr Ezekiel and Mr Lemuel accompanied me, and we informed the District Comissioner, a khaki-uniformed youngish Bengali with a mustache, of my plans. 'I am here as a tourist,' I assured the District Commissioner.

'Mirante is an artist who likes to observe our culture,' Mr Lemuel added.

'But you must have a letter requesting permission to be here in Bandarban,' the District Comissioner told me with a raised eyebrows.

'Oh, the Home Ministry said that I could come here now without any permit—when I visited them in Dhaka...' I said, feeling double-crossed.

'Of course you do not need a permit. You need only a letter requesting permission, that is all,' the District Comissioner explained. He gave us a sheet of paper and Mr Lemuel wrote out a letter for me in the appropriate flowery English: 'I beg to state that I am an American lady and I have arrived here at 1:30 PM today for visiting some picnic spots, tribal villages so as to study tribal culture and social life.' That got photocopied, one for the District Comissioner, one to be dropped off at the police station by Mr Lemuel, and the original was for me to keep. We had a cup of tea with the

District Comissioner, and biscuits, and chatted about the potential for 'eco-tourism' in Bandarban, and he apologized for the lack of proper hotels. I was to stay at a guest house for travelling officials, on a ridge overlooking the town. The Baums had arranged everything. We left the District Comissioner's office somewhat amazed by the ease of it all and the lack of 'tea-money' solicitation.

I paid the van driver, with extra for his lunch, and he went back to Chittagong. Once I got settled into a bubble gum pink room with sea green damask curtains and a Barbie pink mosquito net at the guest house (not too dirty, not too clean), I went for a walk with Mr Lemuel. Our initial destination was the Tribal Cultural Center, which had a small museum on two floors. Costumed dummies demonstrated weaving and standing about in glass cases. A comprehensive collection of baskets, silver ornaments and textiles of the Bandarban Hill Tracts' ethnic groups was on display. Handicrafts of the Baums, Khamis, and Mros, who were also found across the border in Burma, were featured. The walls and shelves also showed articles used by the Rakhines who in Bandarban were known as a tribe called 'Marma'.

In the Center's enviable library of works on indigenous peoples of Bangladesh, India and the world, a painting of the late previous Raja of Bandarban hung on the wall. His gold paisley-embroidered ceremonial coat was on exhibit across from it. In back of the Cultural Center stood four playhouse-sized reproductions of tribal housing. Ethnic craftsmen had built each miniature bamboo dwelling with great care and accuracy. Mr Lemuel showed me where *mithun* skulls should be hung in the anteroom of the traditional Baum house.

Mr Lemuel and I walked down lanes that felt to me like Burma, as had Manipur and Muong Sing. I was glad to see women out in the open again, wandering around in the fresh air, engaged in commerce, drinking soda-pop in shops like regular people. Even though Bangladeshi feminist groups were active and hardworking, and projects like micro-credit banking strove for the economic empowerment of Bangladesh's village women, only in ethnic minority enclaves like Bandarban were women as visible as men. As in Burma, the girls carrying water jugs or schoolbooks wore sarongs and T-shirts and had *thanaka* powder on their faces.

Burgundy-robed Buddhist monks made their unhurried way to a tin-roofed temple guarded by statues of mythical beasts. Bandarban town was '50/50' Bengali/tribal, Mr Lemuel told me. It had two Buddhist monasteries, which were in fierce competition due to sponsorship by two rival Raja succession factions. We had a look at the attractive small white stucco palace of the Raja before last, from its front gate. Then, from the guest house ridge, Mr Lemuel pointed out the newer palace of the recently deceased Raja.

Exhausted and a bit disoriented from being out of the Golden Inn, I listened to the BBC radio in my pink room that night. Bombing raids on Iraq were being threatened, the BBC news reported, and I felt a curious symmetry with my other Bangladesh trip, when the Gulf War, such as it was, had been just winding down. I drank some bottled water, lit a mosquito coil, and got under the pink net. Geckos chased moths in the wordless landscape of a dream.

Mr Lemuel arrived with a hired Bengali driver and assistant driver and their rented boxy dark blue passenger van, at dawn on Friday the 13th. The town was still stroked with wisps of gray morning fog as we went over to Mr Ezekiel's house for breakfast. His place had a cement foundation and woven bamboo walls which were painted green on the inside. In the front room a carved teak cabinet displayed an array of plastic toys, including a play AK47, like museum pieces. Above it real deer antlers were attached to a wooden deer head, as close to a ceremonial *mithun* skull as it got in modern Bandarban town. Mr Ezekiel's small granddaughter, a sprite in a white blouse and plaid skirt, entered the sitting room to present me with a traditional Baum wicker wedding basket. I handed her a box of chocolate Coffee Nips that I just happened to have with me for such an occasion. Mr Ezekiel and Mr Lemuel and I breakfasted on papaya and black sticky rice with coconut. Then we went off for our cultural picnic in the Hills, with Mr Ezekiel's wife and two daughters and the little girl.

Our full van drove upwards, out of town. The Hills were never mountains, and the jungle was never anything but secondary. Kudzu-like creepers and feral banana plants dominated everything else. Turbaned Mro women in striped handwoven sarongs were carrying loads of firewood sticks down to sell in Bandarban's market. We met up with a couple of young Baums out hunting with very old rifles. I asked what they were after and Mr Lemuel translated their reply, 'Deers, monkeys,' adding, 'We have also bears, and of course the wild cows.' Although Bandarban meant 'monkey jungle' in Bengali, I found it hard to believe that with such a sorry excuse for forest remaining, any monkeys or those larger mammals could lurk within range. Perhaps wild chickens, or the odd rodent, civet cat might await a bullet. But never a wild cow, I thought.

We dropped off Mr Ezekiel and his family at a hillside village, except for one daughter, a student who dressed in *salwar kameez* the way Bengali university girls did. One could hardly expect her to go around in a striped Baum mini-skirt. In Bangladesh, the more up-to-date you were, the more you covered up, even in the Hills. We drove along switchbacks to a view point. From the hilltop, where a few Bangladesh Army troops were stationed, we could gaze northeast at India, the mountains of Mizoram. Turning, we glimpsed Burma's peaks, blue in the distance. Another turn faced us west toward Bangladesh's Indian Ocean coastline. In that direction, green scrub-covered hills, interspersed with tribal villages and the Bangladesh Army cantonment, stretched down below to the strip of densely populated rice-growing flat land that led to the seashore.

It was painfully obvious how trapped in the degraded Hills the tribal people were. For the Baums, Mros, and others, there was no place else to go. For anyone fleeing Burma, the outlook was dire. Bengali farmers and their busy market towns were already using up every scrap of level space. While I was happy to look at Burma, a mere thirty miles or so from where I stood, my thoughts were taken up mainly with the demise of the ancestral forest-roaming way of life of Bangladesh's tribes.

Back down the road and a couple of miles up along a steep path in the hot sun, Mr Lemuel brought us into a Mro village. Although it was Friday, the school holiday in Moslem Bangladesh, school was in session there. A few little boys sat at desks in a building that had been damaged by high winds in a more recent cyclone than the one I'd experienced. People were bathing in their sarongs at a village water tank built by the self-help project Mr Ezekiel and Mr Lemuel kept in action in the Hills.

On a shadeless ridge path, we walked among Mro houses made of lashed-together bamboo. A Christian church was built the same way, as was the church of a much newer religion known as 'Gramadi'. The way Mr Lemuel told it, the followers of that upstart faith had something like a cargo cult in progress, in which a savior named Gramadi had been expected to arrive among them in 1995. That he had not appeared was considered due to a shortfall of virtue among the adherents. They would keep trying, hoping and praying for Gramadi's arrival—better late than never. The village's Gramadi priest happened to be at the church, dressed in a white sarong and shawl, his silver hair done up in a topknot. He stepped out of his white tennis shoes to show us the inside of the building. Three bamboo gates led into it, one for men, one for women, and one for priests. Inside, colored paper lace decorated the rafters and the altar table. The priest asked for a donation, and since I didn't have anything of the appropriate size with me, Mr Lemuel had to hand over some small bills, which pained his Presbyterian heart.

We went on to a Baum village, out on another hill ridge. It had a Presbyterian church, and a Baptist one as well. The older villagers were busy erecting instant bamboo meeting halls for a conference of Presbyterians from throughout the Bandarban Hill Tracts, to be held there that very weekend. We went to the headman's house, which was bamboo on wooden stilts, with a verandah and a thatched roof, just like the smaller one at the Tribal Cultural Center. Mr Lemuel and I sat on wooden deck chairs in the front room and children began filtering in for a look at me, followed by their mothers, and then village elders, until the room was full. The headman's family brought us glasses of tea, cookies, bananas and sweet jungle pineapple on bamboo skewers.

'How are you able to come all this way to see us, all by yourself?' one of the women exclaimed, as Mr Lemuel translated for me. 'If we tried to go to your place we would just get lost!'

'Oh, but I have Baum friends,' I replied.

I talked with the older people about World War II, the British aircraft flying overhead back then. A girl gave me a bouquet of magenta clover tied with a strip of cotton. High on the wall, a spider as big as my hand crawled over a framed print of The Last Supper. I got dressed up in a Baum sarong to have my photo taken with a very old, very humorous lady who had spool-shaped golden plugs through her earlobes, an ancient earring style found mostly in museums.

My Burma was the glass of tea in that house, the people who lived in that village, whose people lived also in Burma's Chin Hills. Burma could be found in many places—for instance at a Chin refugee's New Year's party with pots of Burmese fish noodles simmering on the stove, in America. Burma was present at Unocal shareholder' annual meetings in Brea, California, when exiles like Zarni, Khin Omar, Pon Nya, Sai Lape, Steven Dun, Ka Hsaw Wa, Maung and Taw Myo Shwe harangued Unocal CEOs for murdering their people with the gas pipeline scheme. Sometimes when I went hiking in the Pacific Northwest, the moss and mud reminded me of the Kachin State's also temperate rainforests and I would be telling John my old land mine stories from the Thailand/Burma border as we walked. In the Bandarban villages I could feel Burma all around me. I didn't ask the people there if they were refugees from Burma. Mr Lemuel had already told me that some were, and they were trying to keep the Bangladesh Government out of it, having seen the way things had turned out when the Rohingyas sought official help.

Walking through the village, we got a good look down at the Bangladesh Army's artillery testing range, and made jokes about the guns' long-range potential should a Bangladesh/Burma border conflict happen to occur. A group of children posed for pictures in front of an engraved stone memorial slab. In the old days such memorials would be engraved with the animals a great man had hunted in his time (elephants, wild cattle) but now a cross was the usual decoration, sometimes with a powder-horn etched below it to symbolize the tradition of the hunt.

A few village kids put on a 'cultural show' for me. Two young teens dressed in mini-sarongs held bunches of bougainvillea in each hand as they sang in Baum, 'We Are Christian Children.' Then their friends crouched down to bang crossed pairs of bamboo poles in rhythm so the girls could dance through the grid. The girls were very good at the bamboo dance. If it was Baum or Chin, it was also something that Burma's Karens claimed for their culture. It used to be standard at festivals at the old Karen rebel headquarters, Manerplaw. Not only that, but as I watched I could just about feel my childhood ankle bruises from trying the bamboo dance in elementary school. It was a Phys Ed fad one year in the 1950s, and we'd been told it was from The Philippines back then. Maybe it was. I liked the idea of being on a cultural tour and ending up with a dance I'd done myself in the suburban wilds of New Jersey long ago.

Mr Lemuel and I rejoined Mr Ezekiel at the village where we'd left him.

'My little granddaughter is a judge of quality,' Mr Ezekiel commented, 'Even though she has hardly been anywhere, she told me she knew those sweets you gave her were far superior to any she had before. She is a quick mind. We will try to send her to an English-medium school in Dhaka for her later education.'

The family and I ate *hilsa* fish from the Indian Ocean, and drank flat Coca-Cola like it was a glass of brandy after lunch. Then we walked around the village, where two women pounded the husks off rice using an efficient treadle that the Baums had adapted from those used by Bengali settlers. We went into a house where a woman sat weaving a striped blanket on a back-strap loom, and a baby slept under a smaller version of the blanket in a hanging basket-bed.

A man fashioning a split-bamboo rice basket on his front porch greeted Mr Lemuel excitedly: 'Oh, I dreamed that you died! When you went overseas for your project, I dreamed that your airplane crashed! So I prayed for you very hard, very hard indeed!'

'Your prayers kept my airplane in the sky, then,' Mr Lemuel told the basket-weaver, and thanked him with a slightly nervous laugh. Mr Lemuel was a truly unselfish person, whose life was dedicated to helping others, but his existence was fraught with hardship and danger, and he needed all the prayers he could get.

'I am lucky this village man prays to our Lord God above for me,' he sighed. We left to go back downhill to Bandarban in late afternoon, passing an itinerant Bengali popsicle seller with a heavy ice chest of treats balanced atop his turbaned head.

I went to the 'Marma' Rakhine shops in the bazaar at night with Mr Lemuel and his wife, and stopped by their house for pineapple. Fires flashing through the close-packed wood and bamboo quarters of Bandarban town had burned them out of two other homes. Mr Lemuel's manuscripts and documents had ended up in ashes, but he persevered with his Baum survival work. Mr Ezekiel and Mr Lemuel were hanging their hopes on all sorts of small development projects. Agricultural improvements, women's crafts, they had all the plans and proposals. Sometimes they ran into conflict with Bangladesh's forest preservationists, who wanted to protect the Hill watershed by keeping people and their inevitable farms out of it. The only solution I could envision for it was that if Burma was liberated, at least all those 'extra' people from across the border, the refugees, could go home to Burma's more sparsely inhabited mountains, easing some of the population pressure on Bangladesh.

At the guest house I was surprised by a knock on the door and just cracked it open enough to reveal a very polite Bengali plain-clothes officer, who quickly said 'I am Special Branch,' and two colleagues. The Bangladesh FBI.

'Oh, then, you'd like to see my permit letter, I suppose,' I said.

'Of course, if you would not mind, please.' He speed-read the letter and handed it back, asking my occupation.

'Tourist. Artist.'

'Well, thank you, God bless you, goodbye.' And with smiles the Special Branch contingent vanished.

Mr Ezekiel, who had business to attend to in Chittagong, and I took the just less than deluxe bus (velveteen upholstery, no air-con) from Bandarban in the morning. The bus was driven in the bullying fashion common to large vehicles in Bangladesh, in which the driver bears down relentlessly on the horn and gas pedal and all lesser entities had better get out of the way. We left the Hill Tracts as I realized that the only large trees that I'd seen in the Hills were those kept alive for their shade and beauty at the Army cantonment. By the time we reached Chittagong I had an extraordinary stabbing headache. Combined with the tiredness I felt, it made me wonder if I had somehow managed to get malaria. But I knew the headache was really caused by my re-entry to the noise and traffic zone, and the fatigue was the kind that follows the achievement of a goal, getting to Bandarban.

No sooner had I checked back into the Golden Inn, a floor lower, same view, and taken a codeine-tylenol, than the Rohingyas called to take me to lunch. Nurul Islam, Dr Yunus, Salim, Anwar Hussein and Uncle Jilani convened around a table at the Tai Wa, which Nurul Islam said was 'the only truly authentic Chinese restaurant in this city, that is, it actually features the Chinese cooks.' The Bengali waiter brought me chopsticks and the rest got forks. 'He suspects I might possibly be Chinese,' I whispered. Over the best meal I'd ever had in Bangladesh, we discussed democracy for Malaysia, democracy for Burma, and the brewing crisis in Iraq. Some of the Rohingyas were for bombing Saddam Hussein and company to smithereens, some weren't. We lingered over jasmine tea, then parted with the Rohingyas' assurance that their merger announcement would be coming soon, and mine that I would post it on the Internet.

I rushed back to the Golden Inn, where Stephen and Dr S.K. were due to arrive. They came up to my room with a third visitor, a young-looking man with ivory skin and onyx eyes. 'Here is Thomas, our Chin National Front Chairman. I myself did not know where he was, and he is here!' Dr

S.K. told me as I shook hands with the stranger. After a room boy delivered bottles of cold Coca-Cola for all of us and we locked the door, I turned on my tape recorder to interview Thomas for Internet Burma-watchers' consumption. He was in his thirties, and had a law degree, although he looked more like a teenaged jungle fighter. Thomas had not traveled as much as the average 1990s revolutionary leader from Burma, and had not met the press. He understood my questions in English, but answered in Chin and had Dr S.K. translate.

My first question about the CNF seemed to provoke just the opposite of the computer info-bites I wanted. Thomas gave a rather lengthy commentary on Chin oppression starting with background from British colonial times. The Chins were always somewhat defensive about their role as troops in Burma's Army. Like the Kachins, Chin soldiers had served in Burma's pre-World War II Army, under the British, and most of the Chin troops stayed loyal to the Allies during World War II. Units called the Chin Levies were able to devastate Japanese forces far superior in number and arms, by springing clever ambushes, using antiquated flintlock rifles. Chins also served as scouts and guerrillas with the Chindits, and in a 'Free Chin' resistance movement against the Japanese occupiers.

After World War II, many of the Chin soldiers had stayed on in Burma's military, and had been used effectively by the government against the rebellions of other ethnic groups like the Karens. Their loyalties were suspect, though, and the Chin soldiers did not rise to the officer corps. Chin-only units became diluted with other nationalities, especially after brief attempts at Chin rebellion during the 1960s. Many Chins still joined the Tatmadaw, grasping at military service as way out of poverty, but they were just cannon-fodder for it, far from the echelons of power. In 1987, a dormant Chin insurgency had been revived by the CNF's young leaders, who were then joined by urban-educated Chin survivors of the '88 uprising.

After the back-story, Thomas' answers got shorter but more up to date and relevant to the current democracy struggle. I asked the Chairman about the interest Unocal had expressed in building another Burma gas pipeline, one that would stretch though Chin regions to India. 'If the Unocal built the pipeline through the Chinland, we the Chin people will suffer for that,' Thomas replied. 'Like, the forced labor, and forced relocation, and collection of money, and so many things. In order to build this pipeline, they will destroy the environments, in order to set up that pipeline. And we have been suffering a lot about human rights violations. And if they build this pipeline, yeah it will be rampant, it will increase!'

The CNF Chairman explained the nuances of the CNF's military strategy, which was a conceptual departure from that of Burma's more traditional rebel armies with their fixed position battles, hilltop stockades and occasional ambushes of Tatmadaw supply convoys. Small-scale as their capabilities were, the Chin rebels were now trying to take the war right into the Tatmadaw's garrisons. 'In order to reverse their approaching, and the pressure in the remote and the border areas, we create some operations in urban areas. At the same time, we create some confrontation, some operation, where the military regime cannot expect it.' Pausing every few sentences for Dr S.K.'s translation, Thomas continued in his soft but confident voice, 'And we targeted the important one, their main resources. Like their arms and ammunition, in order to attack their camp, but we attack the storerooms of arms and ammunition, like this. And sometimes we target only officers.'

Thomas also described the Tatmadaw's involvement in logging the Chin forests: 'They build their camp and deforest around by their area. And both sides of the chief roads, and any roads were cut off of all trees up to a hundred feet. ...So they are directly enforcing the deforestation. And it badly affects for drinking water in some villages. Because the clear-cut of all that trees, the forest gradually becomes dry and dry, and after some years the villages could not get the drinking water.

'About 1990, some Burmese businessmen came to Chinland, and collect some orchids. And they say that they give a high price. So the people destroy all the forest to collect the orchids. Not that they go and climb up and pick up to collect. But they cut off all the trees and collect the orchids. And still we don't know, that that is a high price, where they sell that orchid. And at the same time the military did not prevent to cut the forest.

'The logging place in Chin State, in Chinland, in far northeastern of Chinland, within the Kalemyo and Tamu township, there is heavy logging! To sell to India. And another one is roundabout in Haka and Surkhua village in the middle east of Chin State. They also are teak logging, and sell to the Burma proper. The third one is the southern one, within the Paletwa township—they cut off the teak and send to Bangladesh through Akyab [Arakan].'

The drug trade in the Chin region was going on with obvious official complicity, according to Thomas, who said of the regime, 'They never interfere with who cultivates this opium. The cultivators have been closely related with these authorities.' The CNF had been gathering proof, he said. Dr S.K. promised me photographs that would reveal the regime's involvement in the western Burma heroin trafficking, pending his translation of accompanying documents from CNF field officers who had gathered the evidence.

Being in that hotel room made me bring up the Tatmadaw's destruction of cemeteries in Burma, one of the regime's many forms of religious persecution. Grave desecration was directed particularly at Christians like the Chins, as well as Moslems, Baha'is, and what was left of Rangoon's Jewish community. 'In Kalemyo, they destroyed the Christian cemetery and built their camp. In Tiddim also,' Thomas told me, referring to towns in the Chin State.

The tape ran out. Then Thomas, who had been stiffly formal during the inteview, warmed up. He told me that he knew about my long time interest in the Chin cause, and thanked me for it. He knew I'd been with the Kachin rebels at Pajau in 1991, not long after he and Stephen had taken military training there themselves. What did I think of the Kachin Independence Organization now, he asked. I wasn't about to give a diplomatic answer. Before I'd left for Bangladesh, I'd heard a report of forced labor in KIO-controlled territory. I was disgusted, I told Thomas, the KIO had sold out their revolution for a stupid sugar mill. They weren't getting anything from the ceasefire, and they wouldn't be fondly remembered for their 'neutrality' when democracy came. I found myself hoping for more from the CNF. Perhaps since they were late in taking up the gun, they would avoid the battle-fatigue which in the end vanquished the Kachins as no Tatmadaw bullets could have. The Chins were still acting like there was a war to be fought, after the world outside had already declared it cease-fired and done with. I found some honor in their stance.

I walked down to the lobby to see the Chins to the door, and there met up with Uncle Jilani, who had brought me another Rohingya visitor, an RSO member I'd met in 1991. The RSO member brought me more historical cultural documents for my Rohingya collection, this time from the Chittagong-based Institute of Arakan Studies. The material included an essay on 'The Muslim Poets of Arakan', a group of sixteenth-seventeenth century literati who particularly intrigued me. My favorite was Sayed Shah Alaol, a scholar and swashbuckler who survived pirate captivity to become a King's cavalryman. Alaol translated epic poems from Sanskrit and Persian for the royal court of Arakan, inserting local interpretations and embroidering the texts in the finest Bengali verse. My meetings with the Rohingyas always carried the implication that theirs was a civil rights struggle which would have to continue even after Burma was rid of its military dictatorship. Somehow the Buddhists of Burma would have to be convinced not just to tolerate this lowly impoverished Moslem ethnic group, but to appreciate that the Rohingyas' connections to the high cultures of Bengal, Persia and Arabia were a gift to Burma that should only inspire profound gratitude.

When the Rohingyas left I turned on CNN, to watch scenes of Indonesian pro-democracy demonstrations, Malaysian pro-democracy demonstrations. Why couldn't there be demonstrations in Burma again, I wondered, I yearned; why couldn't this domino across Southeast Asia like Eastern Europe in '89? Whatever the Chins or anybody else could do in camouflage with their AK47s, the best solution for Burma would still be another popular nonviolent uprising, this time with such force and stamina that it could overcome all the might of the Tatmadaw.

The television news shifted inevitably to Baghdad, where in the background of Christiane Amanpour's pre-bombing report, I could hear the Moslem call to prayer that I heard every few hours in Bangladesh, only now it was coming from a minaret time zones away in Iraq instead of from a loudspeaker over the cemetery.

Uncle Jilani made it to the Golden Inn in the morning, in time to give me photocopies of a few last chapters of his manuscript and see me off on the Dhaka-bound air-con coach. I was seated next to a woman who was completely cloaked for travel in a head-to-toe black *burkha*. I listened to Rahsaan Roland Kirk spacing out on his flute, a tape John had made for me, but I felt headachy and tired all the way. Still, I did not have malaria. I had not contracted typhoid, I had not been lost.

Back in cacophonous Dhaka, I had just enough energy left to rickshaw to the Ambrosia Guest House, buy saris at the self-help handicrafts shop, and sleep. I picked up my jungle rickshaw painting and baby taxied to the airport just ahead of a cross-town BNP protest march aiming its way towards Parliament. I asked for a window seat on the Bangladesh Biman flight to Hong Kong, wanting to look at Burma as we crossed over it. I got a window seat but it was over the wing, so I couldn't see much. Through the dirty scratched-up window I could barely catch sight of mountain ridges, a lake, a fire that could have been a field being cleared for planting or a village being torched by the Tatmadaw.

Burma gave way to China's Yunnan Province, and soon we landed in Hong Kong, where I would only stay three days. I took the silent, cool, spotless, empty rapid train from the new airport to the city center, feeling as though I had landed on another planet rather than another former British colony on the same continent as Bangladesh.

Soon I took that train back to the airport, and with my tin jungle scene, my saris, my interview tapes, a bag of pungent dried fish for Uncle Jilani's exiled relative, and a box of lucky carp white chocolates from the airport gift shop, I left Hong Kong. I was strapped in on a plane with refugee Tibetan lamas, adopted Chinese baby girls and their new parents, soldiers, corporate suits, genuine tourists, and perhaps a fellow spy or two. I flew across the Pacific to my home, to rampant, ferocious, inspired love. To our beautiful dormant volcano. To the dark shelter of the deodar tree, our refugee from the Himalayas. Sometimes from the shuttle flight which followed the trans-Pacific, I could see the deodar's outstretched boughs and topmost branch trident, towering over our house and the other neighborhood evergreens. But now it, and my love, and the volcano, were hidden below the sodden clouds of winter rain. All as invisible and as present as Burma.

Afterword

Since my 1998 Bangladesh border foray, I have touched Burma two more times: on the far-flung island of Guam in 2001, and the very vermillion mud of the Kachin State in 2002.

Around 900 refugees from Burma, mostly Chins, showed up on Guam, a United States territory in the Pacific Ocean in 2000. Desperate political fugitives paid hundreds of dollars for passports and tickets, and made it to Guam on an immigration loophole allowing Southeast Asian tourists to visit without visas. Once there, they applied for asylum from the US, but ended up in bureaucratic limbo, their cases processed ineptly and at a snail's pace. They lived on church charity, crowded in sweltering apartments, unemployed. Some refugee groups in Washington DC were determined to speed up the asylum process, and I decided that since these Chins and others from Burma were stranded practically in my country, I should go see them and hear their stories. Actually they were practically in the Philippines, but after spending 50,000 frequent flyer miles, I joined them on the scruffy island, half US Navy base, half indigenous Chamorro villages, with a crust of luxury resorts for Japanese tourists.

Two of the Chin asylum-seekers, a Dr Lal and a Pastor Lal, drove me around the island and translated for me as I interviewed the castaways in their scattered flats. Pastor Lal himself had been taken into custody by the regime in Chin State more than once. I asked him how he'd been treated, this respected member of the community. 'A number of methods of torture,' he answered, 'One would be, they put a plastic around my head, to suffocate me. Another is, they stripped me naked to be eaten by mosquitoes the whole time. They gave me meals consisting of rice and sand mixed. They literally shot at my head and somehow missed it, whether intentionally or not, the first time I was in prison. They forced me to kneel on the ground, on sharp rocks for hours, put shackles on my legs.'

On Guam I met quite a few Chins who had worked underground, gathering or distributing information for the CNF, as well as an elected member of Parliament, an AIDS prevention activist, and a former policeman who had drawn the line at harassing Aung San Suu Kyi's political party. As well as the Chins, I met Kachin refugees (including former KIO soldiers) and Karens. I asked a Kachin who had been a rebel soldier and then an underground agent, if Burma's regime had given any trouble to his family. It had, especially after he slipped away to Guam: 'My brother was killed in July last year. Because they wanted me, but they couldn't do it to me, so they did it to my brother.'

The Chins told me of the looting of their northern land. Rice crops were being confiscated by the regime's troops, trees and even orchids were stripped from the forests for sale by the army, mountains and river beds were gutted and poisoned by mineral extraction. I learned of the disappearance of the ceremonial mithun (a type of large domesticated ox intrinsic to Chin culture) when a military scheme 'sold all those mithuns to another country. Now there are hardly any left, and almost extinct. Each household used to raise the mithun. It was one of the symbols of the Chin people, and one of our wealths. We killed that animal only when we celebrate a big ceremony, as in ancient times.'

The last person I tape recorded on the island was a Buddhist Burman, who had participated in 1988's student uprising and then done seven years of hard time. For singing in his cell, he had been beaten by the guards until he fell silent for months and faced his parents on one of their rare visits as a speechless creature, 'with my shackles like a slave'. He considered himself lucky to have gotten a prison 'health injection' only once, because the guards 'first inject the AIDS persons and then the political prisoners'. On Guam, he suffered from nightmares: 'It's maybe broken my brain while I was in jail.'

When the Lals and I drove from interview to interview, we passed World War II sites—memorial parks, battlefields, or the caves inhabited by Japanese soldiers (in one case, until 1972). Once again, as in Burma's highlands and the border cemeteries, the war of the 1940s was alive, palpable to me.

On a couple of mornings I managed to visit the beach across the street from my hotel before the days' interviews were to start. I'd wade out towards the coral reef. The Chins, being a far inland mountain people, had a hard time relating to the ocean and the beach, especially when I mentioned that for Americans, long-term idleness on a tropical island was actually what we aspire to. 'You mean you just sit on the sand and look at the water?' Yes, I replied, that was about it. 'Oh... Well, we'll have to try that.' As it turned out, they didn't have to wait on Guam much longer. Wheels turned in Washington, immigration judges flew in, and by that summer, nearly all of the Guam refugees received asylum in the US. They dispersed to Florida, Georgia, Michigan, just in time to watch their new home away from home under televised attack on September 11, 2001.

The next time I flew over the Pacific it was to follow the length of the Kachin/Yunnan border from close to Tibet to the Shan State. I had essentially turned my back on the Kachin Independence Organization since my last visit in 1995. The KIO just didn't seem to be contributing to Burma's revolution. Some colonels had brought about a change in the group's power structure, unseating General Zau Mai, but all remained static. No fighting the Tatmadaw, no standing up for democracy, no human rights reports. But then the Kachins got my attention again with new, immense logging concessions granted to them by Chinese companies. I had to try to talk with them.

Typically, I chose the rainy season in a year of floods, August 2002, to make the trip. August is the Month of the Hungry Ghosts in China, when the dead roam and the living should stay put. I started by flying from Kunming to Baoshan, and from there I took the first of countless minibus rides north along the Salween River (called the Nujiang, 'Angry River', in China) on a twisty, bumpy, hazardous one-lane road. Seated near the driver, I spent the first day second-guessing his every move, worst case scenario-ing every bend in the road, every tumble to the rushing river. By the next day I decided to relax and leave fate in the hands of the minibus professionals. What would happen would happen. At least the whole area was open to foreigners now, so I could travel freely on the Yunnan side of the border.

My first stop was Liuku, a town straddling the Salween with plenty of banks and bars to support the timber industry. From Liuku I took a minibus up the mountain passes to Pianma, a timber depot on the Kachin border. Nothing I'd heard about Pianma really prepared me for the shock of it. I'd expected something like a Pacific Northwest logging town—one or two lumber yards—but Pianma had at least forty. It was a horizontal forest, piled high to the sky. This was Kachin wood. Logging had been banned on the Yunnan side, so each log bore a red stamp certifying that it came from Burma. Pianma was the graphic evidence of the demise of the Kachin forests. A mudslide stopped traffic (big blue logging trucks) at the entrance to Pianma, so I got out of the minibus and walked along the valley rim taking photos of the lumber yards. Buyers in business suits were measuring logs, and there were plenty of big ones. Nobody seemed to mind my presence but I left that afternoon, having to ford the edge of a landslide on foot, along with nomadic logging town 'bad girls' in high heels, on the way down to Liuku.

The following day I went to Fugong, the next big banking and logging center on the river. Fugong was the entrepot for the latest massive logging concession in Kachin State. North of Fugong I saw a brand new bridge across the Salween, built for logging trucks to bring their wood cargo from Kachin State. Past the bridge, the minibus picked up two stranded passengers, and when we got our inevitable flat tire, one of them introduced himself to me. He was from South Korea. He was in 'the timber business'.

To my surprise, given the road conditions, I reached my northern goal, Gongshan, where the last shreds of Kachin forest were due to enter China once new mountain logging roads were finished. The steep, lovely town was close enough to Tibet to have grazing dzo's (yak/cow hybrids.) I ate chanterelle mushrooms there, hiked to a mountaintop Lisu Catholic church, and acquired interesting patterns of flea bites. After Gongshan, I lived through a twelve hour minibus marathon to Liuku. At one of the many rock/mud slide clog-ups I snapped a perfect photo of 'the monster'—one enormous heart-shaped red cedar-like log taking up the entire bed of a truck. Sad, sad, old-growth destruction. All along the Salween road, mud-splattered Chinese trucks carried raw logs of every size (table for two, table for four, conference table.)

I continued further south to Kachin border towns where I'd only ventured surreptitiously, by night, before. I met with some KIO Central Committee members who referred to 'the government' (Burma's military regime) 'allowing' (strong-arming) the KIO to have 'concessions' (their own resources) for 'development' purposes (logging roads/bridges and the empty promise of schools and clinics.) The KIO seemed to have fallen for the Chinese illusion of 'reforestation' as well—as if plantations of spindly pine trees could make up for the incalculable loss of one of the world's most biodiverse temperate forests.

After a fairly bizarre restaurant lunch featuring deep fried jumbo bee grubs and grapefruit wine, the officials and I visited KIO second-in-command Zaung Hra in a Chinese hospital where he was recovering from a minor stroke. I tried to make it clear what my concerns were about resource extraction/destruction. I gave the Central Committee members some documents about gold mining and mercury toxicity, because Chinese companies were dredging for gold in the Kachin rivers, heedlessly dumping or burning the mercury they used, and the local people had no idea how dangerous that could be. That evening when the others went back across the border to Pajau, I visited Madame Brang Seng in her China-side flat. Still beautiful, still tough-minded, she wore a mauve paisley sarong and tortoiseshell spec's. She showed me a video from Chairman Brang Seng's harrowing five-day funeral at Pajau in 1994, which had been sullied by the appearance of some Tatmadaw officers. Madame Brang Seng was quite at odds with the rest of the Central Committee over how everything had gone since. The corruption, the inertia. Her daughter Ja Seng Hkawn had four children now and stayed in Myitkyina, dealing in jade, she told me. When I commented that Ja Seng Hkawn was worth more than all the politician/ officers running the KIO, she replied, 'I may put her in charge some day...'

Following the meetings I went south to the very place where I had first entered Kachinland, exactly eleven years before, in August 1991. I had to take the last bus of the day in order to meet up with my Kachin contacts after dark. After a six hour mountain road trip (including a delay while bus passengers got out to haggle over mushrooms with tribal vendors) I reached my appointed bus stop. A precise insertion at night, by motorbike, got me across the border, and I was back in my element under the stars, breathing the clear air, being brought bowls of the Kachin comfort food—fried potatoes, green chili sauce. It was one of those utopian communities that resolutely spring up in Burma frontier lands. A group of intellectual teachers lived there, with students arriving for the new term at their jungle university. I had long talks there with local officials and a 'founding father' of the KIO.

The perspective from this tiny village was different from that of the KIO 'top brass'. Resentment of resource extraction was pervasive ('all of our trees go to China but no Kachin even has a wooden house'). I was told of forced labor and rape by SPDC troops along the central Kachin State's Ledo Road. The KIO had publicized none of it, silently complicit in their new role of timber warlords.

I gave an environmental workshop for some of the students and I went for a hill-walk above the village. The foliage of those Kachin hills was all secondary—the Chinese had come across the border whenever they felt like it and taken out the good trees. After just a couple of days, I left Kachinland, Burma, in thick predawn fog. I traveled back through western Yunnan, where villages had become towns and towns were becoming cities, where rubber and tea and coffee plantations had replaced the real forests. I was going home on the Burma Road again, the highway's zigzags painted with burnt rubber, Kachin mud in the treads of my hiking boots, face smeared with Tiger Balm for my sinus headache, and no interest in me at those dreaded checkpoints. I was headed for the iced cappuccino cybercafes of Kunming and then Hong Kong, the somewhat degraded city of my dreams.

Now it is November 2004, and I sit in another cafe, in another rainy city, and the news from Burma is today, as every day, a strange collection of despair and hope, defeat and defiance. Aung San Suu Kyi is under arrest, but she symbolizes freedom. Logging and mining continue to ravage the Kachin north, but Unocal is to be put on trial for its Tenasserim pipeline security campaign. Ne Win is dead of disease. Khin Nyunt, head of the junta's dreaded Military Intelligence agency, is under arrest. Min Ko Naing, the eloquent student leader imprisoned since 1988, has just been released at long last.

This book, like *Burmese Looking Glass*, took quite a while to live and write. For their help during that process, many thanks to Wolfgang, Angie, Sally, Linda, Oliver and Mika, Sam and Nanda in Hong Kong; to Geri Thoma for agenting in New York; to Nicole, Louisa and Carol of Santa Monica; to CG, PC and R for the Chittagong contacts; to Trey for 'Blood Meridian'; to Bruce for www.projectmaje.org; to Aunt Edith for the grant; to Uncle George in Ft Bragg for the lieder and to Brigadier George for the leadership. My orchidaceous appreciation to Chris Frape and David Murray for making this book actually happen. Above all, my gratitude to my brother, Rand; my mother, Irma; and my SBS (Supportive Burma Spouse), John.

Free Burma.

Glossary

ACRONYMS

ABSDF All Burma Students Democratic Front, armed group founded by survivors of Burma's 1988 democracy uprising.

ARIF Arakan Rohingya Islamic Front, opposition group of Moslem rebels from Burma, led by Nurul Islam.

BCP Burma Communist Party, formerly large-scale Marxist insurgent group.

BNP Bangladesh National Party, a major political party in Bangladesh (in opposition in 1998) led by Begum Khaleda Zia.

CNF Chin National Front, rebel group of Burma's Chin people.

KIO Kachin Independence Organization, armed opposition group in northern Burma.

RSO Rohingya Solidarity Organization, opposition group of Moslem rebels from Burma, led by Dr Mohammed Yunus.

Slorc State Law and Order Restoration Committee, the junta ruling Burma following its suppression of the 1988 democracy uprising; name later changed to State Peace and Development Council (**SPDC**).

UWSA United Wa State Army, armed group of the Wa people of north-eastern Burma.

ETHNIC GROUPS

Akha A tribal people living in the mountains of Thailand, China, Laos and Burma.

Baum The Chin people living in Bangladesh.

Bangladeshi Any of the citizens of the nation of Bangladesh.

Bengali An ethnic group of India and Bangladesh.

Burman The largest ethnic group in Burma, a mostly Buddhist people.

Burmese Any of the citizens of Burma, or more specifically, the Burman people.

Chakma A hill people of Bangladesh and Burma.

Chin A large, mainly Christian, tribal group of Burma with related groups in India and Bangladesh.

Gurkha Mountain people of Nepal, some of whom settled in Burma.

H'mong A tribal people of Thailand, Laos and China.

Jingphaw One of the Kachin tribes of northern Burma and southern China.

Kachin A group of several tribes living mainly in mountain regions of Burma and China.

Karen A large ethnic group of southern and eastern Burma, and Thailand.

Khami A tribal people living in Burma and Bangladesh.

Kuki A Chin-related people living in Northeast India.

Lahu A tribe of Burma, Thailand, Laos and China.

Laotian The citizens of the nation of Laos.

Lisu One of the Kachin tribes.

Marma *See* 'Rakhine'.

Mon An ethnic group of southern Burma, Thailand and Cambodia.

Mro A tribal people of Burma and Bangladesh.

Naga A tribal people of Northeast India, and Burma.

Pa-O A Karen-related Buddhist tribe of Burma.

Rakhine Buddhist ethnic group of Arakan, western Burma (also called 'Marma' in Bangladesh.)

Rohingya Moslem ethnic group of Arakan, western Burma.

Shan Thai-related ethnic group, living mainly in northern/eastern Burma.

Tai Dam An ethnic group of Laos and Vietnam.

Wa A mountain people of northeastern Burma and southern China.

Zo A large Asian ethnic group which includes the Chins of Burma.

About the Author

Edith Mirante has roamed Southeast Asia for nearly two decades, collecting information on human rights and environmental issues. In 1986, she founded Project Maje, which distributes material on Burma's struggle for freedom. She has investigated abuse and resistance in some of the most remote corners of Burma's frontier war zone.

The author of the acclaimed *Burmese Looking Glass*, Mirante has written chapters in several other books, as well as articles for encyclopedias, *The New York Times*, *Asiaweek*, *Cultural Survival Quarterly*, and *Earth First Journal*. She has testified on Burma before the US Congress, European Trade Commission, and the International Labor Organization. She was instrumental in organizing the campaign for corporate withdrawal from Burma, of the world-wide Free Burma Coalition.

3610 NE 70th Ave.
Portland OR 97213